THE CAMBRIDGE COMPANIO
TO BASEBALL

D0979593

Baseball is much more than a game. As the American national pastime, it has reflected the political and cultural concerns of US society for over 200 years. Baseball thus possesses a rich lore unmatched by any other American sport and generates passions and loyalties unique in American society. This *Companion* examines baseball in culture, baseball as culture, and the game's global identity. Contributors contrast baseball's massive, big-business present with its romanticized origins and its evolution against the backdrop of American and world history. Chapters cover topics such as baseball in the movies, baseball and mass media, and baseball in Japan and Latin America. Between the chapters are vivid profiles of iconic characters including Babe Ruth, Ichiro, and Walter O'Malley. Crucial moments in baseball history are revisited, ranging from the 1919 Black Sox gambling scandal to recent controversies over steroid use. A unique book for fans and scholars alike, this *Companion* explains the enduring importance of baseball in America and beyond.

LEONARD CASSUTO is Professor of English at Fordham University.

STEPHEN PARTRIDGE is Assistant Professor of English at the University of British Columbia.

A complete list of books in the series is at the back of the book

DISCARDED FROM
GARFIELD COUNTY
LIBRARIES

GARFIELD COUNTY LIBRARIES
Parachute Branch Library
244 Grand Valley Way
Parachute, CO 81635
(970) 285-9870 – Fax (970) 285-7477
www.gcpld.org

THE CAMBRIDGE COMPANION TO
BASEBALL

EDITED BY

LEONARD CASSUTO
Fordham University

STEPHEN PARTRIDGE
University of British Columbia

CAMBRIDGE
UNIVERSITY PRESS

CAMBRIDGE UNIVERSITY PRESS
Cambridge, New York, Melbourne, Madrid, Cape Town,
Singapore, São Paulo, Delhi, Tokyo, Mexico City

Cambridge University Press
The Edinburgh Building, Cambridge CB2 8RU, UK

Published in the United States of America by Cambridge University Press, New York

www.cambridge.org
Information on this title: www.cambridge.org/9780521145756

© Cambridge University Press 2011

This publication is in copyright. Subject to statutory exception
and to the provisions of relevant collective licensing agreements,
no reproduction of any part may take place without the written
permission of Cambridge University Press.

First published 2011

Printed in the United States of America by Edwards Brothers Incorporated

A catalogue record for this publication is available from the British Library

Library of Congress Cataloguing in Publication data
The cambridge companion to baseball / [edited by] Leonard Cassuto,
Stephen Partridge.
p. cm. – (Cambridge companion to baseball)
ISBN 978-0-521-14575-6 (pbk.)
1. Baseball–Social aspects–United States. 2. Baseball–United States–History.
I. Cassuto, Leonard, 1960– II. Partridge, Stephen.
GV867.64.R85 2011
796.3570973–dc22
2010046161

ISBN 978-0-521-76182-6 hardback
ISBN 978-0-521-14575-6 paperback

Cambridge University Press has no responsibility for the persistence or
accuracy of URLs for external or third-party internet websites referred to in
this publication, and does not guarantee that any content on such websites is,
or will remain, accurate or appropriate.

CONTENTS

ILLUSTRATIONS

CONTRIBUTORS

LEONARD CASSUTO is Professor of English at Fordham University and the General Editor of *The Cambridge History of the American Novel*. With the publication of this book, he receives an Erdös number of 4.

STEPHEN PARTRIDGE is Assistant Professor of English at the University of British Columbia. He has published research on Chaucerian and other Middle English manuscripts, most recently as a contributor to *The Production of Books in England 1350–1500*, to be published by Cambridge in 2011. He is preparing a book on the manuscripts of Chaucer's *Canterbury Tales*.

RICHARD C. CREPEAU is Professor of History at the University of Central Florida and author of *Baseball: America's Diamond Mind, 1919–1941*. Professor Crepeau teaches courses in twentieth-century American history, the history of American sport, and the history of baseball.

DAVID P. FIDLER is the James Louis Calamaras Professor of Law at the Indiana University Maurer School of Law in Bloomington, Indiana. With Arturo J. Marcano Guevara, he has been active since the late 1990s in raising concerns about problems associated with Major League Baseball's operations in Latin America, including via the co-authored book *Stealing Lives: The Globalization of Baseball and the Tragic Story of Alexis Quiroz* (2002). Professor Fidler is also an internationally recognized expert on global health and international law, biological weapons and bioterrorism, the international legal implications of "nonlethal" weapons, and counterinsurgency and rule-of-law operations.

AL FILREIS is Kelly Professor, Director of the Center for Programs in Contemporary Writing, and Faculty Director of the Kelly Writers House at the University of Pennsylvania. He has published four books, hosts the "PoemTalk" podcast, and is Co-Director of the PennSound archive. He has been a Mets fan since 1962.

DAVID FINOLI is a freelance writer and sports historian who lives with his wife and three children in Monroeville, a suburb of Pittsburgh, Pennsylvania. Finoli has penned eight sports books, the majority dealing with baseball, including four that detail the exploits of his favorite team, the Pittsburgh Pirates. He has also contributed to the *Pirates Game Day Magazine, Pittsburgh Magazine*, and *Baseball Digest* (baseballdigest.com).

STEVEN P. GIETSCHIER is University Curator and Assistant Professor of History at Lindenwood University in St. Charles, Missouri. Previously, he was Senior Managing Editor for Research at *The Sporting News* where he edited the *Complete Baseball Record Book*. He is on the editorial board of *NINE: A Journal of Baseball History and Culture* and is a member of the Baseball Writers' Association of America (BBWAA) and the Society for American Baseball Research (SABR).

DAVID GRANT is a Professor of Mathematics at the University of Colorado at Boulder, where he specializes in number theory. In a previous life he served as Sports Editor of *The Daily Princetonian*.

GEORGE GRELLA is a professor of English and Film Studies at the University of Rochester, and film critic for the *City Newspaper of Rochester* and WXXI-FM. He publishes widely on popular literature (especially detective fiction and related genres), film, and baseball.

LESLIE HEAPHY, Associate Professor of History at Kent State at Stark, has written or edited four books on baseball, including *The Negro Leagues, 1869–1960*, and is editor of the journal *Black Ball*.

MASARU IKEI, born in Tokyo in 1935, is an avid baseball fan, and has played an active role in the sport as a commentator and advisor, serving on the panel for the introduction of the free agent system in Japan, among other appointments. He was the first Japanese to become a member of SABR. Ikei has published several books on baseball and has also carried out research on the role of baseball in politics, based on his expertise in the field of political science. He is currently a professor emeritus at Keio University.

MATTHEW FRYE JACOBSON is a long-suffering Seattle Mariners fan, author of five books on race in America, and chair of American Studies at Yale. When he is not busy despairing of the Mariners' bullpen, he is writing a volume called *Odetta's Voice and Other Weapons: The Civil Rights Era as Cultural History*.

A graduate of Yale and Columbia universities, JONATHAN LEWIN has written on baseball for the *New York Daily News*, the *Huffington Post*, and *The Faster Times*, among others. He has also appeared on SNY-TV's "Mets Weekly" and ESPN radio.

DANIEL LUBAN is a graduate student in Political Science at the University of Chicago.

DAVID LUBAN is University Professor and Professor of Law and Philosophy at Georgetown University Law Center. He writes on professional ethics, international law, and legal philosophy. His most recent book is *Legal Ethics and Human Dignity* (Cambridge). He coached his co-author's Little League team from 1993–1995, with one perfect season.

ARTURO J. MARCANO GUEVARA is a lawyer with an LLM from Indiana University and an MS in Sport Management from the University of Massachusetts. He is an expert on professional baseball in Latin America. Marcano has been at the forefront of generating awareness in the United States and Canada about problems caused by professional baseball in Latin American countries, and he has published extensively on this topic, including the book *Stealing Lives: The Globalization of Baseball and the Tragic Story of Alexis Quiroz*, co-authored with David P. Fidler (2002). Marcano has also served as the International Legal Advisor to the Venezuelan Baseball Players Association.

TIM MORRIS compiles the online *Guide to Baseball Fiction* and is the author of *Making the Team: The Cultural Work of Baseball Fiction*. He is the nonfiction editor of *Aethlon: The Journal of Sport Literature*.

SAMUEL O. REGALADO, Professor of History at California State University, Stanislaus and a 1994 Smithsonian Faculty Fellow, is the author of *Viva Baseball!: Latin Major Leaguers and Their Special Hunger*, and several articles on Japanese American baseball.

USA Today calls CURT SMITH America's "voice of authority on baseball broadcasting." His fourteen books include the classic *Voices of The Game: The Storytellers*, and the new *A Talk in the Park: Nine Decades of Baseball Tales from the Broadcast Booth*. Smith is a GateHouse Media and mlb.com columnist, a National Public Radio affiliate commentator, a frequent Smithsonian Institution and National Baseball Hall of Fame host, and Senior Lecturer of English at the University of Rochester. He also wrote more speeches than anyone else for former President George H. W. Bush.

DAVID F. VENTURO, Professor of English at The College of New Jersey, author of *Johnson the Poet* (1999) and editor of *The School of the Eucharist* (2006), has written extensively on British literature and culture, 1640–1830. He teaches courses on Shakespeare, the long eighteenth century, modern poetry, baseball and American culture, and the Beatles.

ANDREW ZIMBALIST is the Robert A. Woods Professor of Economics at Smith College and has been a visiting professor at Harvard University; Doshisha University in Kyoto, Japan; and the University of Geneva. He has published twenty books, including *Baseball and Billions, May the Best Team Win: Baseball Economics and Public Policy, National Pastime: How Americans Play Baseball and the Rest of the World Plays Soccer, In the Best Interests of Baseball? The Revolutionary Reign of Bud Selig*, and, most recently, *Circling the Bases: Essays on the Business of Sports*. He has consulted extensively in the sports industry for players' associations, teams, league offices, and cities.

ACKNOWLEDGMENTS

The first pitch for this book was accompanied not by hot dogs and beer, but rather by Mexican food and wine – which you can now buy at some ballparks – in the great baseball town of Chicago. We thank Ray Ryan for commissioning *The Cambridge Companion to Baseball* and then for managing the editorial process with his customary efficiency. Thanks also to Rebecca Taylor at Cambridge University Press, Jamie Hood, and Robert Whitelock. In New York, Paul Thifault served as a gold glove research assistant, fielding every task with accuracy and alacrity.

The contributors for this book made up a great team. From the lineup we'd like to single out David Grant and Jonathan Lewin for their all-around play, Leslie Heaphy for help with the illustrations, and David Fidler and Arturo Marcano for their pinch-hit, ninth-inning save.

Rich Klein was a great third base coach, fact-checking as the book rounded its final turn and then waving it home. From the crowd near the dugout, we offer special thanks to Larry Lester, Raymond Doswell of the Negro Leagues Baseball Museum, Toshiyuki Takamiya, George Kirsch, and Daniel Nathan.

In the VIP boxes are our families: Elise Partridge, Debra Osofsky, and KC Osofsky. The front row goes to the older generations: Ike Cassuto, Mary Partridge, and the late Edwin M. Partridge, Jr., and Ann Prichard, who many years ago brought baseball into our lives.

Now let's play ball.

STEPHEN PARTRIDGE

Baseball: a chronology

1845	Knickerbocker Base Ball Club formed in New York. Many versions of the game had been played informally and unofficially up to this point.
1857	Convention representing fourteen New York-area clubs agrees to uniform set of rules based, with some modifications, on the Knickerbocker Club's rules; these become basis for modern baseball.
1858	Convention of New York-area clubs forms the National Association of Base Ball Players (NABBP).
1860s	Baseball is introduced to Cuba.
1869	Cincinnati Red Stockings are first fully professional team.
1871	Professional players from ten clubs break away from NABBP to form National Association of Professional Base Ball Players (NAPBBP). Boston Red Stockings founded; this team later joins National League and in 1908 is renamed the Braves.
1872	Baseball is introduced to Japan.
1876	National League of Professional Baseball Clubs, later known simply as the National League (NL), organized; in subsequent years team owners establish the "reserve clause," which contractually binds each player to his team.
1883	First National Agreement sets up NL and American Association (founded 1882) as major leagues, and Northwestern League as a minor league.
1885	Overhand pitching made legal.
1886	*The Sporting News* begins publication.
Late 1880s	Tobacco companies begin to insert cards with portraits of athletes, including baseball players, into packs of cigarettes.
1890–1911	Major league playing career of Cy Young.

1891	American Association expires after end of season.
1894	Ban Johnson becomes president of minor Western League. He develops plan to make it a major league; in 1899 it is renamed the American League (AL).
1897–1917	Career of Honus Wagner.
1899	The All Cubans are the first Latin American team to tour the United States.
1900	Cuban League admits black players; amateur baseball in Cuba remains segregated until 1959.
	After contraction, NL includes teams in New York, Brooklyn, Boston, Chicago, Cincinnati, Philadelphia, Pittsburgh, and St. Louis; these eight teams remain in these cities until the 1950s.
1900–1916	Career of Christy Mathewson.
1901	AL declares itself a second major league. Eight charter teams of AL include the Boston Americans, renamed the Red Sox in 1908; Baltimore Orioles, who become the New York Highlanders in 1903, renamed the Yankees in 1913; and teams in Chicago, Cleveland, Detroit, Philadelphia, Washington, and Milwaukee (moved to St. Louis 1902). There is no further movement of teams until the 1950s.
1901–1950	Connie Mack owner and manager of Philadelphia Athletics.
1902–1932	John McGraw manager of New York Giants.
1903	First World Series between champions of AL and NL as a result of new National Agreement between the two leagues. Boston Americans (AL) defeat Pittsburgh Pirates (NL), five games to three. By this year most modern rules on balls, strikes, walks, strikeouts, and fair and foul balls are in place.
	Japanese American baseball begins in western United States.
1905–1928	Career of Ty Cobb.
1907–1927	Career of Walter Johnson.
1912	Fraternity of the Professional Baseball Players of America is formed.
1914	Ring Lardner publishes "A Busher's Letters Home," first of six stories that would be collected as *You Know Me Al* (1916).
1914–1915	Startup Federal League lures Major League Baseball (MLB) players with higher salaries and long-term contracts. After

filing antitrust suit against AL and NL owners and MLB's National Commission, Federal League reaches settlement that disbands it, restoring NL–AL monopoly.

1914–1935   Career of Babe Ruth.

1915–1937   Career of Rogers Hornsby.

1917–1918   American participation in World War I.

1919   White Sox lose World Series to Reds; in 1920 eight White Sox players are accused of conspiracy to throw Series games but acquitted in 1921 court case. Wide tabloid coverage of the "Black Sox" scandal tarnishes the image of baseball as the "national pastime."

1920   Negro National League organized.

Babe Ruth hits fifty-four home runs in his first year with the New York Yankees, almost doubling the record he set the previous year. His personal total exceeds that of every other team in baseball but one.

Playing at the Polo Grounds (home of New York Giants), Yankees are first team to reach 1 million home attendance for a season.

Pitchers are forbidden to doctor the ball or apply any foreign substance to it, but active "spitballers" are exempted from this ban; the last retires in 1934.

1921   New National Agreement establishes office of Commissioner of Baseball. Judge Kenesaw Mountain Landis is appointed first holder of the office. Landis bans the eight White Sox players accused of throwing the 1919 World Series from organized baseball for life.

First radio broadcast of an MLB game, from Forbes Field, Pittsburgh.

Babe Ruth hits 139th career home run to set new record. He retires 14 years later with 714 home runs, a mark that would stand for nearly 40 years.

1922   US Supreme Court exempts baseball from antitrust legislation; one effect is to strengthen the reserve clause in players' contracts.

1920s   Branch Rickey organizes "farm" system of minor league teams to supply talent for St. Louis Cardinals. This organization would be widely copied.

1923   Yankee Stadium opens, and is immediately nicknamed "The House That Ruth Built."

1923–1939   Career of Lou Gehrig.

1927	Satchel Paige joins the Birmingham Black Barons; after a long career in Negro Leagues, Paige plays in MLB 1948–1953, returning for a one-game cameo in 1965.
1929	Stock market collapse leads to the Great Depression.
1930–1946	Career of Josh Gibson in Negro Leagues.
1933	First Major League All-Star Game; first Negro Leagues East–West Classic.
1934	Babe Ruth headlines a team of major leaguers who tour Japan, playing twenty-two games there. Japan's first professional team then tours the United States, and in 1936 the Japanese Baseball League is organized.
1935	The first MLB night game is held on May 24 at Crosley Field, Cincinnati.
1936	Baseball elects its first class to the newly founded Hall of Fame: Ty Cobb, Babe Ruth, Walter Johnson, Christy Mathewson, and Honus Wagner. The first induction ceremonies are held in 1939, when the Hall opens in Cooperstown, New York.
1936–1951	Career of Joe DiMaggio.
1939	First televised MLB game, Cincinnati Reds at Brooklyn Dodgers.
	Lou Gehrig's streak of 2,130 consecutive games played ends after he is diagnosed with Amyotrophic Lateral Sclerosis (now also known as Lou Gehrig's disease). On July 4, the Yankees hold "Lou Gehrig Appreciation Day" and in a widely quoted speech, Gehrig declares himself "the luckiest man on the face of the earth." He dies in 1941. In 1942 Goldwyn releases *Pride of the Yankees*, a Gehrig biopic starring Gary Cooper.
1939–1960	Career of Ted Williams.
1941	Joe DiMaggio sets an MLB record when he hits safely in fifty-six consecutive games; Ted Williams is the last player to attain a .400 batting average.
1941–1945	American participation in World War II.
1945	Branch Rickey signs Jackie Robinson of the Negro League Kansas City Monarchs to a contract with the Brooklyn Dodgers; he is assigned to a minor league team in Montreal for 1946 and is named Most Valuable Player (MVP).
1946	Yankees are first team to reach 2 million home attendance.

1947	Integration of MLB. Jackie Robinson is Rookie of the Year; in 1949 he is NL MVP. Larry Doby joins Cleveland Indians later in 1947, integrating AL. World Series is televised for the first time, on four Eastern stations. Hank Greenberg is the first MLB player to reach an annual salary of $100,000.
1949	First annual Caribbean Series, which includes teams that win "winter league" titles in several Latin American countries and Puerto Rico.
1949–1964	Yankees win fourteen AL pennants and nine World Series, including five consecutive World Series from 1949 to 1953.
1950	Vin Scully begins announcing Brooklyn Dodgers games, later moving to California with the team and remaining its voice for more than sixty years.
1950–1953	Korean War.
1951	First national television broadcast of the World Series; in 1953 national broadcasts of the *Game of the Week* begin.
1951–1968	Career of Mickey Mantle.
1951–1973	MLB career of Willie Mays. (He began his professional career in 1947 in the Negro Leagues.)
1952	Publication of Bernard Malamud's *The Natural*.
1953	Braves begin play in Milwaukee, the first of several moves and expansions over the next decade. (The Braves would move again, to Atlanta in 1966.) Owner Bill Veeck sells the St. Louis Browns to investors in Baltimore, where the team begins play as the Orioles in 1954. Players establish the Major League Baseball Players Association (MLBPA).
1954	US Supreme Court's decision in *Brown* v. *Board of Education* outlaws the segregationist practice of "separate but equal."
1954–1976	MLB career of Henry (Hank) Aaron. (Aaron's professional career began in the Negro Leagues in 1952.)
1955	Brooklyn Dodgers win their first and only World Series championship. Athletics move from Philadelphia to Kansas City; in 1968 they move again, to Oakland.
1955–1966	Career of Sandy Koufax.
1955–1972	Career of Roberto Clemente.
1956	Luis Aparicio is first Latin American player to be named Rookie of the Year, in AL.

1957	Dodgers announce move from Brooklyn to Los Angeles and New York Giants announce move to San Francisco. Both teams begin play in California in 1958.
1959	Boston Red Sox are last MLB team to integrate.
1960	Last Negro League folds.
1961	AL expands, granting two new franchises. Los Angeles (later California and Anaheim) Angels begin play in AL. Former Washington Senators relocate to become the Minnesota Twins; an expansion team begins play as new Washington Senators. (The new Senators would move to Texas in 1972.)
	Roger Maris breaks Babe Ruth's single-season home run record.
1962	MLB grants two new NL franchises: Houston Colt .45s (later Astros) and New York Mets.
1963–1986	Career of Pete Rose.
1965	The Astrodome (originally named Harris County Domed Stadium) opens in Houston as the world's first domed sports stadium. After the grass planted in it dies, an artificial playing surface (AstroTurf) is installed in 1966.
	Zoilo Versalles is the first Latin American player to be named MVP, in AL.
1966	Labor economist and unionist Marvin Miller becomes executive director of MLBPA. Sandy Koufax and Don Drysdale stage a joint holdout for higher salaries from Los Angeles Dodgers. They sign shortly before the 1966 season begins – Koufax for $125,000, Drysdale for $110,000.
1966–1993	Career of Nolan Ryan.
1967	Miller negotiates the first collective bargaining agreement between players and club owners.
1969	MLB expands again, adding Kansas City Royals and Seattle Pilots in the AL and San Diego Padres and Montreal Expos in NL. Each league is reorganized into two divisions, and a new round of playoffs, the League Championship Series, between winners of divisions in each league, now precedes the World Series. After just one season in Seattle, the Pilots are sold to a group headed by Bud Selig and moved to Milwaukee, where they begin play as the Brewers in 1970. Curt Flood refuses trade from St. Louis to Philadelphia and files lawsuit challenging reserve clause. The US Supreme Court rules against Flood in 1972.

1970	Publication of Jim Bouton's *Ball Four*.
1971	Satchel Paige becomes the first Negro Leagues player inducted into the Hall of Fame.
1972	Roberto Clemente dies in crash of plane carrying relief aid to earthquake-stricken Nicaragua; in 1973 he is inducted into the Hall of Fame, the first Latin American player so honored.
	Henry Aaron's $200,000 annual salary makes him the highest paid player.
1973	AL introduces the designated hitter (DH), who does not play in the field but bats for the pitcher.
1974	Aaron breaks Babe Ruth's career home run record.
1975	As part of strategy implemented by Miller, pitchers Andy Messersmith and Dave McNally refuse to sign contracts and challenge the reserve clause. Arbitrator Peter Seitz grants them free agency in a decision that allows players to pursue employment with other teams when their contracts expire. Salaries immediately begin to rise.
1977	AL expands, granting franchises to Seattle Mariners and Toronto Blue Jays.
1978	Los Angeles Dodgers become first team to reach 3 million home attendance.
1979	Nolan Ryan becomes first player to earn a $1 million annual salary when he signs with Houston Astros as a free agent.
1979	Entertainment Sports Programming Network (ESPN) is launched.
1981	Season interrupted by players' strike.
	Free agent Dave Winfield signs a ten-year deal with the Yankees for $23 million, then MLB's longest player contract, and its first $2 million annual salary.
1984–2007	Career of Roger Clemens.
1980s	MLB adopts rule against signing Latin American players under 17 years of age.
1985	Pete Rose breaks Ty Cobb's career record for base hits.
1986–2007	Career of Barry Bonds.
1986–2008	Career of Greg Maddux.
1989	Pete Rose banned from baseball for betting on MLB games. Release of *Field of Dreams*.
1989–2010	Career of Ken Griffey, Jr.
1991	Toronto Blue Jays become first team to reach 4 million home attendance.

1992 MLB team owners force Commissioner Fay Vincent to resign; he is replaced by Bud Selig, owner of the Milwaukee Brewers.

For the first time, baseball is a medal sport at the Summer Olympics. (In 2005 the International Olympic Committee votes that baseball and softball will no longer be medal sports after the 2008 Games.)

Opening of Orioles Park at Camden Yards in Baltimore, first of a wave of "retro" stadiums designed primarily for baseball.

Release of *A League of Their Own*.

1993 NL expands to add Colorado Rockies and Florida Marlins.

1994 AL and NL are again restructured so that each now contains three divisions. Another round of playoffs, the Division Championship Series, is added; this round is to include the winners of each division and the best second-place team (or "wild card") in each league.

A players' strike ends the season early, and no playoffs are held. It is the first cancellation of the World Series since 1904.

1994– Career of Alex Rodriguez.

1995 Hideo Nomo becomes first Japanese player to be named Rookie of the Year, in NL. Like most Japanese players crossing over to MLB, Nomo enters with years of Japanese professional experience.

1996 MLB team owners reach their first revenue-sharing agreement.

Free agent Albert Belle becomes first player to earn $10 million per year when he signs a five-year contract with the Chicago White Sox for $55 million.

1997 MLB institutes regular-season interleague games between AL and NL teams.

1998 MLB expands to include Arizona Diamondbacks (NL) and Tampa Bay Devil Rays (AL).

Mark McGwire and Sammy Sosa both break Roger Maris's single-season home run record.

1999 "Posting" system implemented for the transfer of Japanese players to MLB.

Kevin Brown signs first $100 million player contract, for seven years and $105 million, with Los Angeles Dodgers.

2000	Alex Rodriguez signs a ten-year contract with the Texas Rangers for $252 million.
2001	Ichiro Suzuki is named Rookie of the Year and MVP in AL. Barry Bonds sets new single-season home run record.
2002	As part of collective bargaining agreement between owners and players, MLB instates "luxury tax," whereby teams with high payrolls pay money into a fund that is distributed to small-market teams.
2005	Montreal Expos move to Washington and are renamed the Nationals.
	Publication of *Juiced*, in which Jose Canseco recounts his use of steroids and accuses other star players of steroid use. His accusations prompt Congressional hearings at which Rafael Palmeiro denies Canseco's charges; later in 2005 Palmeiro is suspended for testing positive for steroid use. Mark McGwire's testimony is evasive.
2006	Bonds breaks Aaron's career home run record. *Game of Shadows*, which accuses Bonds of longtime steroid use, is published.
	Japan wins the first World Baseball Classic, which brings together teams from different countries.
2007	Bonds indicted for perjury allegedly committed in 2003 when he denied using steroids under oath.
2008	MLB introduces instant replay to judge difficult home run calls.
	Roger Clemens testifies before Congress that he never took steroids or any other performance-enhancing drugs. His former trainer, Brian McNamee, also appears, and contradicts Clemens's account.
2009	After positive drug test results from 2003 are leaked to the public, Alex Rodriguez admits to using steroids from 2001 to 2003. Manny Ramirez is suspended for fifty games after testing positive for a banned drug.
2010	McGwire admits having used steroids for a number of years, including during his pursuit of the home run record in 1998. Roger Clemens is indicted for perjury and obstruction of Congress.

LEONARD CASSUTO

Introduction

Pearls Before Swine, a daily comic strip written by Californian Stephan Pastis and syndicated in more than 500 newspapers, ran a series of strips in 2005 in which one of the characters, a bear, goes on a cross-country trip to "try and find the one person who can bring this divided country together." That person turns out to be Willie Mays. "You were baseball, Mr. Mays," says the bear. "You were the greatest player in the history of the game and an icon of a past era that somehow seems better than today."[1]

The bear's view of baseball – and its inverse – lie at the heart of this book. Like many observers, the bear sees baseball as special compared to other games, and he sees baseball's glorified past as mythically different from, yet somehow still deeply connected to, its fallen present. Moreover, baseball history somehow corresponds to American history in the bear's mind: the game's great past is also the nation's. So he thinks the person most qualified to rescue the country is a long-retired baseball player.

This link to national character sets baseball apart from other American sports. It arises from baseball's much-heralded reputation as the "national pastime," but the meaning of that epithet is as hazy as that of "American Dream," another pneumatic concept that floats in the same precincts. ("National pastime" is in fact the older of the two terms, dating back to baseball's nineteenth-century beginnings. "American Dream" was coined during the Depression.) Like "American Dream," the idea of a national pastime conjures up inchoate yet idealized visions – equal parts myth and pastoral fantasy. These visions always inform, and frequently distort, views of past and present together. Murray Ross, in a well-known 1970 essay, suggests that baseball was "conceived in nostalgia" and was thus "old-fashioned from the start." The game does, says Ross, "what all good pastoral does – it creates an atmosphere in which everything exists in harmony."[2] Historically, professional baseball has exploited such associations with extraordinary dexterity.

The reality is that baseball is part sport and part business – big business. From its humble roots in boys' sandlots and men's amateur club fields, the game has become a multi-billion-dollar worldwide entertainment enterprise whose audience (and participants) extend from South America to Japan. Professional baseball players, once racially segregated, middle-class workers, are now unionized, much-scrutinized, multicultural, and wealthy. Professional baseball teams, once concentrated in the eastern United States, now spread over the continent, with leagues all over the world.

The cultural theorist Pierre Bourdieu links sports to class distinctions, with people's choices tending to "express all the differences sociologically pertinent at that moment: oppositions between the sexes, between the classes, and between class fractions." Bourdieu suggests that the more accessible a sport is, the more the "dominant class," which wants distance for itself, will disdain it – hence the elitist reputations of sports like skiing and tennis. It's striking how poorly baseball fits Bourdieu's model, for the game tends to collapse such sex and class distinctions. Baseball appears to have far more female fans than other male sports, and its male stereotypes range from loud, beer-drinking rooters to highbrow intellectuals like the political commentator George Will, who has written two books on baseball and follows the game avidly as a fan. One might say, following Bourdieu's reasoning elsewhere, that baseball possesses a kind of "cultural capital" unique among American sports that allows it to break down barriers rather than reinforcing them.[3] Truly, baseball is America's game. It's also America's prism, reflecting (and refracting) the concerns of US and greater American society over nearly two centuries. The game has received serious attention from artists, storytellers, and scholars, giving it a voluminous lore that is also unmatched in American sport.

The Cambridge Companion to Baseball sets one foot in baseball's past – both its idealized and real versions. Both are crucial, for in baseball, a deep and rich mythology not only accompanies its reality but also greatly affects it. That mythology is notably interwoven with national ideology in a way that sometimes makes the two hard to separate. (The character of Babe Ruth is a case in point: he's both a baseball legend and the hero of a quintessentially American upward mobility story, two identities that have had real-life effects on real-life people.[a]) This book also locates itself in baseball's present, as a ubiquitous social, economic, and even political presence in the culture.

The story of baseball is, in an important way, the story of the interaction between the myth of the national pastime and the reality of the baseball business. The tension between the two is what drives this book.

---

[a] See the interchapter on Babe Ruth in this volume, 45–48.

The fantastic lore of baseball begins with its founding myths, the most famous of which has Abner Doubleday inventing the game before going on to become a Civil War general. (That story, and others related to it, are debunked in the first chapter of this book, which traces the early evolution of the game's rules.) The romance of baseball's origin myths laid the foundation for a likewise romantic past full of whitewashed heroes (and I use the term "whitewashed" advisedly) from Ty Cobb to Mickey Mantle. Almost everything a boy could learn about baseball during the first half of the twentieth century was wrapped in gauze and perfumed with diamond dust. A bird flies out from under Casey Stengel's cap. St. Louis Browns owner Bill Veeck sends a midget up to hit in a major league game. (He wears uniform number 1/8.) Owners and players gallantly put aside their bats and balls to fight for freedom when Uncle Sam calls them to battle. Joe DiMaggio marries Marilyn Monroe. Jimmy Piersall runs around the bases backwards. Gambling taints baseball once in 1919, but the game expunges it. Racism is invisible until Jackie Robinson suddenly appears to defeat it.

All of these things are true – more or less. They're the kernels of some of the game's great stories. They also promote the notion that baseball is in essence a boy's game possessing a lovable innocence that it is somehow able to identify and celebrate. (This is a contradiction in terms because if you know what innocence is, then you're no longer innocent.) Baseball's place in American culture owes much to sleight of hand like this, which keeps the sport's stories clean and simple. Nevertheless, those stories have an underside that for years rarely saw the light. As Richard Crepeau details in Chapter 6, baseball's response to war was much more venal than advertised, even if Ted Williams was an actual flying ace. The little person Eddie Gaedel worked as a mascot after his one turn at bat for the Browns, drank heavily, and died young. DiMaggio's marriage didn't last long. Piersall was hospitalized for mental illness. The 1919 "Black Sox" gambling scandal harbors mysteries that have never been solved. And through it all, African Americans had to play in their own leagues because Major League Baseball was segregated – and as Matthew Jacobson demonstrates in his interchapter in this volume, racism hardly disappeared even after the game was thoroughly integrated. The Boston Red Sox, for example, didn't sign their first black player until three years after Jackie Robinson retired.

Baseball became a business almost as soon as the rules were agreed upon in the mid nineteenth century. Labor disputes were suppressed, and accounts of them downplayed. Who but the most historically immersed fans know of the challenge to Major League Baseball by the upstart Federal League in 1914? (Andrew Zimbalist discusses it in Chapter 14.) The game has zealously guarded its mythology – and its economic hegemony, which includes an antitrust exemption. It has done so even as franchise relocations have exposed the bottom-line relation of baseball teams to cities and made the economic realities of the professional game more obvious. The most notorious such move was of course the relocation of the Brooklyn Dodgers to Los Angeles in 1958, considered by David Finoli in Chapter 7 as part of a larger survey of this subject.

But the story of baseball is more complicated than a group of capitalists running a lucrative, private, and mostly secret business. Baseball really was a tool of Americanization, with all the power its mythology implies. It really did help immigrants find a place in the culture, as Samuel O. Regalado details in his account in Chapter 4 of Japanese and Mexican Americans in the early twentieth century. Baseball really has maintained a romance with its fans. It really did underlie historian Doris Kearns Goodwin's relationship with her father, as she has recounted – and, as Al Filreis points out in Chapter 9, those ties create a powerful community among fans. And as Leslie Heaphy shows in Chapter 5, the integration of baseball really did set the pace for the integration of everything else in the United States. Moreover, the US major leagues remain a holy grail for many Latin American boys today – though as Arturo J. Marcano and David P. Fidler show in Chapter 12, the search for that grail is fraught with old and new pitfalls. It's easy to be cynical, especially these days, but baseball has a special magic evident in the abundance and special character of the literature and film that surround it; these are surveyed in Chapters 2 and 8 of this book.

The essence of baseball lies in the interaction – sometimes competing, sometimes meshing – of the myth and the reality of the game against an evolving backdrop. The game's economic landscape, and with it the competition on the field, shifted drastically when arbitrator Peter Seitz granted free agency to baseball players in 1975, a series of events recounted in the interchapter following Chapter 14.

But everything had already changed for baseball a few years earlier, in 1970, when a journeyman player named Jim Bouton published a book called *Ball Four*. Bouton, a former star pitcher for the Yankees in the early sixties, lost his fastball in mid-decade and by 1969 was struggling to hang on with the Seattle Pilots, a first-year expansion club staffed by other teams' discards. During rebellious times for the nation, Bouton showed sympathy for rebellious youth ("They're concerned about the way things are and they're trying to change them") while he mounted his own rebellion against the sanitized narratives that had governed baseball up to that time.[4]

Ball Four revealed a side of baseball that no fan had ever seen. Baseball players, it turned out, drank, caroused, abused drugs (especially amphetamines, which they called "greenies"), and chased skirts – who knew?

Sportswriters knew, of course, but they had kept their knowledge under wraps. Bouton unwrapped everything with principled hilarity: he wanted baseball to be seen as it was really played, and lived. That meant revealing how general managers would squeeze player salaries before free agency gave players their economic freedom. It also meant telling on great players like his former teammate, Mickey Mantle. Bouton tells of how Mantle once hit a home run while hung over (he had gotten drunk the night before because he didn't expect to play the next day). When he got back to the dugout, Bouton reported, Mantle "squinted out at the stands and said, 'Those people don't know how tough that really was.'"[5] After *Ball Four*, they did. Nor did Bouton limit himself to prurient matters. He noted, for example, that baseball's top hitters were disproportionately black – meaning that African Americans had to be extra skillful to make it to the major leagues.

A generation of young readers grew up with a different view of baseball because of *Ball Four*. I was one of them. I read my father's copy when it was still warm off the press and hot from the scandal surrounding it. I loaned it to my friend and fifth-grade classmate, David Grant (who later became the co-author of Chapter 3 of this book). When David brought the book to school, the principal confiscated it.

"Sportswriters were upset with *Ball Four*," said Bouton in a recent interview. "They had been portraying ballplayers basically as boy scouts and now here was a guy, who obviously had better access, that was showing that they weren't boy scouts. They were angry at me for drawing new boundary lines."[6] Reviewing the book for the *New York Times*, Christopher Lehmann-Haupt said that Bouton "tells you things you never dreamed of when your father took you out to the old ballgame and bought you some peanuts and Cracker Jack."[7]

The reader "will never see the game quite the same way again," said *Times* sportswriter Robert Lipsyte, "unless he is an accomplished fantasist or thinks Jim Bouton lies."[8] Baseball Commissioner Bowie Kuhn did his best to encourage the latter view and thus preserve baseball's elastic sense of innocence. Soon after the book appeared, Kuhn summoned Bouton to his office and, Bouton says, tried to get him to sign a statement saying that his book was a "bunch of lies."[9] This call to a different kind of principal's office had an effect opposite to what Kuhn intended. The meeting, along with Bouton's open lack of contrition, was widely publicized, and generated even more press for the author and his bestselling book. For once, baseball could not restore its reliable pastoral balance. Coverage of the game changed forever, becoming more frank, more critical, and finally more human. A quarter-century after its publication, the New York Public Library named *Ball Four* one of its "books of the century."[10] Bouton, who was once widely shunned (including being banned for years from Yankees Old Timers' events), has been forgiven his honesty.

More than one writer has drawn a line that extends from *Ball Four* to *Juiced*, Jose Canseco's sensational 2005 account of steroid use in professional baseball.[11] Like Bouton, Canseco was reviled as a liar – and like Bouton, Canseco is gaining a reputation as a truth-teller, a canary in baseball's coal mine.

Bouton was an idealist, Canseco less so. Accordingly, Canseco endorses steroids, while Bouton exocoriates them as much worse than the amphetamines that players gobbled in his own time. Steroids, Bouton said in 2006, have caused "a crisis of confidence among fans that has put the integrity of the game at stake. This is worse than the 1919 Black Sox scandal. Far more games have been compromised by steroid use than ever by gambling."[12] Perhaps Bouton is right, perhaps not. Baseball's steroid era is history that is still under construction, and it's considered in this book from two overlapping angles: the history of baseball cheating (Chapter 13) and of the game's peculiar fascination with numbers (Chapter 3).

Baseball's numbers fancy led more recently to another literary exposé, Michael Lewis's 2003 *Moneyball*.[13] Lewis's description of the number-crunching that goes on in baseball teams' inner sanctums gained him some resentment for disclosing trade secrets, but nothing like the criticism that Bouton received. If *Ball Four* described players in a new light, then *Moneyball* did the same for baseball executives. It described a new reality: the twenty-first-century business of baseball.

That new reality gains full expression throughout this book, always in juxtaposition with baseball's pasts – the mythical and legendary one, and the real one. *The Cambridge Companion to Baseball* ends with two panoptic chapters that essentially recount the history of baseball's massive present, from the important perspectives of economics (Chapter 14) and mass media (Chapter 15). They bring this book's cultural tour of the game to a close.

The Cambridge Companion to Baseball is a book for fans and aficionados, but it's also for readers interested in viewing American culture through one of its most storied pursuits. Each chapter of this book reflects on a different social, historical, economic, or artistic aspect of baseball. Some chapters overlap chronologically as they focus on their particular histories (for example, Chapter 11, on Japanese and East Asian baseball, runs from the mid nineteenth century to the present, and crosses in time with most of the others). Together, the book traces a loose chronological arc that takes the game from its antebellum liftoff to its twenty-first-century on- and off-the-field turbulence. And because a book about baseball would be incomplete without the people in the game, there are a series of interchapters dispersed throughout that focus on characters who have made important contributions to the game.

None of the chapters of this book requires any prior expertise, and they may be read in many possible sequences. But a newcomer to baseball might start with Chapter 1 (which reflects on some of the game's more important rules), Chapter 14 (which traces its development as a business, along with the interchapter that follows), and Chapter 5 (a capsule history of the Negro Leagues), before going on to Chapters 2 and 8 (on literature and film). We have also placed intertextual footnotes in the volume to indicate where stories and analysis cross paths in different chapters. For example, when David F. Venturo considers the meaning of stadium design in Chapter 10 on material culture, we have provided a footnote to refer the reader to the financial battles over stadiums discussed in Chapter 7, on the changing relation between teams and cities. One may follow these notes from chapter to chapter to create alternative paths through the book.

"Get back in centerfield," the bear begs Willie Mays in *Pearls Before Swine*. "I want to return to 1957 when this was one nation." To which Mays (whose career began in the Negro Leagues) replies, "When I couldn't eat in certain restaurants?" He refuses, and the bear concludes that, "We're doomed to work this out for ourselves."[14] As I have been stressing throughout this introduction, "this" applies to baseball and the national scene at the same time. As to the baseball part, we can begin working it out by understanding the sport as a cultural phenomenon both broad and deep – and still, for all that, a fun game to watch and play. Batter up.

NOTES

1. Stephan Pastis, *Pearls Before Swine: The Crass Menagerie* (Kansas City: Andrews McNeel, 2008), 128.
2. Murray Ross, "Football Red and Baseball Green: The Heroics and Bucolics of American Sport," *Chicago Review* 22.1 (1970), 31, 32.
3. Pierre Bourdieu, *Distinctions: A Social Critique of the Judgment of Taste*, trans. Richard Nice (London: Routledge, 1984), 223, 214.
4. Jim Bouton, *Ball Four: My Life and Hard Times Throwing the Knuckleball in the Big Leagues* (New York and Cleveland: World Publishing, 1970), 145.
5. *Ibid.*, 30.
6. Shotgun Spratling, "Q&A w/Former MLB Pitcher Jim Bouton," *The Blue Workhorse*, January 20, 2010, www.blueworkhorse.com/articles/mlb/qaa-w-former-mlb-pitcher-jim-bouton.
7. Christopher Lehmann-Haupt, "Not All Peanuts and Cracker Jack, Exactly," *New York Times*, June 19, 1970, 33.
8. Robert Lipsyte, "Ball Four," *New York Times*, June 22, 1970, 67.
9. Jim Bouton, *Ball Four, Twentieth Anniversary Edition* (Hoboken: Wiley, 1990), 408.

10. Elizabeth Diefendorf, ed., *The New York Public Library's Books of the Century* (Oxford and New York: Oxford University Press, 1996), 119.

11. Jose Canseco, *Juiced: Wild Times, Rampant 'Roids, Smash Hits, and How Baseball Got Big* (New York: William Morrow, 2005).

12. Larry Stone, "Jim Bouton (seriously) raps steroids," *Seattle Times*, July 1, 2006, http://seattletimes.nwsource.com/html/mariners/2003097905_sabr01.html.

13. Michael Lewis, *Moneyball: The Art of Winning an Unfair Game* (New York: W.W. Norton, 2003).

14. Pastis, *Pearls Before Swine*, 128.

I

STEVEN P. GIETSCHIER

The rules of baseball

The roots of American baseball and the origins of the rules by which it is played remain elusive. For most of the twentieth century, casual fans were often content to accept as fact the legendary tale that Abner Doubleday had invented baseball in the village of Cooperstown, New York, in 1839. (That tale had romantic appeal because of Doubleday's later service as a Civil War general.) More serious students embraced the alternative version sportswriter Henry Chadwick first advanced in 1860: that baseball derived from rounders, a game Chadwick saw as a youth in England. Late in the twentieth century, well after scholars had discredited the Doubleday myth while leaving Chadwick's explanation intact, new research not only refuted Chadwick's rounders thesis but also presented persuasive evidence about how baseball might have begun and when its rules might first have been set in type.[1]

Rule 1.01 in the *Official Baseball Rules*[2] defines baseball as "a game between two teams of nine players each, under direction of a manager, played on an enclosed field in accordance with these rules, under jurisdiction of one or more umpires." Generically, baseball is a stick-and-ball game with the principal offense–defense confrontation matching the batter against the pitcher, who has the statistical advantage. Since baseball's rules were first codified in the nineteenth century, various rules committees have made adjustments to maintain a suitable competitive balance between offense and defense.

Simple stick-and-ball games, using either curved sticks to move a ball along the ground or straight sticks to propel a ball through the air, go back in time at least to ancient Egypt and probably further. Some scholars have attempted to connect these early activities to the modern game of baseball, but not persuasively. More advanced stick-and-ball games played in England and in Europe apparently occupy significant places in the nexus of baseball's antecedents, but exactly how the game evolved is uncertain. By the middle of the eighteenth century, children of both sexes, and perhaps adults, too, were playing a game called "base-ball" in England and maybe elsewhere. Played sometimes with a bat and sometimes without, this game existed several decades before anyone, so far as is known, published an account of its rules.

Using the word "base-ball" in print dates at least to 1744, and in 1796, a German physical educator, Johann Gutsmuths, published a description of *Ball mit Freystaten (oder das englische Base-ball)*, which translates as "ball with free station (or English base-ball)," in a comprehensive guide to the games and sports popular in his day. The game Gutsmuths described was a precursor of the modern game of baseball, albeit on a smaller scale. The pitcher stood only five or six steps from the batter, and the bases (or stations) were but ten to fifteen paces apart. The batter, using a bat about two feet long, had three tries to hit the ball and, after doing so, ran counterclockwise from base to base, the number of which depended upon the number of players. Each team got only one out before being retired. Fielders could put a batter out by catching the ball on a fly, throwing the ball to the appropriate base, or touching or hitting the runner with the ball. European settlers in North America brought this game or variations on it with them. The first description of a baseball-like game in English appeared in William Clarke's *The Boy's Own Book*, published in London in 1828 and in Boston a year later. In North America, playing base-ball did not remain solely a children's activity. By the time of the American Revolution, men had taken it up in significant numbers and were modifying how they played it to suit adult abilities.[3]

Both those who clung to the Doubleday myth and those who preferred Chadwick's version agreed that credit for first codifying baseball's rules belonged to the Knickerbocker Base Ball Club, an organization formed in New York in 1845 by merchants, lawyers, clerks, doctors, and others at liberty to leave work in mid-afternoon. Alexander Joy Cartwright, Jr., a bank teller-turned-bookseller and a charter member of the Knickerbockers, often received credit for formulating the club's rules, fourteen covering the playing of the game and six concerning administrative matters. Indeed, the National Baseball Hall of Fame inducted Cartwright in 1938 for this accomplishment as well as for his supposed efforts to spread the game to the American West. Cartwright's Hall of Fame plaque calls him the "Father of Modern Baseball" and recognizes him for three significant rules innovations: "Set bases 90 feet apart, established 9 innings as game, and 9 players as team." Later research revealed that Cartwright did not compose the club's rules, and that these rules did not include the improvements listed on Cartwright's plaque. Evidence strongly suggests that when the Knickerbockers played their version of baseball, the distance between the bases and the number of innings varied from game to game, while the number of players per side could be as few as seven or as many as eleven.[4]

Since scholars agree that several other clubs playing baseball preceded the Knickerbockers, the exact achievements of Cartwright's club and his precise role have been further muddied. He did suggest that his comrades, who had been playing ball informally since at least 1842, form themselves into a club, and he may have had a hand in writing the club's constitution and bylaws. These alone were valuable contributions, for when New Yorkers and others formed new baseball clubs in the 1850s, they followed the Knickerbockers' lead. Similarly, while the Knickerbockers' playing rules did not "invent" baseball, they did serve to improve existing practices in several ways, including establishing foul territory and outlawing the painful technique of "soaking" or "plugging," i.e., putting a runner out by hitting him with a thrown ball. Other clubs took notice. In January, 1857, fourteen clubs playing some variety of baseball in and around New York City sent representatives to a convention. Using the Knickerbockers' code as a template, the assembled delegates agreed to a uniform set of playing rules while making three major changes: fixing the distance between bases at ninety feet, setting the pitching distance at fifteen yards, and declaring the winner of a game to be the club that scored the most runs after nine innings. Although the rules have been modified many times since, these 1857 rules remain the basis for the modern game of baseball.

The setting of the rules in no way interfered with their continuing evolution, a process that continues to this day. The shape of the field and the positions of batter and pitcher illustrate aspects of that evolution, which meets the changing needs of both competition on the field and entertainment value for the fans.

The baseball infield, i.e., the area circumscribed by the four bases, has always been called a diamond, but in reality it is a square with one base located at each of its four corners. The 1857 rules defined what these bases should look like, saying that "the first, second, and third bases shall be canvas bags, painted white, and filled with sand or sawdust" and that each base had to cover a square foot. Home base and the pitcher's point, as they were then called, were marked by circular iron plates painted or enameled white. Home base became a twelve-inch square in 1868, and in 1874 it was turned forty-five degrees. In 1877, home base was moved completely into fair territory with its two rear sides lying flush along the foul lines. In the same year, the other three bases became fifteen-inch squares, and in 1887, first base and third base were moved inside the foul lines, while second base remained centered upon its corner of the diamond. Finally, in 1900, the four-sided home base became the familiar five-sided home plate, making it easier for the umpire to judge whether the pitcher had thrown the ball over the plate.[5]

The pitcher's place on the diamond was also redefined several times before it reached its modern conformation. The pitcher's position, forty-five feet from home base, was further delineated by a straight line extending two yards to each side of the pitcher's point. The pitcher had to remain behind this line as he delivered the ball, although he was not required to stand directly behind the pitcher's point. In fact, he was not required to stand still at all, and some pitchers, risking lack of control, took a short, preliminary run before releasing the ball, an approach similar to what we see today in cricket. In 1863, in an effort to restrain pitchers somewhat, the pitcher's point became a box formed by two parallel lines, four yards in length, having their mid-points at two iron plates placed fifteen and sixteen yards distant from home base, with modifications made over the following years. Over the next few years, as home base was slightly repositioned more than once, the pitcher's box also moved slightly to maintain the forty-five-foot distance to the center of home base.

Throughout the 1870s, pitchers had the advantage, and scoring declined. Since fans have always enjoying scoring, the width of the pitcher's box was reduced in 1879 from six feet to four feet, in an effort to prevent the pitcher from moving too far from side to side. For the 1881 season, the entire pitcher's box was moved back five feet, putting its front line fifty feet from home base, and in 1886 the rear line was pushed back a foot. A year later, since run scoring had continued to decline, the depth of the box was reduced to five-and-a-half feet, and the pitcher was required to begin his delivery with one foot on the back line, fifty-five feet, six inches from home base. This restriction prevented the pitcher from getting a running start. In 1893, the rules committee decided to eliminate the pitcher's box entirely, replacing it with a rubber plate, the familiar pitcher's rubber of today, fixed at today's distance of sixty feet, six inches from the back corner of home base.[6]

During these same years, the batter's position was also altered several times. The 1857 rules made the batter stand directly on "the line of the home base." In 1868, the batter was required to stand astride this line, and in 1874, the line was replaced by the batter's box, "a space of ground – located on either side of home base – six feet long by three feet wide."[7] As home base moved over the next few years, the batter's box was adjusted accordingly. In 1885, the batter's box was enlarged to six feet long by four feet wide and moved six inches closer to home base, its present configuration.

These changes to the playing field were subtle, often involving inches rather than feet, but they were meant to fine-tune the competitive relationship between the team in the field and the team at bat. Alterations to the game's basic equipment were more haphazard and often came about at the instigation of particular players.

The Knickerbockers' rules did not include specifications for the bat, but the 1857 rules did, saying that it must be round, made of wood, not more than two-and-a-half inches in diameter and "of any length to suit the striker [batter]." The bat's maximum length was set at forty inches in 1868 and forty-two inches a year later. Its maximum diameter was increased to two-and-three-quarter inches in 1894. (There have never been restrictions on its weight.) The evolution of the baseball itself is much more convoluted. The size and weight of the ball have changed many times, and the exact method of its construction, including how resilient it should be, has often been shrouded in secrecy. The 1857 rules required the ball to weigh "not less than 6 nor more than 6¼ ounces" and to measure "not less than 10 nor more than 10¼ inches in circumference." Further changes came in 1859, 1861, 1868, and 1871. In the 1872 rules, the ball's weight was set at five to five-and-a-quarter ounces and its circumference at nine to nine-and-a-quarter inches, specifications that remain to this day.[a]

The quest for equilibrium between offense and defense also involved protracted tinkering with the playing rules, including, among other provisions, how the pitcher was to deliver the ball, how batters and runners could be put out, and how such crucial concepts as balls and strikes and fair and foul balls would be defined. Under the 1857 rules, as in earlier versions of the game, pitchers had to deliver or "pitch" the ball with a locked-wrist, underhand motion, the intent being for the pitcher to lob the ball toward home base so that the batter could easily put it into play, and the fielders could demonstrate their skill. Shortly thereafter, Jim Creighton, playing for the Niagara Club in New York, developed a low, swift delivery that became known as "speed pitching." In technical violation of the rules, Creighton imperceptibly snapped his wrist as he brought his right arm around. Since Creighton pitched with both speed and accuracy, he and his imitators changed the game dramatically. Pitchers began to challenge batters and chafed at the rules that confined their deliveries. Their desire to carve out a larger competitive role for themselves transformed baseball from casual recreation to intense contest.

In an effort to restrain pitchers, the rules changed in 1863, introducing (along with the pitcher's box) a requirement that the pitcher have both feet on the ground when delivering the ball. Interpreting this rule was hard, and many games ended prematurely with one team leaving the field in protest.

---

[a] For more on the changing materials, sizes, and shapes of balls, bats, and gloves, see "Baseball and material culture" in this volume, 141–143.

Figure 1. An artist's rendering of a game between the Brooklyn Atlantics and Cincinnati Red Stockings in 1870. Note the positions of the players and umpire, and the pitcher's underhanded delivery. Transcendental Graphics/theruckerarchive.com.

Rules makers had no recourse but to grant pitchers additional leeway. In 1872, the rules were amended to permit a bent-arm delivery and to allow pitchers to release the ball sidearm from as high as their hips. Pitchers persisted in pushing the limits, and when catchers began to wear protective equipment (such as masks in the 1870s and chest protectors in the early 1880s), overhand throwing, as opposed to underhand pitching, became practical. The 1883 rules allowed pitching from shoulder height, and in 1885, the rules legalized overhand deliveries. Coupling these modifications with the change from a pitcher's box to a mound in 1893 resulted in the kind of pitching we see today.

The pattern illustrated by these rules changes – of frequent adjustment to achieve a desirable balance between offense and defense – is also reflected in the evolution of rules on strikes and balls. The 1857 rules allowed the umpire to call strikes but not balls. The batter was supposed to request a pitch in a precise location. If the pitcher complied and the batter swung and missed, that was a strike; if the pitcher complied and the batter did not swing, the umpire could opt to call a strike; and if the pitcher missed the requested spot, he simply had to deliver again. Soon, pitchers began to tempt batters with pitches deliberately wide of the mark, and batters retaliated by declining to swing at all, sometimes for minutes on end, threatening the entertainment value of the spectacle. The first attempt at resolving this impasse came in 1863. If the pitcher repeatedly failed to deliver hittable pitches, the umpire could warn him and call the next unsatisfactory pitch a ball. If the pitcher persisted, the umpire could call two more balls after which the batter would be awarded first base (a "walk"). Since umpires were reluctant to issue such warnings, the waiting game continued. In 1874, the rules makers expanded the definition of an unfair pitch. By 1875, every third "ball," however delivered, became a called ball, so that a batter, in effect, would walk on nine balls. Over the next few years, the number of balls and strikes allowed changed several times until, in 1889, the rule book settled on the familiar four balls and three strikes.

Concurrent with this tinkering came the development of the strike zone. After umpires gained the power to call balls as well as strikes, they were still disinclined to call a strike even if the pitch was very good. In short, no one knew exactly what a called strike looked like. Starting in 1871, the rules forced a batter to call either for a "high pitch" or a "low pitch," creating, in effect, two strike zones. If the pitcher delivered the ball into the requested area and the batter did not swing, the umpire had to call a strike. In 1885, calling for high or low pitches was eliminated, and batters had to defend one standard strike zone stretching from the shoulder to the knee. Both the top of the strike zone and its bottom have been adjusted several times since.

The 1857 rules also declared that any batted ball initially hitting the ground in fair territory was a fair ball. This rule gave rise to the "fair/foul," a ball landing first in fair territory and then spinning away into foul territory. "Fair/fouls" were controversial because they were difficult to defend and because umpires found them hard to judge. In 1877, the rules were changed: "A batted ball striking in foul territory and then in fair is fair; a batted ball striking fair and then foul is foul." This, with some clarifications, is the modern rule. Batters were also advantaged because neither the Knickerbockers' rules nor the 1857 rules counted a foul ball as a strike. Batters thus could try to avoid strikes by attempting to drive good pitches foul. Rules makers introduced the batter's box in an attempt to confine the batter and make hitting deliberate fouls more difficult, but adept batters could still do so. The rule that any foul with fewer than two strikes on the batter had to be called a strike was late to appear. It entered the National League in 1901, and the American League in 1903.

By the turn of the twentieth century, the basic rules of modern baseball were almost entirely in place. Significant changes since then have come sporadically. Starting in 1902, for example, umpires were empowered to call an automatic ball if the pitcher failed to deliver a pitch within a certain amount of time, at first twenty seconds. (The time today is set at twelve seconds, but the rule is rarely enforced, so games can run long. One may expect this threat to entertainment value to be addressed in coming years.[b]) The 1903 rules first limited the height of the pitching mound to fifteen inches. Starting in 1920, pitchers were forbidden to doctor the baseball or apply any foreign substance to it, with an exemption granted to all "bona fide spitball

---

[b] For a related discussion of the length of current games, see "Baseball and mass media" in this volume, 237–238.

pitchers" then active. The last legal spitballer was Burleigh Grimes, affectionately called "Ol' Stubblebeard." He threw his last spitball in 1934. In 1931, fair balls bouncing into the stands became two-base hits instead of home runs, and fly balls leaving the playing field were declared to be fair or foul (that is, home runs or foul balls) according to their position when they left the field.

Several twentieth-century rules changes concerned players' safety, while others, once again, addressed the delicate balance between batter and pitcher. Some batters had begun wearing protective headgear in the 1940s, but using a batting helmet did not become mandatory until 1971. (Even then, a grandfather clause allowed current players who had not worn helmets to refuse to wear one.) By the end of the first decade of the twenty-first century, some batters were wearing helmets with two flaps plus additional devices to shield their forearms, elbows, and ankles.

In 1969, following several years of declining offensive production, rules makers handicapped pitchers by lowering the height of the pitcher's mound to ten inches. The American League took an additional step toward boosting offense in 1973 by introducing the designated hitter, a tenth player assigned to bat for the starting pitcher and all relief pitchers "without otherwise affecting the status of the pitcher(s) in the game."[8] Starting in 1978, umpires were given authority to judge whether or not a pitcher had deliberately thrown at a batter. In this situation, the umpire was to warn both teams that the next such attempt would result in an ejection. In 1988, this authority was extended to permit ejection on the first offense.

These various restrictions on pitchers altered the balance between offense and defense. Pitchers became reluctant to throw inside (i.e., close to the batter), and batters felt more confident about digging in at the plate. Umpires compensated by shifting the de facto borders of the strike zone, moving it lower and off the outside edge of the plate. By the late 1990s, critics complained that umpires had gone too far. Too many pitches once called balls were now strikes, in this view, and individual umpires had too much freedom to define their own strike zone regardless of what the rule book said. In 2001, Major League Baseball began to install electronic technology in some ballparks to help standardize each umpire's conception of the strike zone. This procedure appeared to work, at least to the extent that it mitigated criticism of called balls and strikes, but televised replays of other close and controversial calls exposed umpires to additional scorn. In 2008, Major League Baseball introduced instant replay, allowing umpires to consult television monitors to help judge difficult home run calls. It seems likely that the role of technology in regulating the play of the game is still in flux.

Even before it became a professional sport, baseball created an administrative structure beyond the playing field to govern who could play the game and under what conditions. In 1858, one year after fourteen New York clubs held their first convention, twenty-two clubs from the New York area sent representatives to a second convention. Besides amending the playing rules, these delegates organized the National Association of Base Ball Players (NABBP), the sport's first governing authority, run by players. The constitution and bylaws established the conditions under which other clubs could seek admission. A club needed at least eighteen members to join the Association. Applicants approved by a two-thirds vote were allowed two delegates and two votes, and club dues were set at five dollars per year. In this fashion, the Association grew rapidly to become a true national organization, adding clubs from all over the country and forming state and regional associations. The tenth convention of the NABBP, held in December, 1866, attracted representatives from hundreds of clubs, mostly from the northeastern USA but some as far away as Kansas, Oregon, and Tennessee. The following year, the convention accepted a report from its nominating committee barring the admission of any club with one or more African American members.[c] The Association's code also governed the eligibility and conduct of individual players, each of whom had to be a member of a club for thirty days before being allowed to play in a game against another Association club. No player was allowed to bet on the outcome of a game. The players remained amateurs: no one could play who had received compensation to do so. This latter rule proved difficult to maintain. The best players began to realize that their sport no longer had to remain an amateur endeavor, and in succeeding years baseball evolved from amateur entertainment to professional business.

The NABBP remained baseball's central administrative body through the 1870 season, but it was unable to manage changes transforming the game. People were willing to pay to watch baseball games, and clubs, amateur in name only now, proved willing to compensate players for their talent. At first, paying players was illegal under Association rules and was done surreptitiously, but after a while some clubs paid players openly. Moreover, as clubs de-emphasized fellowship and put more stress on winning, professional baseball was infected by three ills: gambling; "revolving," i.e., players moving suddenly from one club to another offering more money; and "hippodroming," two clubs taking turns losing to one another while giving the impression of competing honestly, in an effort to boost fan interest. The

---

[c] African Americans went on to develop their own baseball organizations. For an account of these, see "Baseball and the color line" in this volume, 61–75.

Association had no enforcement mechanism for dealing with these problems, especially given its commitment to amateurism. So, in 1871, professional players from ten clubs broke away from the NABBP to form the National Association of *Professional* Base Ball Players (NAPBBP) to govern their own affairs. Amateur clubs endured, but the best players gravitated toward the professional game.

The NAPBBP, better known as the National Association, was run by players like its predecessor, and it suffered from some of the same problems. Nine clubs formed a league, and each pledged to play about thirty games against other league clubs. However, the National Association had little authority to ensure that games be played as scheduled. Clubs pleading lack of funds often declined to travel to distant cities, especially near the end of a season. Players felt free to engage in rowdy play, and gambling, revolving, and hippodroming continued. After five seasons, the National Association was in shambles, and William A. Hulbert, who had a financial interest in one club, the Chicago White Stockings, led a movement to form the National League of Professional Baseball Clubs. This was an organization of clubs, not players, run by owners, not athletes. Baseball had evolved from a game into a business.

Hulbert invited only strong clubs to join the League, and each became a franchise within a monopoly. Every club played a set schedule under pain of expulsion, and each respected the others' territorial rights, eschewing any games against non-league clubs in any other league city. The League also eliminated revolving by prohibiting any club from signing a player under contract to another league club. Within a few seasons, clubs gave themselves an additional weapon: the option to renew a player's contract for the following season without his consent. Inserted into the standard contract was a "reserve clause" that rolled over the contract automatically, thereby depriving players of the right to change clubs freely. In 1883, the League signed the first National Agreement setting up itself and the American Association as major leagues and the Northwestern League as a subordinate minor league. This hierarchical structure, still intact, marked the beginning of Organized Baseball. The American Association expired after the 1891 season, and the American League joined the National League as a second major league in 1901.[d]

The reserve clause gave major league club owners complete control over baseball's labor supply. Clubs decided to whom they would offer employment and under what conditions. Over several decades, organized baseball

---

[d] These developments are chronicled from a different perspective in this volume, in "Baseball's economic development," 201–203.

devised elaborate regulations to govern player recruitment, movement from one club to another and, once minor leagues proliferated, from one level of competition to another. Clubs asserted that the reserve clause bound players in perpetuity, and when the United States Supreme Court decided in 1922 that baseball was not a business subject to antitrust regulation, players had little legal recourse. Even after the Major League Baseball Players Association, a union founded in 1953, negotiated its first collective bargaining agreement in 1967, the reserve clause still held sway. Players gained some leverage when the 1970 collective bargaining agreement mandated arbitration of disputes. After the 1974 season, two pitchers, Andy Messersmith and Dave McNally, challenged the reserve clause.[e] After that season, both players filed grievances arguing that the reserve clause in a signed contract could not be enforced beyond one option year. The arbitrator agreed, granting players the right to play out their options and become free agents. Over the next several collective bargaining agreements, the leagues and the union negotiated the terms under which players could become free agents, eventually arriving at a system that basically allowed free agency after six major league seasons.

This evolving balance of power between labor and management parallels the one between offense and defense on the field. Indeed, one may say that the story of how organized baseball is played, and by whom, constitutes a dynamic, and malleable history that has always been under construction. It is a history that permeates American culture, as the following chapters in this book will show.

NOTES

1. Historical research into the origins of baseball and its antecedent games is ongoing. Readers who want to explore the refutation of the rounders thesis should start with David Block, *Baseball before We Knew It: A Search for the Roots of the Game* (Lincoln: University of Nebraska Press, 2005) and then examine the work of Project Protoball (www.retrosheet.org/Protoball/index.htm), an attempt to build and maintain an online database documenting "baseball-like" games up to the time of the American Civil War. The Doubleday myth is omnipresent in twentieth-century baseball literature. See, for example, Robert Smith, *Baseball: A Historical Narrative of the Game, the Men who Have Played It, and Its Place in American Life* (New York: Simon and Schuster, 1947). The first researcher to question the Doubleday story was Robert W. Henderson, *Ball, Bat, and Bishop: The Origin of Ball Games* (New York: Rockport, 1947). Chadwick's contributions are thoroughly discussed in Andrew J. Schiff, *"The Father of Baseball": A Biography of Henry Chadwick* (Jefferson, NC: McFarland, 2008).

[e] The interchapter on Andy Messersmith, Charlie Finley, and George Steinbrenner, 216–20 in this volume, traces the eventual dissolution of the reserve clause at this time.

2. Available at http://mlb.mlb.com/mlb/official_info/official_rules/foreword.jsp.

3. Block, *Baseball before We Knew It*, 67–75. Other scholars render "Gutsmuths" as "Guts Muths."

4. Harold Peterson, *The Man who Invented Baseball* (New York: Charles Scribner's Sons, 1973) lays out the case for Cartwright, but contains little documentation. Monica Nucciarone, *Alexander Cartwright: The Life behind the Baseball Legend* (Lincoln: University of Nebraska Press, 2009) is a much-needed corrective, weighing all the evidence with great care.

5. On all of these adjustments to the playing field, see Tom Shieber, "The Evolution of the Baseball Diamond," in *Total Baseball*, ed. John Thorn and Pete Palmer with Michael Gershman, 4th edn. (New York: Viking, 1995), 113–124.

6. Peter Morris, *A Game of Inches: The Stories behind the Innovations that Shaped Baseball*, 2 vols., Vol. 1: *The Game on the Field* (Chicago: Ivan R. Dee, 2006), 100–107.

7. Shieber, "Evolution of the Baseball Diamond," 116.

8. The National League stood alone among professional leagues by declining to adopt the designated hitter, but, starting in 1978, the designated hitter was mandated for use in World Series play on an every-other-year basis. In 1986, the rule changed with the designated hitter used in every World Series game hosted by an American League club.

2

STEPHEN PARTRIDGE AND TIMOTHY MORRIS

Baseball in literature, baseball as literature

It's hard to read an American classic without finding some mention of baseball. The most famous reference is in *The Great Gatsby* (1925), where Nick Carraway marvels at how Gatsby's associate Meyer Wolfshiem fixed the 1919 World Series "with the single-mindedness of a burglar blowing a safe."[1] In the great novel of the American Dream, it seems inevitable that Nick Carraway's musings on innocence and disillusionment should encompass baseball. Allusions to baseball range from a mention of Arnold Rothstein – the real-life model for Fitzgerald's Wolfshiem – in Dashiell Hammett's *The Maltese Falcon* (1930), to a chapter relating a rowdy game at the Polo Grounds in E. L. Doctorow's *Ragtime* (1975). Marianne Moore and Robert Pinsky, among many others, have written poetry about baseball, and a leading character in one of August Wilson's most important plays, *Fences* (1983), is a former player in the Negro Leagues. A rich tradition of American nonfiction about baseball includes work by Donald Hall and John Updike.

While baseball allusions and work in other genres offer rewarding venues for criticism, this chapter focuses specifically on fiction devoted to the game. It will introduce the most accomplished examples from the relatively small canon of literary fiction about baseball, but will suggest that these can best be understood in relationship to a much larger body of juvenile, pulp, and genre fiction about baseball. Baseball writing existed largely in the realm of the popular in the first half of the twentieth century, but after World War II there evolved a recognizable high-art tradition as well. Although these high and low traditions of baseball writing have often been discussed separately, they have proved to be mutually enriching, with the literary evolving out of the popular, and in turn providing further models for its predecessor, particularly in the area of children's fiction of the past generation. Considering

Timothy Morris wishes especially to thank Trey Strecker for bibliographical advice, and Gyde Martin for teaching him some frameworks for reading juvenile literature.

these two strands together shows more clearly the work that baseball fiction does in American culture.[2]

Baseball's literary tradition in America began with the juvenile fiction and sports reportage and pulp fiction for adults that emerged in the latter years of the nineteenth century and the early years of the twentieth. Juvenile baseball fiction flourished in the first three decades of the twentieth century. The most entertaining and influential baseball juveniles from the 1910s and 1920s are the Baseball Joe series. Published under the pseudonym "Lester Chadwick" (perhaps Howard R. Garis, perhaps syndicate-master Edward Stratemeyer himself), the Baseball Joe books combined a boys'-adventure core with unbelievable baseball action.[3] The series, which began in 1912 and eventually ran to fourteen volumes, follows the career of hero Joe Matson from the sandlots to boarding school, Yale, the minors, into the majors, and on to many championships with the New York Giants.

"Matson" was a thinly veiled version of the surname of the great Giant pitcher Christy Mathewson, whose experiences provide the template for the early books in the series. After *Baseball Joe in the World Series* (1917), however, the exploits of the fictional Matson and the historical Mathewson parted company. Joe Matson would continue to star agelessly in series fiction until 1928, three years after Mathewson's death. When the real-life game began to emphasize slugging over pitching in a pinch, Joe reinvented himself as *Baseball Joe, Home Run King* (1922). In this and subsequent volumes, he not only leads the league in all pitching categories, but breaks all major league home-run records, even those newly set by Yankee slugger "Kid Rose," an obvious *nom à clef* for Babe Ruth.

The game scenes in the Baseball Joe series are both rudimentary and preposterous. Triple plays, perfect games, and other rarities of the baseball world occur on a regular basis. The game sequences take the form of manager McRae (a genial version of scrappy and profane Giants manager John McGraw) exhorting his team to try their hardest, and the team proceeding to do just that on their way to victory. The Baseball Joe novels set a pattern for subsequent baseball fiction, in that what is really of interest are the off-field exploits of the hero. Joe Matson courts and wins the beautiful Mabel Varley, but when he marries Mabel, he gives a hostage to fortune – or, more precisely, a hostage to various kidnappers who abduct her in hopes of throwing Joe off his game. When kidnapping loses its appeal, Joe's enemies resort to trying to run him over, forcing his car off the road, braining him with rocks, beating him up in dark alleys, and eventually sending him venomous snakes via parcel post and inventing a ray gun to drain the power from his pitching arm.

In a succession of early Baseball Joe volumes, the villain of the piece is a jealous teammate. On team after team as he rises from amateur ball to the majors, Joe must displace the resident pitching ace in order to achieve glory. The rival typically resents his displacement, and resorts to increasingly out-landish skulduggeries to avenge himself on Joe. As the series matures, Joe becomes the undisputed ace of the champion Giants, and there's nobody left to resent him. The locus of villainy shifts to gamblers, especially in the wake of the 1919–20 Black Sox scandal, leading to Joe's stand against game-fixing in *Baseball Joe Saving the League* (1923). Amazingly, Joe's unimpeachable conduct is not proof against future fixers. He fends off further gamblers in *Baseball Joe, Captain of the Team* (1924) and *Baseball Joe, Champion of the League* (1925), spurring their more-and-more desperate attempts to do away with him. By mixing baseball action with informal crime-fighting, the Baseball Joe novels establish a presence both in boys' sport fiction and boys' detective fiction – a mixing of genres that has characterized much of base-ball literature in the subsequent century. Moreover, for all their corniness and unrealistic portrayal of baseball action, the novels provided baseball literature with an array of plots and characters known to most male writers who grew up in the first half of the twentieth century. These authors might choose to resist rather than adopt the series' clichés, but the patterns estab-lished by Baseball Joe exerted great influence on the shape of subsequent baseball fiction.

Sometimes duplicating, sometimes adding to this stock of conventions for baseball fiction was the adult pulp story. Magazine and newspaper writers like Charles Van Loan, Ring Lardner, and Heywood Broun produced briskly written, formulaic sport fiction for the popular press in the early 1900s.[4] Van Loan, Lardner, and Broun aimed their stories at middlebrow or higher audiences, but the failure of the literary mainstream to use them as models suggests that its artists found even the best baseball stories indistinguishable from the formulaic fiction that appeared in adult publications like *Sport Story Magazine* in the 1920s. When Lardner died in 1933, F. Scott Fitzgerald remarked that "Ring moved in the company of a few dozen illiterates play-ing a boys' game,"[5] a dismissal that revealingly brought together the juvenile and the sub-literate.

Contra Fitzgerald, Lardner today is regarded as the first to write a sub-stantial body of true literature about baseball. He did belong, however, to a generation of writers who moved readily among pulps, juveniles, sports writing, and serious fiction.[6] Tales by the likes of Harold de Polo, Stanley Frank, and others center on a few tried-and-true elements: the fresh busher ready to crack the major leagues, the grizzled veteran out for a last come-back, the oddball player (often a spy, cop, grifter, or genius in disguise), and the averting of gambling scandals. The shifting nature of baseball team rosters enabled a standard formula for an early-century baseball story like

Van Loan's "Mister Conley" (1919) or Lardner's "The Poor Simp" (1915), where veterans torment a rookie from the sticks. Lardner's *You Know Me Al* (1916) offered the definitive "busher" character in the person of Jack Keefe, the garrulous, conceited overreacher whose charm lies in his aggressive innocence. In Gerald Beaumont's "Tin Can Tommy" (1921, where he is potrayed comically), and Lardner's "My Roomy" (1914, where he is more sinister), the "busher" character reveals extraordinary quirks that threaten his teammates' composure or even their well-being.

We can detect in Lardner's Jack Keefe certain characteristics that will survive in other fictional ballplayers. A country boy gone to the big city, he is in some ways innocent but not harmless. He is overconfident in his ability to manage opponents, booze, women, teammates, managers, and owners. Lardner, who began as a sports reporter, portrays Keefe as a fictional character in completely recognizable major and minor leagues. He faces opponents such as Ty Cobb, with whom he has a special rivalry; tangles with manager McGraw during an all-star team's tour of the American West; and negotiates his contracts with the shrewd and stingy White Sox owner, Charles Comiskey. But there are elements of caricature in Lardner's portraits of all of them, and they reappear either as themselves or as stock types in later fiction. Lardner makes topical issues into important elements; during the years of the Federal League challenge, Keefe several times threatens (unsuccessfully) to jump teams, and in one sequel ("Call for Mr. Keefe!" [1918]), he is drafted for service in World War I. The final sequel, "Along Came Ruth" (1919), reveals Lardner's prescience that the players of the dead-ball era, which we now regard as one golden age of baseball, were about to give way to the sluggers of a new day. Keefe recounts a game against the Red Sox when he remained on the pitcher's mound too long to avert disaster: "Well Al I didn't get one anywhere near close for Strunk and walked him and it was Ruth's turn. The next thing I seen of the ball it was sailing into the right field bleachers where the black birds sets. And that's all I seen of the ball game."[7]

As pulp fiction has evolved into the ever more specialized genres of contemporary mass-market fiction, writers (and publishers) have readily appropriated baseball themes. The pulp-like energy of the Baseball Joe series was channeled in the first baseball mystery novel for adults, Cortland Fitzsimmons's *Death on the Diamond* (1934), but it was after World War II that the market for mysteries, including those about baseball, really flourished. Aaron Marc Stein, writing as George Bagby, kicked off the postwar baseball-mystery genre with *Twin Killing* (1947), establishing the inexhaustible potential of baseball puns for mystery titles. Leading crime fiction writers have turned their hands to baseball mysteries, including Rex Stout, who set a baseball puzzle for Nero Wolfe to solve in 1953 ("This Won't Kill You"). This baseball-mystery genre-mixing has continued to the present. Paul Auster, before achieving fame, published the mass-market mystery *Squeeze Play* in 1982. Mystery is not the only genre that has taken up baseball. There have also been baseball romances – where the reuse of *Squeeze Play* as a title by Kate Angell (2006) has perhaps lost the advantage of surprise – along with baseball westerns, Civil War novels, science fiction, and vampire/werewolf stories and novels.[8]

As for the evolution of popular fiction, the years immediately after World War II were crucial for the rise of baseball fiction to literary respectability. Frank O'Rourke's stories and novels, including the collection *Flashing Spikes* (1948) and the novel *The Team* (1949), combined gritty realism and whimsy (usually not in the same story). Murrell Edmunds, in *Behold, Thy Brother* (1950), provided a serious look at integration in the majors. Lucy Kennedy's *The Sunlit Field* (1950) was the first exhaustively documented historical treatment of the sport in fiction, recreating pre-Civil-War baseball in Brooklyn, with cameos by figures like Walt Whitman.

Bernard Malamud's Pulitzer-winning *The Natural* (1952) is, however, the baseball novel from this period that remains best known (thanks in part to the 1984 film adaptation, considered elsewhere in this volume[a]), best regarded, and most clearly indebted to the stock narratives and characters of popular baseball stories. In a spirit of affectionate parody, Malamud packs his novel with pulp motifs, such as covers torn off balls, outfielders killed by fence crashes, improbable heroics and failures on the field, and a gambling fix – elements that provide much of the book's energy. *The Natural* begins as a story of the country boy, Roy Hobbs, on his way to Chicago for a tryout. But it turns to tragedy, failure, and disillusionment. First, at one of the train's stops, Hobbs strikes out The Whammer, an obnoxious batting champion he has met on the train to Chicago, but his third pitch accidentally kills his catcher, the scout who has mentored him and arranged the tryout. Then, after his arrival, Hobbs is shot in his hotel by an obsessed female fan. Having lost his big chance – and his innocence – he only returns to the majors fifteen years later, when he is signed to bolster the woeful New York Knights. Although he is now older, wary, and cynical, Hobbs experiences familiar rookie trials and triumphs. These include practical jokes by veteran teammates, the contempt of an arrogant rival, and skepticism from manager and coaches, until he is finally given a chance to crack the lineup when that rival, Bump Bailey, makes his fatal charge into the outfield wall.

---

[a] See "Baseball at the movies" in this volume, 111–124.

In the same spirit of excess that characterizes his use of pulp-fiction motifs, Malamud loads the book with allusions to deep cultural myths. Early on, for example, Hobbs is compared to Perceval, who in medieval romance comes from rustic origins to become the greatest of King Arthur's knights and achieve the quest of the Grail.[9] Just as Perceval is the only knight with the power to make the waste land fertile again, Hobbs's home runs seemingly pierce the sky to bring rain (and victory) after weeks of drought, literal and figurative, that have afflicted the Knights. Moreover, Malamud draws on a third source of allusion, namely major league baseball history. Here too, as David McGimpsey has pointed out, Malamud's allusions are many: the Black Sox scandal, a woman's shooting of a pro player in 1949, the 1908 baserunning error by a New York Giants rookie immortalized as Merkle's Boner (about which more below). Malamud's version of Merkle's boner is "Fisher's Flop," a years-ago tumble by Hobbs's manager halfway to home plate in a crucial game.[10] The star's brief, hyperbolic speech on Roy Hobbs Day (held so fans could urge the stubborn Giants owner, a stock type, to raise Hobbs's rookie salary) evokes Lou Gehrig's farewell to New York Yankees fans at a famous ceremony held in his honor after he was diagnosed with a fatal illness. A reader begins to see every element in the book carrying the weight of multiple allusions: when Hobbs, who was first scouted as a pitcher, enjoys his biggest success as a slugger, we recall not only the career of Babe Ruth but also the fictional trajectories of Baseball Joe and of Roy Tucker, protagonist of John R. Tunis's darker juvenile fiction, *The Kid from Tomkinsville* (1940).

While Malamud's narrative regularly invokes the magical, Mark Harris follows a very different path in his Henry Wiggen series. These books include *The Southpaw* (1953) and *Bang the Drum Slowly* (1956) – the latter, like *The Natural*, given additional fame by a film adaptation (1973) – as well as a novella and a coda novel in the 1970s. Unlike Hobbs, Wiggen plays a recognizable game of baseball in a realistic, if thinly fictionalized, major league. One consequence of Harris's insistence on realism is that his novels draw significant meaning from the details of their fictional contests. Wiggen's narrative voice blends Lardner's Jack Keefe and James Farrell's proletarian everyman of the 1930s, Studs Lonigan, with debts to Huckleberry Finn and other literary voices of the American vernacular. Like many juvenile heroes before him – very much like Baseball Joe – Henry succeeds by dint of plain speaking and a strong pitching arm. But his world is unlike Baseball Joe's in that friends go their own ways or even die, women prove more nuisance than consolation, and children disappoint.

In the decades since *The Natural* and *The Southpaw*, the serious baseball novel has ranged between the magical and realistic, with many of the best-known instances combining elements of both. Furthermore, the theme of innocence and its loss has continued to figure prominently in this tradition. Significant new trends have also appeared, including a shift toward the perspective and experience of the spectator, rather than the player, and an interest in revisiting baseball's (and America's) history. In one of the best postmodern novels about baseball, Robert Coover's *The Universal Baseball Association* (1968), there is no actual baseball, just a dice game that a certain J. Henry Waugh plays on his kitchen table – a game that becomes more real than life itself. A motif in this and in several other notable postmodern novels is that of a team or league of misfits, a page of baseball's past that has been discarded or suppressed by official historians.

The most familiar such foray into revisionist history is *Shoeless Joe* (1982) by the Canadian author W. P. Kinsella. *Shoeless Joe* is one of many baseball fictions that aim to redeem, rather than revile, the "Black Sox" players who threw the 1919 Series.[11] Again, a film adaptation (*Field of Dreams* [1989], discussed in Chapter 8) has greatly increased the novel's popularity. In *Shoeless Joe*, protagonist Ray Kinsella hears a voice saying "If you build it, he will come." Instead of seeking therapy, Ray proceeds to construct a baseball diamond in a cornfield, where the ghosts of Joe Jackson and other old-timers do appear to play. Building "it" enables Ray to revisit and rewrite baseball's past together with his family's past, as he is reunited with his estranged brother and his father, a former minor leaguer who in his ghostly form finally gets to play with Jackson and other greats. Kinsella invokes baseball's rural myth and its associations with innocence when Ray's farm, which he is fighting to hold onto, becomes a refuge for Jackson the naive Black Sox scapegoat and a venue for the psychic healing of Ray and his family.

Baseball novels identified more with the realistic tradition have also addressed baseball's past and indeed have often taken the form of historical fiction. There may well be pragmatic reasons for this. Readers are so familiar, through media coverage, with contemporary baseball that it may be more difficult for writers to create persuasive fictions set in the present day. In baseball novels set in the distant past, by contrast, writers have more freedom to make it up and have it still sound true.

Moreover, writers increasingly have employed the traditional baseball theme of lost innocence to explore change not only at a personal but also at a collective level. A few examples will illustrate the range of ways writers juxtapose themes of mutability in the lives of individuals, in the game of baseball, and in American society generally.

Perhaps the most distinguished of all realistic baseball novels is *The Celebrant* (1983), by Eric Rolfe Greenberg. Like the Baseball Joe series,

The Celebrant is based on the career of New York Giants pitcher Christy Mathewson, but Greenberg's technique is obsessively realistic. Every aspect of Mathewson's career and context is painstakingly recreated: dress, cuisine, transport, baseball equipment, and the fluent profanity of manager McGraw. The protagonist and narrator, however, is not Mathewson himself but Jackie Kapp, Jewish jewelry designer, who admires Mathewson from a discreet distance, fashioning rings for him that commemorate his Baseball-Joe-like triumphs. (In a metafictional touch, Greenberg has Jackie's Yiddish-accented Uncle Sid continually refer to the pitcher as "Matson.") Near its end, the Baseball Joe series lapsed into anti-Semitism, and Greenberg's treatment of Kapp and his family seems another aspect of his response to Baseball Joe's fictional version of Mathewson. While Kapp and his brother Eli, in particular, experience ugly prejudice from some ballplayers and others, Mathewson's generous appreciation of Kapp's artistry distinguishes him and forms another aspect of his heroism.

Drawing on historical accounts, Greenberg narrates, from Kapp's perspective, five games, around which he organizes the novel's narrative and thematic structures. The first two are among Mathewson's most notable triumphs: a no-hitter pitched against St. Louis in 1901, and one of his three shutouts for the victorious Giants in the 1905 World Series. The third is the 1908 late-season game against the Cubs that ended in a tie – a real-life instance of a baseball oddity – because of the baserunning blunder that sportswriters dubbed "Merkle's Boner." The mistake, and the Cubs' second baseman's clever appeal to an obscure rule that persuaded the umpire to call Merkle out, ultimately allowed the Cubs to beat out the Giants for the National League pennant. The fourth game recounted by Greenberg is one Mathewson lost to the Boston Red Sox in the 1912 World Series. Finally, there is a 1919 World Series game between the Reds and the White Sox, when the retired Mathewson, sitting with reporter Hugh Fullerton, records apparently intentional physical and mental errors by the players who would become infamous as the "Black Sox."

This summary makes clear the book's trajectory of decline: decline in Mathewson's powers, in the team he plays for, and in baseball's integrity as it fails to purge itself of gamblers and corrupt players. The decline is first gradual, then precipitous and catastrophic. Mathewson, after he retires from playing, manages the Reds for only a short time before resigning in the wake of a gambling scandal (in which he is not implicated) that presages the Black Sox episode. Then, when he enlists to fight in World War 1, he is gassed in a training exercise, and disabled; only after a long convalescence is he able to attend the 1919 Series. A "Coda" to the novel acknowledges his premature death in 1925. While the Kapps' jewelry business thrives, Jackie

Kapp suffers terrible family losses, including the death of his child in the influenza epidemic that follows the war. Jackie's brother Eli is forced out of the family firm for gambling and is then ruined and driven to suicide by his wager on the White Sox in the fixed Series.

Philip Roth's *American Pastoral* (1997) is not strictly a baseball fiction, but it shares a number of themes with *The Celebrant*. The narrator, Roth's alter ego Nathan Zuckerman, recounts the life story of "Swede" Lvov, who stars as a slugging first baseman for his New Jersey high school and then for military teams and a local college team before he gives up baseball to work in his family's glove-making business. The Swede's heroics become a locus for the aspirations of Zuckerman and other Jewish fans toward assimilation into American society. Moreover, they provide a means of escape from the terrible realities of World War II, as the bloody South Pacific campaign of 1945 – with the abrupt end of the Asian war not yet in sight – coincides with Lvov's final and finest high school season. While Roth contrasts these last days of an adolescent golden age with the horrors that loom beyond it, the novel also portrays the 1940s and 1950s as a lost youth for America, as the Swede suffers in the 1960s – especially in his relationship with his daughter Merry, a countercultural revolutionary who is lost to a fugitive life after being involved in a deadly bombing. At the same time, an early episode casts doubt on the notion that baseball ever offered a version of paradise. As a boy, Zuckerman relates, he discovered Tunis's *The Kid from Tomkinsville* and its sequels, and was staggered by their vision of "playing up in the majors" as "yet another form of backbreaking, unremunerative labor." Zuckerman is shocked: "I was ten and I had never read anything like it. The cruelty of life. The injustice of it. I could not believe it."[12] He loses his innocence when on the cusp of adolescence, and reads the Swede's life through the lens of Tunis's stories.

Roth's allusion to Tunis's series acknowledges adult literary fiction's debts to early baseball writing for children. It comes at the same time that juvenile baseball fiction of high quality has flourished, partly because writers for children have drawn on adult literary novels such as *The Natural* and *The Celebrant*. This new wave of juvenile baseball fiction often features social themes, many of them shared with adult baseball fiction and with other children's fiction. Among these new books have been historical novels in a range of settings. In *The Brooklyn Nine* (2009), a metafiction that charts a family's involvement with baseball over a century-and-a-half, Alan Gratz uses baseball lore and memorabilia to speculate on the nature of continuity and memory. Bette Bao Lord's *In the Year of the Boar and Jackie Robinson* (1984) uses the Dodger's pathfinding experience to parallel that of a young Chinese immigrant in 1947, who learns to become American via the game of baseball. Virginia Euwer Wolff, by contrast, takes a grimmer view of the Asian immigrant experience in *Bat 6* (1998). In Wolff's novel, set shortly after World War II, a girls' softball game in a Pacific Northwest community becomes fraught with repercussions of the wartime internment of Japanese Americans. Also set in the 1940s, M. J. Auch's *One-Handed Catch* (2006) introduces another common theme from young adult fictions of recent years: that of disability. The protagonist is a young man who loses a hand in an accident and must learn to relate to the world anew – even to the extent of playing baseball again. Drawing on the magical strain in baseball fiction, Dan Gutman's Baseball Card Adventure series sends hero Joe Stoshack where he likes in time, because when he handles old photographs – preferably baseball cards – he is at once transported to the year the photo was taken. This series had its inception with *Honus & Me* (1997), where Joe handles the most famous of all cards, the T-206 Honus Wagner card, and is whisked back to the 1909 World Series.[b] Like so much baseball fiction, the Baseball Card Adventures series is an eclectic enterprise that at its best uninhibitedly embraces the genre's clichés.

Eclecticism also characterizes Don DeLillo's *Underworld* (1997). This novel begins with a detailed recreation of one of baseball's most famous contests, the final game of a 1951 playoff between the Giants and the Brooklyn Dodgers to decide the National League title. Bobby Thomson's home run in the bottom of the ninth inning won the game for the Giants. The newspapers called it "The Shot Heard Round the World." Film of this moment appears in virtually every documentary of baseball's history, and Thomson's homer always appears high on any list of the most dramatic finishes in sports. DeLillo therefore faces the challenge of narrating an event that his readers believe they already know. He finds imaginative space to create the elements of that day not captured on film: teenagers jumping the turnstiles to gain entry to the Polo Grounds; spectators throwing paper to distract the Dodger outfielders; obscene repartee in the broadcasting booth away from the microphones; the fierce struggle in the left-field stands for Thomson's home run ball (which in fact seems to have disappeared).

DeLillo clearly works against some of baseball fiction's clichés. This game is decidedly an urban one and, far from being innocent, has its own underworld. Yet the novel's historical sweep means that DeLillo, in a familiar strategy, can invoke baseball to write of mutability in the lives of individuals and society. *Underworld* moves on to other settings as it pursues the meaning of twentieth-century American life – the neighborhoods of fifties

---

[b] For a detailed account of the origins and rarity of the Wagner T-206 card, see the interchapter in this volume, 152–154.

Brooklyn, the New York art world, the offices of multinational corporations, the Arizona suburbs. The threat of nuclear annihilation that hangs over the entire period becomes real on the day of the famous game, when DeLillo shows J. Edgar Hoover of the FBI, who is attending at the Polo Grounds, receiving word that the Soviet Union has successfully tested a nuclear bomb. Periodically throughout the novel, however widely he ranges, DeLillo returns to the motifs of the home run ball's afterlife and the collective experience of those who watched and listened to the game. The reader learns that Nick Shay, who emerges as the protagonist and sometime narrator, lost his faith in the Dodgers and much else when he listened on the radio to Thomson's winning "shot."

Years later, when Shay sits in an antiseptic lounge at Dodger Stadium in Los Angeles with business colleagues, the conversation turns to "where were you when?" Another character remembers it thus:

> When JFK was shot, people went inside. We watched TV in dark rooms and talked on the phone with friends and relatives. We were all separate and alone. But when Thomson hit the homer, people rushed outside. People wanted to be together. Maybe it was the last time people spontaneously went out of their houses for something.[13]

As Al Filreis's chapter in this book makes clear, this memory is not literal, even in the limited history of baseball spectatorship.[14] But the passage shows how DeLillo, in a way that is readily recognizable from the tradition of baseball fiction he inherits, uses baseball to write about change and loss – this time of an authentic social and political life.

NOTES

1. F. Scott Fitzgerald, *The Great Gatsby* [1925] (New York: Scribner, 1992), 70.
2. While this chapter will focus, with one exception, on American writers, other literatures, such as Japanese, include distinguished fiction with baseball themes.
3. Stratemeyer was a writer and publisher of children's books who created and sometimes wrote for such series as the Bobbsey Twins, Tom Swift, the Hardy Boys, and Nancy Drew. Garis wrote Tom Swift books and some of the Bobbsey Twins series, and also wrote the Uncle Wiggily Longears books.
4. Trey Strecker, ed., *Dead Balls and Double Curves: An Anthology of Early Baseball Fiction* (Carbondale: Southern Illinois University Press, 2004), xviii.
5. Quoted in Christian K. Messenger, *Sport and the Spirit of Play in American Fiction: Hawthorne to Faulkner* (New York: Columbia University Press, 1981), 204.
6. In addition to Strecker, *Dead Balls and Double Curves*, see Andy McCue, *Baseball by the Books* (Dubuque, IA: William C. Brown, 1991); and Noel Schraufnagel, *The Baseball Novel: A History and Annotated Bibliography of Adult Fiction* (Jefferson, NC: McFarland, 2008).

7. Ring Lardner, *Selected Stories*, ed. Jonathan Yardley (New York: Penguin, 1997), 140.

8. For a survey of over 1,000 books on baseball themes, see Timothy Morris's web page, www.uta.edu/english/tim/baseball/.

9. An influential article by Earl Wasserman pointed out mythical patterns in the narrative: "*The Natural*: World Ceres," in *Bernard Malamud and the Critics*, ed. Leslie Field and Joyce Field (New York: New York University Press, 1970), 45–66.

10. David McGimpsey, *Imagining Baseball* (Bloomington: Indiana University Press, 2000), 70.

11. Kinsella has written a number of baseball fantasies, some of them, like Malamud's *The Natural*, drawing on deep cultural myths. *The Iowa Baseball Confederacy* (1986) takes up the motif of a league expunged from the records, and includes a ballgame that lasts forty days and forty nights, while *Box Socials* (1991) is a mock-Homeric epic of baseball in the Canadian West.

12. Philip Roth, *American Pastoral* [1997] (London: Vintage, 1998), 8, 9.

13. Don DeLillo, *Underworld* [1997] (New York: Scribner, 1998), 94.

14. See also Vin Scully's recollection of the scene in Brooklyn after the Dodgers won the World Series in 1955: Tyler Kepner, "Sixty Years in Dodgers' Booth, and Scully is Still in Awe," *New York Times*, June 24, 2010. Available online at www.nytimes.com/2010/06/25/sports/baseball/25scully.html.

3

LEONARD CASSUTO AND DAVID GRANT

Babe Ruth, sabermetrics, and baseball's politics of greatness

We begin our discussion of baseball greatness by considering Harriet Beecher Stowe, whose career record should speak for itself. Stowe is the author of the abolitionist novel, *Uncle Tom's Cabin* (1852), the bestselling American book of the entire nineteenth century and probably the most read work of American literature ever. It's also the book that the phrase "the great American novel" was invented to describe.[1] Yet despite Stowe's overwhelming popularity and immense influence in her time and beyond it, literary arbiters – critics and scholars – didn't respect her work, so she was read in few American literature classrooms until a generation ago. Simply put, her work wasn't considered worthy of inclusion in the American literary canon, not considered sufficiently "great" to assign to the nation's youth.

Babe Ruth never had this problem. The most famous baseball player in history, Ruth has been the very measure of greatness in baseball, and also in other sports. Even a contemporary giant like Michael Jordan has often been called the "Babe Ruth of basketball."[2] Ruth was canonized from the start, and even though all of his most famous records have been broken, his iconic status has never been threatened.

Our goal in this chapter is to talk about greatness itself: who defines it, and who is defined by it. The examples of Ruth and Stowe show how greatness is an overarching concept that pervades our perception of our society. We apply it to our leaders of business and war, to our artists and writers, and (heaven help us) to our politicians. Arguing over who or what is great is therefore more than a consistent entertainment. It is a crucial part of the operation of the American public sphere. It's also crucial to the way that baseball is played and consumed in America.

We would like to thank Jonathan Lewin for helpful suggestions. This chapter grew from a talk that the authors delivered jointly at the Babe Ruth Centennial Conference at Hofstra University in 1995. We thank the organizers for giving a rostrum to two old baseball card collectors.

In baseball, greatness is inseparable from the numbers. That is, if you want to know the role that baseball plays in the history and consciousness of American culture, you have to study the role of baseball statistics in the understanding of the game, and in the creation of baseball greatness. We will focus our analysis on the canonical example of Babe Ruth, but we seek to show more generally how numbers operate in our appreciation of baseball greatness – and also, crucially, to show that the standards of baseball greatness, statistically based though they are, remain highly malleable.

Stowe's greatness is determined by literary evaluation, which, one might argue, ought to be relative, for literary greatness is and always will be a matter of opinion – perhaps the quintessential example of a subjective value. There is no doubt that by any reasonable definition, Babe Ruth was a great baseball player. We know, or believe we know, that Ruth was great in large part because of his numbers.

Baseball is the most statistically analyzed American sport, so it seemingly provides the easiest domain in which to test greatness. As in all team sports, there are quantifiable things to measure. Last time we looked, the team that has the highest score wins. Great teams are great because they win more often than lousy ones do. And great players make statistically measurable contributions to the success of their teams. But in recent years, debate has risen over how to best measure those contributions.

Indeed, there are lots of different things that good players can do to help the team's cause. The extraordinary role of statistics in baseball may be due to the game's history, but it may also be traced to baseball's unique balance of individual and collective performance, for a baseball game is the aggregate sum of multiple iterations of an individual act: a single batter facing a pitcher, who is backed by a defensive squad.

The Society for American Baseball Research, along with its acronym SABR, was founded in 1971, but it was Bill James who coined the term "sabermetrics" (also spelled "sabrmetrics") and who (along with John Thorn and Pete Palmer) brought the serious quantitative study of baseball performance into popular culture, and eventually into the baseball hierarchy.[3] *The Bill James Baseball Abstract*, which James published annually from 1977 through 1988, along with James's other books, provided the foundation for more rigorous statistical analysis since then.

This preoccupation with quantitative measures should be considered something of a renaissance, for baseball brought the spirit of numerical analysis with it from its nineteenth-century womb. Many of the well-known statistics, like batting average and fielding percentage, were early inventions, and arguments over their efficacy surfaced immediately after their appearance and were then forgotten, only to be reprised in light of saber-metric interventions of recent decades.

The emphasis on numbers actually changed the way the game was played on the field, even in baseball's early days. Players, conscious of their statistics (such as batting average) and the value of those statistics during contract negotiations, began to disdain acts of teamwork (such as sacrifice bunts) in favor of efforts that would inflate their individual statistics (such as swinging for home runs). As early as the nineteenth century, Henry Chadwick, a journalist who originally helped popularize the use of baseball statistics, complained that players now "played for their record." By the early twentieth century, John Heydler, the secretary of baseball's National League, declared that statistical records gave "a permanency to the game which it could never otherwise enjoy." The endorsement of statistics by the game's authorities soon led to the creation of now-commonplace statistics like earned run average (ERA). Journalists steadily bought into the use of numbers to track performance, and by the second decade of the twentieth century, Al and Walter Elias, the founders of the still-extant Elias Sports Bureau, were retailing daily lists of league leaders in a variety of statistical categories to newspapers around the country, a service that proved wildly popular among readers.[4]

Today there are three natural cohorts of consumers of baseball statistics:

(1) Baseball professionals, including general managers of baseball teams (who are in charge of putting together the best roster for the smallest amount of money) and field managers of baseball teams (who must manipulate that roster to greatest advantage during actual games).

(2) Baseball writers (including all chroniclers of the game, in print, on television and radio, and, more recently, in the blogosphere).

(3) The fans: both the rabid ones (for example, those who play fantasy baseball, a popular game that allows fans to form their own "teams" made up of real-life players, whose performance is measured by the real-life day-to-day statistical performance of those players in their own teams' games), and the merely avid fans, who are not rabid but who still care about statistics.

The last group is especially numerous, its members maintaining statistical awareness by reading box scores, attending to a player's quest for a particular record, and so on. Indeed, players are presented to the public using statistics, both at the ballpark and on television and radio. Every turn at bat is preceded by an announcement of the player's offensive statistics. Baseball professionals use statistics to make decisions, trying to predict future success based on past performance. They do this in two ways: first, by measuring the performance of individual players; and second, by determining how individual performance leads to aggregate performance of the whole team. The first task is hard enough. For example, let's say that you want to make a decision based upon a player's batting average. One must first assume that players behave in predictable ways (so that each player has what might be called an "intrinsic batting average" – allowing us to say of someone, for example, "He's a .300 hitter"). Then you have to gather enough data so that the statistical Law of Large Numbers gives you sufficient confidence of what that batting average is. Then you have to take into account that this batting average is a conditional statistic: dependent on the pitcher, the number of men on base, who's on deck, the dimensions of the ballpark, the quality of the defense, the number of hours of sleep the player has gotten, etc.

There are too many conditions for you ever to be certain of how a player is likely to perform in a given situation. The job of the statistician is to determine which conditions are most salient in determining a player's performance. This is what sabermetricians (and their forebears before the term was invented) do: they come up with statistics that, they hope, accurately predict actual player performance.[5] Thanks to the work of sabermetricians, many old statistical measures have been marginalized or retired, while new statistical categories have proliferated in recent years, and caught on with baseball's fan base. "OPS," for example (meaning the sum of on-base percentage plus slugging average) has come to be seen by professional number-crunchers and avid fans alike as a truer measure of a hitter's value than the venerable batting average. With this explosion of research into new statistics and statistical analyses, both fans and managers alike can see that much traditional baseball orthodoxy is not supported by reliable data.[6]

Baseball's general managers have also started making good use of sabermetricians. (Though this too is not exactly new: baseball writer Alan Schwarz details how legendary general manager Branch Rickey employed statistician Allan Roth long ago.)[7] Among recent baseball team employees, Craig Wright was the first to hold the title "sabermetrican" (with the Texas Rangers), while general manager Theo Epstein of the Boston Red Sox hired Bill James and Eric Van, and Keith Woolner works for the Cleveland Indians. Michael Lewis describes in detail in his influential *Moneyball* (2003) how general manager Billy Beane and the Oakland Athletics adopted a quantitative approach to fielding a team. Beane disciple Paul DePodesta went to work for the San Diego Padres in 2006 after a stint with the Los Angeles Dodgers.

The sabermetrics that general managers need as they move from predicting individual performance to predicting team performance may be too difficult to do with just formulas. Some professionals, like Tom Tippett of the

Red Sox, use computer simulation techniques to generate a large number of possible results with a given baseball lineup, to see how the individual statistics of the players combine to predict the performance of the team.[8]

But our main concern here centers on writers and fans, for they are the ones who mainly fuel the questions and debates over baseball greatness. And their need for statistics is different from those of the professionals within the sport, for their attachment to numbers links inextricably to their desire to define greatness in baseball. It is for them we ask: who determines which criteria define greatness?

To answer this question, let's first look back to the literary realm. Stowe's reputation as a great writer has grown in recent years for a lot of reasons, but one of these is because she has benefited from extensive critical re-evaluation of the criteria that have gone into the selection of canonical authors – a theoretical reconsideration of what we're looking for when we look for "greatness." Literary critic Jane Tompkins has influentially argued that discussions of literary quality must take place in cultural context, and that books do "cultural work," with this being the most appropriate measure of whether and how we should read them. We should read *Uncle Tom's Cabin*, says Tompkins, not according to our own contemporary criteria (which privilege a certain kind of interpretive difficulty), but instead according to what Stowe herself was trying to do, which was to change minds by first changing hearts, and her success in doing so.[9] By this measure – which has been widely adopted by literary critics in succeeding years – Stowe's greatness derives from the effect of her book on its readers and in society, and the resulting way in which these changes affect the way we look at the literature produced by her and her peers.

Babe Ruth's greatness comes from a similar source: he changed his world and the choice of statistics we use to measure it. Viewed in this light, it is this non-quantitative accomplishment of Ruth – the way he changed the measure of success in baseball – that should define him as "great." In other words, Ruth's greatness derives not just from his numerical greatness, but also from his "cultural work."

Similarly, even if he had had fewer stolen bases, Jackie Robinson would be great because his greatness as a man gave him the strength to forever break baseball's color barrier.[a] And an example from another endeavor: once ballerina Marie Taglioni mastered dancing on her toes in the early nineteenth century, it became compulsory for every future ballerina (but fortunately

---

[a] For more on Jackie Robinson's heroics, see "Baseball and the color line" in this volume, 72–73, 76.

not every future ballplayer) to do so. It is the ability to effect lasting change in a discipline that characterizes greatness in a wide variety of fields.

We know that Ruth changed the game by swinging from his heels and aiming for the fences. His contemporaries in 1920 were still mired in the old bunt-and-run style of play. When Ruth's long-ball style was widely copied in the 1920s and 1930s, Lou Gehrig, Jimmie Foxx, Hack Wilson, Chuck Klein, Rogers Hornsby, and Mel Ott each hit a comparable (albeit lower) number of home runs. It follows that Ruth, and those he inspired, made the home run a measure of greatness, and hence changed the game forever. (Ron Shelton's eponymous film biography of Ty Cobb – a ferocious competitor and prolific base-stealer, considered the greatest offensive player before Ruth, and still the holder of the highest lifetime batting average ever – has some memorable footage of Cobb complaining bitterly about his own eclipse as a consequence of just that change.)[10] What better evidence of the effect that Ruth had on the way that the game was played?

The effect of this change on how players were valued was put succinctly in a quip from the 1940s, variously attributed to the great home-run hitter Ralph Kiner or one of his teammates: "Home run hitters drive Cadillacs. Singles hitters drive Fords."[11]

There are other nonquantitative measures of Ruth's greatness as well. Indeed, Babe Ruth has been associated with the idea of greatness in every sense of the word – his deeds have been brilliant, but also large, larger than life. In 1925 he suffered "the stomachache heard 'round the world." And Ruth's widely reported defense of his $80,000-per-year salary in 1930 as being higher than President Herbert Hoover's because, Ruth may have said, "I had a better year than he did," has gained the status of legend.[b] There's an entire mythology that surrounds Ruth, much of which is closer to actual fact than one might expect.[12] Improbable as it may seem, for example, Ruth deserves fair credit for the genesis of professional baseball in Japan.[c]

To this real-life mythology should be added the real-life fact that Ruth's success changed the way that baseball writers and fans followed the game. Because of Ruth, they now looked at statistics to an extent that they never had before.

Ruth's astonishing success as a long-ball hitter surprised followers of baseball. Games had been mostly low-scoring affairs during the 1910s, depending more on pitching prowess than on prodigious feats of hitting. Then

---

[b] Babe Ruth's personality and celebrity receive more attention in "Interchapter: Babe Ruth," this volume, 45–48.

[c] For more on Ruth's contribution to Japanese professional baseball, see "Global baseball: Japan and East Asia" in this volume, 155–167, esp. 159–160.

Ruth started hitting home runs in record numbers, bringing a new focus to offense, and to his own records. Ruth broke the single-season home-run record in 1919 when he hit twenty-nine homers, and then he shattered his own record in 1920, when he hit fifty-four. Then he broke it again in 1921, with fifty-nine. The charisma of his big swings proved infectious – and influential. Baseball attendance skyrocketed, but more important, the *kind* of attention that Ruth received marked a shift. Sportswriters and fans alike became caught up not only in Ruth's record-setting performances, but also in the record-setting itself. "While thousands cram the grandstands" to watch Babe Ruth, reported journalist F. C. Lane in 1921, the numbers of those who followed Ruth's statistics to "see what Babe has done" numbered "literally millions."[13]

In other words, Ruth was not only one of the primary beneficiaries of baseball's numbers game; he also created it in its modern form. The national fascination with Ruth's record home-run-producing seasons in 1919–1921 and 1927 (when he again broke his own record, this time with sixty homers) was replayed in 1961, when Maris broke Ruth's single-season record by hitting sixty-one home runs; in 1974, when Hank Aaron broke Ruth's career home run record; again in 1998, when Mark McGwire and Sammy Sosa both surpassed Maris; in 2001, when Barry Bonds set the new single-season mark; and in 2007, when Bonds surpassed Aaron's lifetime total.

All of these occasions have proved in retrospect to be embarrassing moments for baseball, for reasons that have both very little and very much to do with numbers. Maris had the misfortune of battling the more popular Mickey Mantle for the home run title in 1961, and found himself in the even more unfortunate position of breaking a record set by a man who was more beloved than he, which led to death threats and an almost inhuman level of stress as he pursued Ruth's prized total. Complicating his feat, Maris achieved it in the first year the American League played a 162-game season, whereas Ruth played in a 154-game schedule in 1927.* Aaron faced death threats as well while he chased Ruth's lifetime home-run total, not only from crazies who cherished Ruth's record, but also from racists aghast that baseball's most cherished record would be broken by a black man.[d] Baseball statistics and what they symbolize had reached the stakes of life and death.

---

* Baseball Commissioner Ford Frick, whose affection for Ruth extended to his presence at Ruth's deathbed, called attention to the eight-game difference, but he did not, as popular belief holds – and Maris himself believed to his death – attach an asterisk to Maris's record. See Allan Barra's excellent corrective account at www.salon.com/news/sports/col/barra/2001/10/03/asterisk/index.html.

[d] For more detail on baseball racism after Jackie Robinson, see "Interchapter: Jackie Robinson and Curt Flood," this volume, 76–80.

On the other hand, the general baseball population was thrilled in 1998 when McGwire (of the St. Louis Cardinals) and Sosa (of the Chicago Cubs) engaged in a fierce but friendly battle for the year's home-run title. Each wound up surpassing Maris's record (no talk then about a 162-game season), with McGwire ending with 70 to Sosa's 66. There are notable parallels between this battle and Ruth's record-setting achievements three-quarters of a century earlier. In Ruth's day, baseball was emerging from the shame of the notorious Black Sox scandal resulting from the collusion of eight members of the 1919 Chicago White Sox with gamblers to throw the World Series. In McGwire's and Sosa's time, baseball was in the doldrums following a player's strike that shortened the 1994 and 1995 seasons and canceled the 1994 World Series. The McGwire–Sosa home-run derby brought many disillusioned fans back to the game.

The glow the public received from this epic rivalry began to fade almost immediately, when in 1998 McGwire admitted to using the legal performance-enhancing drug Androstenedione. It was extinguished altogether for many fans in 2005 when former teammate Jose Canseco accused McGwire of taking illegal performance-enhancing anabolic steroids.[14] Canseco's accusations of McGwire and others provoked a Congressional inquiry the same year at which appeared a number of high-profile players, including McGwire and Sosa. When asked directly about his alleged steroid use at those hearings, McGwire refused to answer. "I'm not here to discuss the past," he said, citing the advice of his lawyers.[15] Most observers took this as an admission of guilt. Sosa, who had exhibited great facility with the English language while basking in the light of his earlier celebrity, suddenly required an interpreter at the hearings, and acted very confused. It surprised few when Michael S. Schmidt of the *New York Times* reported on June 16, 2009 that Sosa had tested positive for steroid use in 2003. This confirmed long-held suspicions, and contradicted Sosa's own testimony.[16] Perhaps even fewer were surprised when McGwire finally admitted in 2010 to steroid use.[17]

No account of baseball statistics and baseball greatness would be complete without mentioning former San Francisco Giants slugger Barry Bonds. Bonds currently holds the single season home-run record of 73 (set in 2001), the career home run record of 762, the single-season walks record of 232 (set in 2004), the career walks record of 2,558, and the single-season slugging percentage record of .863 (set in 2001) – and no one seems to credit them. (These are all records once held by Ruth.)

The reason that Bonds's numbers lack credibility is, of course, because he has long been suspected of steroid use. The 2006 book, *Game of Shadows*, by *San Francisco Chronicle* reporters Mark Fainaru-Wada and Lance

Williams, gives a detailed indictment going back to 1998, when Bonds, already considered an all-time great player, apparently became jealous of the accolades McGwire and Sosa were garnering (despite the rumors circulating even then about their steroid use). The authors claim that Bonds then became a user himself, with dramatic results. There's much to be said about the Bonds steroid saga (and more is said elsewhere in this volume[e]), but we will content ourselves to note that Bonds was indicted for perjury in 2007 for denying steroid use under oath, and Schmidt of the *Times* reported on January 28, 2009 that federal prosecutors were in possession of urine samples tying Bonds to more extensive steroid use than he had admitted publicly.[18] These sobering stories provide another reason why baseball statistics, even in the age of sabermetrics, are not in and of themselves the true measure of greatness.

Finally, we want to discuss another way that statistics play a role in determining which players are great enough to be canonized: they are the main determinants considered by the baseball writers who vote on who will be enshrined in Baseball's Hall of Fame in Cooperstown, New York. Although later copied by other major sports, the Hall of Fame is something of a peculiar institution to baseball.[19] The Hall, one might say, plays the role of legendary baseball writer Grantland Rice's "One Great Scorer," giving players entry for whether they won or lost, and, in rare cases, also keeping them out for how they played the game.[20]

The Hall of Fame compares readily to a literary canon. Arguments about who should and who should not be in the Hall of Fame are familiar to baseball fans, and particularly revealing of the Hall of Fame's canonical aspect. We say that those who are in the Hall must be great and, that if they're great and not yet in, that they should be, that election will validate their greatness. Bill James has written an excellent book, *The Politics of Glory* (1994), that showcases a sabermetrician's view of how players should be selected for the Hall. James develops a "similarity score" measuring players against those already enshrined. Babe Ruth was a member of baseball's first Hall of Fame class in 1936, and James notes that being statistically similar to Babe Ruth essentially merits automatic entry into the Hall. James also suggests a "black ink" test to see how often a player has been one of his league's leaders in a recognized statistical category, giving a measure of a player's worth against his peers, which offers one way to compare players of different eras.[21]

But a telling story is the difficulty McGwire is having – and that Sosa and Bonds will soon have – entering the hallowed halls of Cooperstown. Their careers are being measured on a nonstatistical, moral yardstick. Lifetime

---

[e] See "Cheating in baseball" in this volume, 189–195.

statistics have long been vital to judging a player's Hall of Fame candidacy, and McGwire's career numbers would ordinarily merit swift enshrinement. But in four years on the ballot, his vote totals have been embarrassingly low. In effect, the baseball writers who elect players to the Hall of Fame were declaring McGwire's statistics to be illegitimate because of his then-alleged steroid use.[22]

The fact that there are Hall of Fame voters at all (rather than automatic entry for players upon their reaching certain numerical milestones) suggests a subjective factor to the admission decision. For decades harmony reigned between record keepers and Hall of Fame voters, with subjectivity entering only to adjudicate statistical ambiguity (for example, I know that he has over 400 home runs, but his on-base percentage is only .323; is that high enough for the Hall of Fame?). Generally speaking, players who gained important numerical thresholds (such as 3,000 lifetime hits), were duly elected to the Hall of Fame when they became eligible after their retirement. The steroids controversy has provoked a disequilibrating numbers problem in the Hall of Fame voting, and that problem reflects a larger one in the game itself.

Hall of Fame voters ordinarily validate a player's numbers, but now they are refusing to do so. McGwire's failure at the ballot box is only the first scene of what some believe will be a long-running drama as baseball tries to reconcile its love affair with statistics with a set of distinctly skewed numbers from what is already being called "the steroid era," a period that may still be going on. Bill James, still the most respected sabermetrician, finally weighed in on the steroid controversy in 2009, asserting that McGwire, Sosa, Bonds *et al.* will eventually be elected to the Hall of Fame because voters will never be able to untangle the question of who was cheating during those years and who was not, and will eventually be forced to give in and elect the best players of the time, regardless of steroid use. But James believes that the day of their enshrinement will not come until 2040 or 2050.[23] Until that day, and probably beyond it, their place in baseball history will remain in doubt.

We know that Babe Ruth was a great baseball player. He's the center of this chapter because he was a great player. But we're not discussing his greatness because he scored 177 runs in a season (a record that stood for more than 75 years), or even because he was a great pitcher before he was a great hitter. (Though we admit that this latter fact is compelling. Others have remarked that Ruth is the only big leaguer who could do what the best player on every little league team does: both pitch and bat cleanup.) We're writing about him because he did more than anyone else to set the criteria by which everyone – including baseball players themselves – measure the performance of everyone else. We're writing this because he created the paradigm, because he set the mold that future players have all looked at and tried, with varying degrees of success, to fill. His greatness lies not just in putting up the numbers but in setting the categories that the numbers go in. Greatness is not, we suggest, merely a matter of numbers. Nor is it purely a matter of knowing it when we see it.

When Abraham Lincoln met Stowe for the first time, during his presidency, legend has it that he greeted her by saying, "So this is the little lady who started the big war." Ruth was the big slugger who started baseball's long and ongoing war of long balls. He was the epitome of baseball greatness, the drink that holds the straw.

NOTES

1. John W. De Forest, "The Great American Novel," *The Nation* 6 (January 9, 1868).

2. See, for example, www.hofmag.com/content/view/673/29/.

3. See John Thorn and Pete Palmer, *The Hidden Game of Baseball* (New York: Doubleday, 1985).

4. In this and the preceding paragraph, we rely on the account in Alan Schwarz's important *The Numbers Game* (New York: Thomas Dunne Books, 2004), 17 (Chadwick), 25 (Heydler).

5. See David Grabiner, "The Sabermetric Manifesto" for a fuller statement of the calling of sabermetricians: www.baseball1.com/bb-data/grabiner/manifesto.html.

6. See Tom Tango, Mitchel Lichtman, and Andrew Dolphin, *The Book: Playing the Percentages in Baseball* (Dulles, VA: Potomac Books, 2007).

7. Schwarz, *The Numbers Game*, 54–59.

8. See Alan Schwarz, "Answering Baseball's What-Ifs," *New York Times*, April 7, 2009, D1. For more on Tippett, see www.diamond-mind.com.

9. Jane Tompkins, *Sensational Designs: The Cultural Work of American Fiction 1790–1860* (New York: Oxford University Press, 1985), esp. Chapter 5.

10. *Cobb* (1994), written and directed by Ron Shelton. Based on Al Stump's biography of Ty Cobb.

11. This line is attributed to Kiner in popular lore, and in various sources like the *Baseball Almanac*: www.baseball-almanac.com/yearly/yr1947n.shtml. But the *Baseball Biography Project* quite plausibly attributes it to Kiner's teammate Fritz Ostermueller, who reportedly made the comment after Kiner did indeed buy a Cadillac: http://bioproj.sabr.org/bioproj.cfm?a=v&v=a&bid=1066&pid=7516.

12. See John Eisenberg, "Ruthian Myths Don't Stray Far from Facts," *Baltimore Sun*, February 3, 1995, 3E.

13. F. C. Lane, quoted in Schwarz, *The Numbers Game*, 49.

14. Tyler Kepner, "LaRussa Disputes Claims in Canseco's Book," *New York Times*, February 7, 2005.

15. Duff Wilson, "McGwire Offers No Denials at Steroid Hearings," *New York Times*, March 18, 2005, www.nytimes.com/2005/03/18/sports/baseball/18steroids.html?_r=1.

16. Michael S. Schmidt, "Sosa Is Said to Have Tested Positive in 2003," *New York Times*, June 17, 2009, B11.

17. Tyler Kepner, "McGwire Admits that He Used Steroids," *New York Times*, January 12, 2010, B10.

18. Michael S. Schmidt, "Urine Samples Said to Link Bonds to Steroids," *New York Times*, January 29, 2009, B18.

19. For an interesting discussion of halls of fame, see Richard Rubin, "Mall of Fame: Even in Neglect, a Shrine to Our Society's Values Embodies Them Still," *Atlantic Monthly*, July, 1997, 14ff..

20. Grantland Rice quoted in Suzy Platt, ed., *Respectfully Quoted: A Dictionary of Quotations Requested from the Congressional Research Service*. Available online at www.bartleby.com/73/.

21. Bill James, *The Politics of Glory: How Baseball's Hall of Fame Really Works* (New York: Macmillan, 1994).

22. It is worth noting that steroids were not officially banned by major league baseball at the time that McGwire, Bonds, and Sosa were putting up record-breaking numbers. Hall of Fame voters, though, evidently see steroids as cheating.

23. James's essay is available online at www.actapublications.com/images/small/PressReleases/Cooperstownandthe%27Roids_F2.pdf.

LEONARD CASSUTO

Interchapter: Babe Ruth

Seventy-five years after playing his last game, George Herman "Babe" Ruth endures as the Atlas of baseball's storied lore. He was a great baseball player who anchored championship teams and set famous records, but what makes Ruth extraordinary is the way that his life fits so snugly into so many well-worn American narrative grooves.

Ruth's life fits the pattern of the classic American rise from rags to riches. "I had a rotten start," he wrote in his autobiography, and as a boy he was sent to reform school, which became an emotional home to him.[1] Brother Matthias Boutlier, the head of discipline at the St. Mary's Industrial School for Boys, rescued the wayward Ruth and introduced him to baseball. Ruth's rise was meteoric, but he never lost touch with his inner child. (It seems appropriate that Ruth, whose fame brought him into contact with more people than he could ever learn names for, adjusted by calling everyone "kid.") Ruth's devotion to children made headlines, as when he promised to hit a home run for a sick child, Johnny Sylvester, in the 1926 World Series, and then hit three in a game, propelling Sylvester into his own place in history. Suffering from a painful cancer and speaking in a gravelly rasp on "Babe Ruth Day" at Yankee Stadium shortly before he died in 1948, Ruth declared that "this baseball game of ours comes up from the youth. That means the boys ... You got to let it grow up with you ... And if you try hard enough, you're bound to come out on top." Ruth's finish on top makes him the hero of the ultimate boy's story.

"No one," says Ruth biographer Leigh Montville, lived "a more public life" than Babe Ruth.[2] Ruth's theatrical feats on the baseball diamond inspired rapturous accounts that turned into instant folk tales. The length of his home runs inspired raconteurs even before Ruth was promoted to the major leagues. One right fielder reportedly refused to retrieve a ball hit by the young Ruth unless he was given cab fare.[3] Ruth's feats also inspired statisticians bearing tape measures in pursuit of more precise records. (The

Figure 2. Babe Ruth. © Bettmann/CORBIS.

aforementioned blast was measured at exactly 428 feet. Such calibration of home runs continues today, and breeds esoteric specialists in the length of batted balls of both past and present.[4])

Before television provided a permanent visual record, Ruth's exploits gained in the retelling, and attained the status of legend in his own time. Much ink has been spilled over whether Ruth actually "called his shot" in the 1932 World Series – that is, whether he predicted the timing and location of his own home run – but observers agree that Ruth milked the situation for all of its drama, holding up one finger after letting strike one go by and then another for strike two, before he launched his drive.

Babe Ruth played at a time when the baseball media – mainly print reporters – protected players and concealed their off-field indiscretions. But when coverage of baseball later expanded to include what had previously been held off-limits, Ruth's Rabelaisian appetites made him the cynosure of a new canon of prurient stories. Stories of Ruth's prodigious appetite for hot dogs and beer (the so-called "Babe Ruth diet") are now rivaled by priapic tales of his sexual prowess. "Everything about him reflected sexuality," wrote biographer Robert Creamer, "the restless, roving energy; the aggressive skills; fastball pitching; home run hitting; the speed with which he drove cars; the loud, rich voice; the insatiable appetite, the constant need to placate his mouth with food, a drink, a cigar, chewing gum, anything."[5]

Ruth fit the national narrative in times of plenty and poverty alike. His outsized embodiment of reckless consumption made him an ideal avatar of the Roaring Twenties. Yankee Stadium, constructed in 1922–1923, quickly became known as "The House that Ruth Built." But Ruth's fame continued to expand even after the Great Depression hit. At that point he became part of the media-driven dream factory that manufactured hope for a stricken population, frequently appearing in movies as himself when he wasn't playing baseball.

In short, Babe Ruth was no mere baseball player. He lies at the center of American mythology. "To hell with Babe Ruth," Japanese soldiers would scream when they charged US troops during World War II. Ruth had been retired from baseball for years by then, but he remained a symbol of the national character. And a character he was, the central character in an array of American stories, and the most monumental and extraordinary character in a sport full of both monuments and characters. He was, as one baseball scribe put it, "the greatest icon of the game's joy."[6]

NOTES

1. Babe Ruth with Bob Considine, *The Babe Ruth Story* [1948] (New York: Signet NAL, 1992), 2.
2. Leigh Montville, *The Big Bam: The Life and Times of Babe Ruth* (New York: Doubleday, 2006), 15.
3. *Ibid.*, 36.

4. See, for example, William J. Jenkinson, *The Year Babe Ruth Hit 104 Home Runs: Recrowning Baseball's Greatest Slugger* (Cambridge, MA: Da Capo Press, 2007).

5. Robert W. Creamer, *Babe: The Legend Comes to Life* [1974] (New York: Simon and Schuster, 1992), 322.

6. Richard Ben Cramer, *Joe DiMaggio: The Hero's Life* (New York: Simon and Schuster, 2000), 254.

4

SAMUEL O. REGALADO

Not the major leagues: Japanese and Mexican Americans and the national pastime

In the United States, baseball's reputation as the country's national pastime has largely come from its history as a professional institution. Major league stars from Harry Wright in the 1870s to contemporary celebrities like Alex Rodriguez, along with legendary clubs like the New York Yankees, have long been the face of baseball and have overshadowed the game at the amateur level. One reason is because many standout amateurs ended up in the majors. Additionally, large media outlets and corporate sponsors used their resources to create larger-than-life figures. Finally, generations of mainstream fans took to the professional game, attracted by its seeming egalitarian characteristics. Marketed as a display of democracy, professional baseball has had no equal when it comes to its symbolism of American values. After all, claimed its partisans, in what other forum could a person like Babe Ruth rise from humble origins to international stardom?

Even in the nation's black community, the professional game had an avid following. Deprived of the opportunity to play in the major leagues until 1947, African Americans created their own leagues by 1920.[a] In their heyday, the strongest ball clubs played in major league stadiums, got national attention from the black press, and drew respectable crowds. To match their counterparts in the majors, black baseball had its share of legendary figures who gained international fame, particularly in the Caribbean. But while professional baseball's heartbeat was strong and steady, the game outside these ranks, particularly in many of the nation's ethnic communities, was vibrant and culturally significant.

On the western periphery of the United States, the situation of baseball in the neighborhoods of both Japanese Americans and Mexican Americans before the 1950s best portrayed the game's impact beyond the diamond. In each case, baseball had a large presence as it served as a chief mechanism for

---

[a] For a history of professional black baseball, see "Baseball and the color line" in this volume, 61–75.

the demonstration of "Americanness" and the creation of working class unity, and as an expression of these communities' cultural attributes. Moreover, the game was among the means for both reinforcing cultural tradition and easing the transition into a new national environment. Unlike in other institutions such as college baseball, where participants played the game solely out of competitiveness and school spirit, young adults of Japanese and Mexican heritage played baseball with a larger sense of purpose. "Whenever I put on my uniform," said Takeo Suo, "I felt like I was putting on the American flag."[1] For people in these ethnic communities, local baseball that operated well outside the ranks of the major leagues was the national pastime.

At that level, where admission was free, attendance rarely numbered in the hundreds and only small local papers reported on the contests. Still, baseball thrived in this environment. Teams and the players were often the "face" of their enclaves to the mainstream public. For many of these immigrants, the baseball games and leagues proved to be an especially significant forum in which to exhibit their competitive abilities and their patriotic virtues without undermining their cultural identity.

Some say baseball at this level was the purest form of the game. Historians have traced the relationship between game and community long before baseball was professionalized. Even before the 1860 Currier and Ives lithograph popularized the notion that baseball was the country's "national pastime," in many areas this was already an understatement. With the game taking shape in the 1830s and entering its recognizable so-called "modern" phase in the 1840s, baseball captivated both urban and rural followers in its pre-professional era. Hundreds of clubs were founded in the antebellum period, and reconvened after 1865. Of this era, historian Harold Seymour writes, "Players and spectators alike showed an intensity of interest which approached zealotry. Workingmen would get up at four or five o' clock in the morning to practice before going to work."[2] The emergence of organized baseball also presented an opportunity for civic marketers to promote their towns. "Older eastern cities could ... take their eminence for granted," writes historian Benjamin Rader, but "a smaller city might see in its baseball team an opportunity to embarrass a larger neighbor."[3] At the end of the century, baseball, in the opinion of many, had come to represent the ideals of the nation. "It's our game," said poet Walt Whitman, "the American game."[4]

As baseball euphoria gained momentum, the United States aggressively stepped up its commercial and military advances abroad and became a global power. The impulse to "democratize" those in the colonized regions led to the introduction of American culture beyond the nation's borders. To that end, American ministers, teachers, and other adventurous sorts sought to teach baseball in their schools, businesses, and even at military bases. As a result of exchanges that took place between the United States and both Latin America and Asia in the late nineteenth century, baseball landed in each region no later than the mid 1880s.[5] But while American ambassadors of "good will" mentored many in both regions on the virtues of the game, baseball made its strongest appearance in the Caribbean and Japan as a result of activism on the part of Latin American students returning from the United States who were intrigued with the new American "fad," and of Japanese diplomats who ambitiously sought mechanisms to help modernize their nation. As interest grew in the northern sector of Latin America and in Japan, teams and leagues were organized and, by 1900, baseball had become a fixture in both areas. Thus, it is little wonder that between 1890 and 1910, as migrants from both regions entered the USA, baseball returned to the country with them.

The case of Japanese Americans

Baseball's "claim" on the Japanese started during the height of the Meiji Period in the 1870s when westernization dominated Japan's crusade to increase its global prominence.[b] For Japanese migrants who left their country for the United States, the popular game also helped to unify them as they settled into their new environs. Additionally, the activity of baseball in their community aided their quest to create an American identity.

Zoruku Obata arrived in San Francisco in 1902, in the midst of the first wave of Issei migration to the United States. Having adopted the trade name of Chiura ("a thousand bays"), Obata gained notoriety as a painter. Young, energetic, and optimistic, after only one year in San Francisco Obata in 1903 brought together other like-minded Issei (those born in Japan), and formed a baseball team called the Fuji Athletic Club. It was the first United States mainland baseball team made up entirely of Japanese players. Though his own playing skills are not entirely clear, the artistic and ambitious Obata designed the team uniforms and logos. This pioneering enterprise drew the attention of other Issei, many of whom were already familiar with the game.

Only a year after the Fuji Club was formed, a rival outfit, the KDC, came into existence. The team, which like many early Issei clubs adopted a name that reflected its prefecture,[6] competed against teams of varied ethnic groups. In an era of overt anti-Japanese hostility, however, contests against mainstream white teams were played with caution. "A lot of these white teams didn't take losing very well. As the game got closer to the end and we were winning,

---

[b] For an account of these developments in Japan, see "Global baseball: Japan and East Asia" in this volume, 155–156.

we would start gathering up our equipment and as soon as the game ended, we would grab our gear and run," said one man, recalling what his Issei father had told him about his experiences.[7]

In 1906, a devastating earthquake hit San Francisco, killing thousands and leaving many more homeless and unemployed. Though some Japanese had already migrated to other locales, the disaster drove many others to relocate in Sacramento, San José, and other outer bay area locations, and new clubs emerged in these new locales. San José saw its first Issei team in 1910. Further east, in the Sacramento neighborhood of Florin, Issei settlers initiated their baseball activities in 1912. And in Oakland, the game appeared in the Japanese enclave as early as 1915. Still other clubs formed in California's inland region and in the Los Angeles basin.

In the Pacific Northwest, baseball had also taken hold of the tiny Seattle Japanese community. As early as 1904, first-generation immigrants formed the "Nippon" baseball squad, which initially played games against mediocre Caucasian teams. Baseball interest in that area greatly increased when a Japanese team from Tokyo's Waseda University visited the United States a year later and played an array of opponents, including some in the Puget Sound area. This trip was significant for two reasons: first, it greatly stimulated Issei baseball interest in the Pacific Northwest; and second, it increased the nostalgia of the Japanese sojourners for their homeland. On both counts, Frank Fukuda, born in Japan, played an important role.

Fukada played for a notable Issei team, the Mikados. "The Mikado team dominated the Japanese baseball league the next few years and Fukuda became a premier second baseman in the league," claims historian Ryochi Shibazaki.[8] In fact, so skilled were the Mikados that the *Seattle Post-Intelligencer* published a picture of the club with the caption "Japanese Baseball Champions of the Northwest," after a 1910 victory over the Columbias of Tacoma, another Issei team.[9] In an assessment of the club's parity with Caucasian teams, the daily was gracious but cautious. "The Japanese team is not the best amateur aggregation in the city, but it can give any of [their opponents] a battle," the paper announced. "[They] have shown that they rank well with the American players. While a little weak in batting, the little fellows are wonderful fielders, fast, and good base runners."[10]

But Fukuda's significance as a player paled before his eventual role as a motivator for the expansion of Japanese American baseball in the Pacific Northwest. An important step in that direction took place when, in 1909, Fukuda founded a young Nisei club that he called the "Cherry" team, akin to today's Little League. (Nisei refers to the children of the Issei, i.e. the first generation born in America.) In 1912, Fukada christened the Cherry team the "Asahi Club," and promoted it as a social organization for young men.

Figure 3. Asahi baseball team at their clubhouse in Seattle, *c.* 1920. University of Washington Libraries, Special Collections UW23721z.

Social or athletic clubs like the Asahis were common in Issei communities. Though the names carried recreational connotations, these institutions had a much broader appeal. Most included those Issei who saw themselves as "refined." "The Asahi club," Ryoichi Shibazaki points out, "was not a baseball team in the strict sense. It was an organization consisting of Japanese students and the main purpose was to produce the future leaders of Japanese society in Seattle through various activities like baseball."[11] The clubs also served as an important bridge between the first and second generations. Kenji Kawaguchi, a Seattle Nisei, recalled with passion his early desire for inclusion in one of the clubs: "We wanted to belong. Everybody wanted to be part of the Taiyo Athletic Club. We wanted to be affiliated with the older boys so as to get their support."[12]

Strong on initiative, Fukuda, then a clerk and eventually a vice-president in Seattle Japanese Bank, took the Asahi club and expanded its largely social functions to include recreation. Given Fukuda's upbringing in competitive-minded Meiji Japan, it is not surprising that he and others like him saw sport as a key factor in the process of assimilating in their new surroundings. And as had been the case in the San Francisco region, Seattle's Issei between 1905 and 1910 "were moving toward genuine immigrant status rather than [being] simply transient workers from Japan."[13] Therefore, it seems reasonable to assume that most if not all of Fukuda's Asahi Club's goals were long-range. In keeping with that orientation, Fukuda was the catalyst for several baseball teams that emerged from that club. Other Japanese Americans who encouraged baseball in their communities soon followed.

In 1928, Jimmy Sakamoto, a Nisei from Seattle, had only recently returned to the Pacific Northwest after a few years in New York City. Blinded by blows to the head during his brief career as a professional boxer but determined not to let his disability hamper his ambition, Sakamoto turned his attention to the civic activities of the Nikkei (all persons of Japanese ancestry living in the United States) community in Seattle. He launched the first exclusively Nisei newspaper in the United States, the *Japanese American Courier*, in which he was not shy about expressing his advocacy of Japanese cultural assimilation. A co-founder in 1929 of the assimilation-minded Japanese American Citizens League (JACL), Sakamoto drew on his athletic ambitions to create formulas by which the Nisei might parlay community strength into a model of cultural uplift that Caucasian powerbrokers could view as admirable and patriotic. Eventually, he settled on sport, especially baseball, as the vehicle to help the Nisei reach such goals.

The *Courier* echoed the affinity the Nikkei held for the national pastime. Enthusiasts routinely expressed their sentiments about the game and its heritage within their community. *Courier* writers also included brief stories of major league players, commentary on professional baseball, and even touted the "rosy" scenario of possibly seeing Japanese teams in the major leagues.[14]

That baseball took center stage was no accident. To be sure, it was popular, but Sakamoto's concerns transcended the game. At the time the *Courier* came into existence, sports were already a fixture, at times a divisive one, among the Seattle Nikkei. Football drew the publisher's attention in particular for the partisanship it inspired among its fans. The less aggressive quality of baseball, however, made it much better suited for Sakamoto's leanings toward unification. Initially, the publisher pressed to construct a single "all star" type of team, but gave way to the organizers who opted instead to form an all-Nisei league. For the young Nisei at that time, this arena was important. "I made the high school [baseball] team when I was a freshman. I played the whole season, every game, every inning," remembered Kenji Kawagawa. "But outside the ballgame, [Caucasians] weren't friendly with you. So I realized that was not the kind of situation I'd give my efforts to. So, after my freshman year, I quit [the team] ... to play Sunday ball with my [Nisei] friends."[15] Nisei baseball aficionados gravitated to the new leagues, but Issei support was also apparent. "The older people were interested ... [T]hey came to the games to watch their young ones play.

It was community involvement," said Kawaguchi.[16] Indeed, affection for the game came from both generations. "Baseball served to bring together the two generations and lessen the generation gap between the immigrant fathers and their American-born sons," observed historian Gail Nomura. "In baseball the immigrant fathers could come together with their sons in a shared passion."[17]

The baseball division of the Courier League began in 1928 with ten teams, all from Seattle proper. By 1941, its final season, the league had expanded to over thirty teams and four different classifications based on skill level.[18] Affiliate teams of the Courier League could be found 200 miles east in Wapato, Washington, and as far south as Portland, Oregon. As the league caught on, in any given year over a thousand players participated, and the *Courier* sponsored traveling all-star clubs who played in Oregon, California, and even Japan. The paper also hosted Japanese clubs who toured the United States mainland.

The future did not unfold exactly as planned. Following the Japanese attack on Pearl Harbor on December 7, 1941, paranoia over possible Japanese saboteurs operating in the United States led to the adoption of Executive Order 9066 and the incarceration of ethnic Japanese. Remarkably, in all of the ten internment camps, they managed to continue their baseball activities and constructed elaborate leagues. In the years immediately after World War II, the Nisei resumed their baseball agenda and continued to hold tournaments and leagues until the early 1950s. But age caught up with the Nisei, and their Sansei (i.e., third-generation) offspring no longer played in exclusively ethnic-Japanese leagues. But the evaporation of their "golden era" of baseball did not kill their legacy. By the mid 1990s, descendants of the players and social historians generated new studies on prewar Nikkei baseball. As a result, major league clubs paid tribute to the surviving players with days held in their honor, artifacts of their leagues landed in museums, and a traveling exhibit was temporarily displayed at the Baseball Hall of Fame in Cooperstown in 1998. And perhaps most important, there is today a flow in both directions of players between the Japanese and American major leagues, with Japanese players achieving fame and fortune in the American game.

Baseball in Mexican America

Like the Nikkei in Seattle, Mexican Americans in the Los Angeles area engaged in their own struggles to empower themselves in a region where they had little clout. In many respects, their greatest struggles were internal, as many coped with the dual identities of Mexican heritage and US nationality. Unlike the Nikkei, Mexicans in the southwest possessed a distinctive and exclusive Mexican identity long before the region fell into US hands. Nonetheless, as the demographics shifted in favor of a new Protestant-Caucasian majority, Mexican American civic leaders at the turn of the century drew from their community ideas, agendas, and programs that would serve their needs, preserve their cultural identities, and create bridges to the majority culture. Baseball was an important component in this activist blueprint.

In 1930, only one year after the founding of the JACL in Seattle, *Tejanos* (literally "Texans") came together in Corpus Christi, Texas and created the League of United Latin American Citizens (LULAC). Having pledged to protect the interests of United States citizens of largely Mexican descent, LULAC leaders sought a mainstream American profile. They targeted education and civil liberties as their chief goals, but these objectives did not always resonate with their constituents, so LULAC leaders were often seen as out of touch with the working class. But sport garnered attention. Indeed, even as LULAC drew its blueprint for unity and inclusiveness, other community leaders in the US southwest had already established amateur baseball clubs, many of which effectively displayed the virtues of the Mexican American identity that LULAC leaders sought.

Baseball's origins among Hispanics in this region had several roots. Developments in the late-nineteenth-century era of Mexican President Porfirio Diaz, for instance, played a significant role in advancing the game, first in Mexico proper and later to its northern frontier. To modernize the country, the Diaz administration adopted measures to draw the attention of foreign industrialists so that they might invest in Mexican products and resources. The government also sought greater productivity from its laborers, and so it encouraged baseball, a "modern" game with an emphasis on team play.[19] Though the game initially caught on with the elites – particularly in the Yucatán area – in the 1890s, a decade later its popularity had expanded among urban and rural proletariats.[20] As Mexican industry grew in the country's northern periphery, laborers who had engaged the game in the south migrated with the help of the railroad and, once they settled in their new environs, eventually sought to satisfy their appetite for baseball.

On the US side of the border, agricultural productivity expanded greatly during this time. This development proved a magnet for Mexican job seekers, some of whom played baseball. But the game in the southwest did not only arrive with Mexican migrant workers; baseball had become a national phenomenon by the end of the nineteenth century. As early as 1884, the game had already caught the attention of the citizens of Laredo, and from there, it likely spread to Mexico's Nuevo Laredo.[21] By 1900, baseball's gravitation to the borderlands of the American southwest was complete. All along the international border from the Gulf of Mexico to the Pacific coast area, local newspapers routinely reported game results. Fourth of July tournaments were common and "nines" in the Texas area were reported in such towns as Laredo, San Antonio, and Corpus Christi.

Further west, the booming citrus industry also helped to promote the game in Southern California. "US companies subsidized baseball teams on both sides of the Rio Grande to increase worker productivity and foster company loyalty," observes historian José Alamillo.[22] Sunkist Growers, Inc. spearheaded the movement to introduce baseball programs into their companies. G. B. Hodgkin, the director of Sunkist's Industrial Relations department during the period of World War I, wrote that Mexican workers "have to become a member of a local society or baseball team ... to increase their physical and mental capacity for doing more work."[23] To that end, the company even employed Keith Spalding, son of baseball pioneer A. G. Spalding, to build baseball facilities in a company community on a ranch site in Fillmore, California.[24]

To be sure, between 1900 and 1945, the national pastime had captivated the Mexican American *barrios* and *colonias* even outside the realm of the company "towns." A tremendous interest in sport and competition in general provided the stimulus for the baseball activities. "[A]mateur enthusiasts of 'baseball,' have begun practicing this lovely sport in the lawn tennis patio of the club," wrote *El Heraldo* in 1916 about the Mexican elites who had recently arrived in Los Angeles. But as historian Douglas Monroy has discovered, the working class produced the most competitive games.[25] With the increase of Mexican migration into the United States by the mid-to-late 1920s, in part due to the vicious civil war that claimed nearly one million Mexican lives, several southwestern cities – including San Antonio, El Paso, and Los Angeles – grew greatly. By 1925 the Mexican population of Los Angeles had surpassed every city in Mexico other than the national capital.[26]

In the Mexican *barrio* of East Los Angeles, baseball thrived. Mexican small-business owners sponsored several teams that competed against each other and clubs outside of their enclave. Such team names as El Paso Shoe Store, the El Porvenir Grocery, and the Ortiz New Fords provided good advertisements for sponsoring businesses. Their support provided an avenue of respect and social position for those who wore their uniforms, and also a sense of Mexican identity within the surrounding mainstream society. Douglas Monroy argues that baseball in the *barrios* in this era gave Mexican Americans "an identity as Mexicans, a way for Mexicans to garner respect in the eyes of the americanos, and a public reinforcement of the traditional manly family values of forceful, dynamic activities."[27] Proud displays of their dual identity were evident in games played on US holidays, when fans brought US and Mexican flags to the games, and ceremonies were conducted in English and Spanish.[28]

The vibrant baseball culture in the Mexican urban and rural communities also aided networking on both sides of the border. In the 1920s and 1930s, athletic clubs were abundant within Mexican and other ethnic immigrant enclaves. These clubs served as social centers akin to the mutual aid organizations that existed in the late–nineteenth-century *colonias*. The clubs drew attention and support from local businesses, the Spanish-language press, the Catholic Church, and labor unions. "These sporting networks established during away games and tournament matches became important for community organizing and labor struggles," says Alamillo.[29] Moreover, in their support for baseball, club leaders often arranged games against similar organizations in other regions, and against clubs from Mexico. "Mexican American baseball was a transnational phenomenon" asserts Alamillo, "straddling both sides of the border to entertain spectator crowds who filled the stands to cheer their favorite teams."[30]

As a result, not only did players compete against each other, but families also came together when teams caravanned to games en masse. In that setting, *mariachi* musicians and Mexican cuisine created a festive backdrop for the weekend contests. Moreover, when clubs from across the border competed, the pre-game promotions on local Spanish-language radio often commenced with a salute to both the US and Mexican flags.[31] As I have observed elsewhere, "Baseball in the barrios more than helped to preserve a strong sense of Mexican heritage within the communities. It wielded a sense of unity amongst the people."[32] Indeed, so meaningful were these games that players often went to extraordinary lengths to play in them. For instance, on one such trip in 1931, the Corona Athletics Baseball Club, a team made up largely of Mexican American field hands, rode to a game in the back of a fertilizer truck. "By the time we arrived to play, we all smelled like fertilized fields. We did it because we loved the games," recalled one player.[33]

Particularly before the age of television during the 1950s, baseball thrived in such communities as the Nikkei and Mexican American enclaves. It enabled both groups to express their athletic skills and, in some cases, advanced their transition to life in the United States. But it also helped them to preserve their own cultural identity. In baseball, they got the best of all worlds: an expression of patriotism that did not sever the roots of their Asian or Mexican heritage. Indeed, the game, as they saw it, championed both forms of their transnational identity. Finally, it delivered to them a greater sense of presence and respect as they dealt with the social, political, and legal barriers that tempered their opportunities for success. Far beyond the limelight of the major leagues, early Japanese and Mexican American baseball carried the game's amateur tradition into the twentieth century and, in doing so, created a more inclusive vision of an American national pastime.

NOTES

1. Kerry Yo Nakagawa, *Through a Diamond: 100 Years of Japanese American Baseball* (San Francisco: Rudi, 2001), 27.
2. Harold Seymour, *Baseball: The Early Years* (New York: Oxford University Press, 1960) 24–25.
3. Benjamin G. Rader, *Baseball: A History of America's Game*, 2nd edn. (Urbana and Chicago: University of Illinois Press, 2002), 32.
4. Whitman, quoted in *ibid.*, 1.
5. For more on the origins of baseball in Latin America and Asia, see Roberto González Echevarría, *The Pride of Havana: A History of Cuban Baseball* (New York: Oxford University Press, 1999).
6. According to Nakagawa, each letter in "KDC" had a different meaning: "K" for Kanagawa-ken, their prefecture; "D" for *Doshi*, a loose translation for "a bunch of guys"; and "C" meaning "Club" (Nakagawa, *Through a Diamond*, 32). The use of team names drawn from cities or regions from where their organizers had migrated was not unusual. For instance, in the Mexican American *barrio* of East Los Angeles in the 1920s, among the most successful clubs was one named "El Paso Shoe Store."
7. *Ibid.*, 32.
8. *Ibid.*, 79.
9. *Seattle Post-Intelligencer*, May 23, 1910. Clipping in Frank Fukuda Collection, Special Collections Archives, University of Washington, Seattle.
10. *Ibid.*, n.d. Clipping in Frank Fukuda Collection.
11. *Ibid.*
12. Kenji Kawaguchi, unpublished interview with author, Seattle, Washington, June 15, 1993.
13. Robert A. Wilson and Bill Hosokawa, *East to America: A History of the Japanese in the United States* (New York: William Morrow, 1980), 45.
14. *The Japanese American Courier*, May 26, 1928.
15. Kenji Kawaguchi interview.
16. *Ibid.*
17. Gail M. Nomura, "Beyond the Playing Field: The Significance of Pre-World War II Japanese American Baseball in the Yakima Valley," in *Bearing Dreams, Shaping Visions: Asian Pacific American Perspectives*, ed. Linda A. Revilla (Pullman, WA: Washington State University Press, 1993), 18.
18. *Japanese American Courier*, March 1, 1941.
19. William Beezley, "Bicycles, Modernization, and Mexico," in *Sport and Society in Latin America: Diffusion, Dependency, and the Rise of Mass Culture*, ed. Joseph L. Arbena (Westport, CT: Greenwood Press, 1988), 25.
20. Gilbert Joseph, "Forging the Regional Pastime: Baseball and Class in Yucután," in Arbena, *Sport and Society*, 36.

21. Alan M. Klein, *Baseball on the Border: A Tale of Two Laredos* (Princeton: Princeton University Press, 1997), 35.

22. José M. Alamillo, *Making Lemonade out of Lemons: Mexican American Labor and Leisure in a California Town 1880–1960* (Urbana: University of Illinois Press, 2006), 101.

23. Hodgkin, quoted in *ibid.*, 101.

24. *Ibid.*

25. Douglas Monroy, *Rebirth: Mexican Los Angeles from the Great Migration to the Great Depression* (Berkeley, CA: University of California Press, 1999), 46.

26. Matt S. Meier and Feliciano Ribera, *Mexican Americans/American Mexicans* (New York: HarperCollins, 1972), 120.

27. Monroy, *Rebirth*, 47.

28. See Samuel O. Regalado, "Baseball in the *Barrios*: The Scene in East Los Angeles since World War II," *Baseball History* 1 (Summer, 1986), 7.

29. Alamillo, *Making Lemonade*, 110.

30. José Alamillo, "Peloteros in Paradise: Mexican American Baseball and Oppositional Politics in Southern California," *Western Historical Quarterly* 34.2 (Summer, 2003), 195.

31. Regalado, "Baseball in the *Barrios*," 57.

32. *Ibid.*

33. Alamillo, "Peloteros in Paradise," 198.

5

LESLIE HEAPHY

Baseball and the color line: from the Negro Leagues to the major leagues

Following the Civil War, people expected many things to change across America, especially race relations. Reconstruction policies were designed to help the newly freed slaves adapt to their new lives and to help America adjust to changes in the North and the South. For example, the Freedman's Bureau was created to help with education and jobs for the freedmen. All aspects of life would be affected by these changes, including sports and entertainment. The fastest growing sport of the day was baseball, now spreading across the country. As baseball grew in popularity it did not discriminate. It became important in all elements of society, with African Americans adopting the game like everyone else. With the success of the Pythians, the first black baseball club, in the late 1860s, the stage was set for baseball to become an important form of entertainment for African Americans.

America's national pastime spread during the war and became a professional sport in 1869 when the Cincinnati Red Stockings paid all their players and had a perfect season. The Red Stockings' success led other clubs to move into the professional realm and this created a need for increased organization. The National Association of Professional Base Ball Players provided rules and regulations but also posed the question of who would be able to play on the member clubs. Would African American ballplayers be accepted or not? From the 1880s until 1947 the answer was no, until Jackie Robinson and the Brooklyn Dodgers changed existing practice and opened the doors to the majors for African American players. The color line that was created in the sport kept the two races from playing together in organized leagues and left the history of black baseball lost in the shadows until recently. Though its role was often lost in the telling, baseball became a vital part of the life of many African-American communities, with businesses supporting teams and fans turning out everywhere teams played. Teams such as the Kansas City Monarchs and Homestead Grays became sources of pride for their local communities.

By the 1870s, baseball was flourishing across America with professional, semi-pro, and amateur clubs playing in small towns and the fast-growing cities. Teams such as the Troy Haymakers, the Philadelphia Excelsiors, and many others gave young men the chance to make a living on the baseball diamond, but it was not an equal chance as Jim Crow laws gradually spread across the country, overturning the progress of Reconstruction. For baseball this meant a gradual segregation and the creation of separate teams and even leagues. The Cuban Giants became the first professional African American baseball team in the 1880s, and in 1887 the first attempt at a colored baseball league was undertaken. While the league never really got off the ground, lasting only a week, it spotlighted the changing racial landscape in America that made such a segregated league both a necessity and an eventual reality by 1920.

The Cuban Giants were organized by Frank Thompson in 1885 to entertain guests staying at the Argyle Hotel on Long Island. Thompson hired waiters who could play ball, and these men took on all challengers. The Giants tried to overcome some of the racial attitudes of the time by passing themselves off as Cubans and not as blacks. They reportedly spoke gibberish on the field to add to the illusion that they were not American players. The Cuban Giants' success encouraged other teams to follow in their footsteps. Many independent black teams developed across the country, some even entertaining hotel guests such as those at the Flagler Hotels in Florida. As the number of black teams grew, the desire to organize them into a formal league also became stronger.[1]

The League of Colored Baseballists was established in 1887 because a new "gentlemen's agreement" had been created in white professional leagues forbidding integrated play. Managers such as Cap Anson and John McGraw refused to play teams with African American players, leading to the decision to segregate that gradually pushed all black players out of the majors and minors by the turn of the century. When Anson refused to have his White Stockings play when George Stovey was slated to pitch for the Newark Little Giants, the gentlemen's agreement was born. The new league included such teams as the Louisville Fall Citys, Philadelphia Pythians, Boston Resolutes, Washington Capital Citys, New York Gorhams, Pittsburgh Keystones, Lord Baltimores, and Cincinnati Browns. The league failed because it lacked financing and leadership. Teams also did not have their own stadiums and travel was difficult because segregation had taken hold again after Reconstruction. Scores of only thirteen games appeared in local papers before the league folded.

The only remaining opportunities for black players became their own teams without league affiliations, such as the Philadelphia Giants, the

Pythians, the Acme Colored Giants, the Chicago Unions, and the Cuban X-Giants. There were over 100 players on these teams and their history was chronicled by future Hall-of-Famer Sol White in his *Sol White's Official Baseball Guide* published just after the turn of the century.[2] White introduced baseball fans to black stars such as Dell Matthews, Clarence Lytle, and Big Bill Gatewood. Matthews pitched for the Leland Giants during their much-touted fifty-six-game winning streak and Lytle pitched for the Chicago Unions in the 1890s. White's history challenged the idea supported by organized white baseball that African Americans did not want to play baseball or did not have the talent to play. He introduced people to the stars and the lesser players, showing most importantly that interest in baseball in the black community was alive and well. Sol White, Frank Grant, George Stovey, Moses Fleetwood Walker, Bud Fowler, and other players like them had the chance to play on integrated teams but were eventually forced off these teams, joining many hundreds of young black men playing in the shadows of organized baseball.[3]

Moses Fleetwood Walker played for a number of teams before giving up on baseball and going to work as a barber. Walker is the best known of the few African Americans to play in the majors in those early years. Walker and his brother Weldy played for the Toledo entry in the American Association, which was considered a major league in 1884. Fleet Walker caught for Toledo and struggled through a season of injuries and insults as his teammates did not welcome him and his pitchers ignored his signs behind the plate. At the conclusion of the 1884 season both Walkers found themselves let go and the American Association lost its major league status, making Walker the last black player in the majors until 1947. The gentlemen's agreement kept this segregation going even though some tried to change it. This agreement did not stop African Americans from playing baseball, though. Instead, baseball gradually grew within black communities, giving them their own heroes and stars to follow just like white fans had.

Charlie Grant almost broke the agreement in the early 1900s when John McGraw signed him to play. McGraw's love of winning overcame his concerns over the color of his players. He thought he could get around the segregated practice by signing Grant to a contract as "Chief Tokohama," but white fans saw through the ruse when black fans showed up to cheer for him in his first game. The ruse was immediately up; no one believed Grant was an Indian and his contract was voided before he ever played. Other managers told players such as Andrew "Rube" Foster, a pitcher from Texas, that if they had not been black the clubs would have loved to sign them but could not, because of the agreement and also because of prevailing racial attitudes in the United States.

As segregation became more ingrained in American life – condoned by court decisions such as *Plessy* v. *Ferguson* in 1896, which established the doctrine of "separate but equal" – other black leagues were attempted in 1890, 1907, 1910, 1915, and then successfully in 1920. Earlier attempts failed, not because of a lack of talent or players, but owing to factors such as a lack of finances and ballparks to play in, travel difficulties, and fears of what might occur if mixed audiences came to games. Local business leaders, sports promoters, and politicians all tried to launch leagues, but the timing never seemed to be right. Nevertheless, lack of league play did not stop black teams from barnstorming around the country, entertaining all fans.[4]

Chicago politician Beauregard Moseley announced the establishment of his new National Negro Baseball League in 1910. Moseley wanted to begin with ten teams paying $300 for the privilege of joining, with a stipulation that teams would be replaced if they did not pay all their expenses. Moseley was elected president and he put out an appeal to the public through the *Chicago Broad Ax*, but even with all this planning the league failed before it ever really began.[5]

The playing talent was certainly there when one considers the play of such greats as John Henry "Pop" Lloyd, who starred with teams such as the Leland Giants and Philadelphia Giants; John Preston "Pete" Hill, who started his Hall of Fame career in 1899; Louis "Big Top" Santop, who caught for teams such as Fort Worth during his long career; and many others. John Donaldson pitched his way across the Midwest, compiling a record that is still being discovered today. Recent scholarship suggests he won more games than major league record holder Cy Young, and struck out batters at a pace that would have made strikeout king Nolan Ryan take notice. Fans could also watch the impressive play of second baseman Frank Grant, who played for six years in the minor leagues before being pushed into segregated play with the Leland Giants and Philadelphia Giants. Grant's fine play earned him induction into the National Baseball Hall of Fame in 2006 with Pete Hill.

One of the key pieces missing from the unsuccessful leagues was effective leadership. Rube Foster finally became the leader required for success. Foster grew up playing baseball, even when his preacher father tried to discourage him because, he told his son, baseball was not a real job. Foster left home to play and found himself a star for a variety of teams in Texas, Philadelphia, and Chicago. Foster became the mainstay of the pitching staff for Frank Leland's Giants in the first decade of the 1900s. The Leland Giants enjoyed success on and off the field, leading Foster to challenge owner Frank Leland over better pay for the players. Eventually Foster split with Leland over the issue and created his own team. After some internal fighting Foster won the rights to his team, and they became the Chicago American Giants, one of the mainstays of the Negro National League (NNL) when it began in 1920. Foster used his team, their leased stadium, and the contacts he had made to invite owners, newspaper men, and lawyers to Kansas City to create a Negro League. Foster wanted to give black players a chance to play until the day the majors opened their doors to them, and from this point until 1960 there was always at least one Negro League in operation.

The NNL founders met at the YMCA in Kansas City, established a constitution, and collected $500 membership fees from the first eight entrants in the league. The original members of the NNL included Foster's American Giants, the Chicago Giants, the Kansas City Monarchs, the Cuban Stars, the Indianapolis ABCs, the Detroit Stars, and the St. Louis Giants. "Giants" was the common moniker of many teams, building on the popularity of the name used by major league teams. Foster served as president and booking agent from 1920 until he became ill in 1926. With Foster at the helm and C. I. Taylor of Indianapolis serving as vice-president, the NNL began play in May, 1920, flourished, and saw an expansion in league play in 1923, with the addition of a second league. Other teams participated as associate members, which gave them some benefits, but their games didn't count in the league standings, and they could not play in any championships.[6]

The Negro Southern League (NSL) also began play in 1920, with eight teams paying a $200 franchise fee to join their new association. Led by the Birmingham Black Barons, this league operated into the 1960s, playing their own league games, an occasional all-star competition, and even an occasional championship series. The NSL was generally thought of as the minor league to the NNL and other northern-based leagues.

Owing to high travel costs for the eastern clubs, Ed Bolden, owner of the Hilldale Daisies, decided to branch out on his own in 1923 to form a second league called the Eastern Colored League (ECL). Bolden and the other eastern owners charged a membership fee, worked with booking agents, and governed their league with a group of commissioners rather than one president. Part of the reason for that decision was the belief by some owners that Foster had too much power as president of the NNL, and made choices for the benefit of his American Giants and not the league. The original entrants in the ECL included the Hilldale Daisies, the Eastern Cuban Stars, the Brooklyn Royal Giants, the New York Lincoln Giants, the Bacharach Giants, and the Baltimore Black Sox. The ECL lasted through the decade before folding during the Great Depression. With the addition of a second league, the ECL and NNL owners decided they could stage their own World Series, which started in 1924 with Hilldale challenging the Kansas City Monarchs. The Monarchs won that inaugural series led by the stellar play of future Hall-of-Famers José Méndez, Bullet Rogan, and others. Hilldale came back the following season and won the rematch, after each team won its respective league title.[7]

With two leagues in operation, the Negro Leagues now resembled the majors, but without the finances. Salaries were often dependent on the money that came from ticket sales on any given day, so anything from weather to bad publicity could affect a team's pay. Teams in both leagues struggled to stay afloat, resulting in franchises changing hands regularly and players jumping their contracts. Often teams could not meet their pay-rolls so players left for the promise of a regular pay check. League meetings were dominated by discussions about contracts, membership, and umpires. For example, Cleveland had over ten different teams in the Negro Leagues between 1920 and 1948. The Dayton Marcos spent only one season in the NNL before returning to independent play.

Finding and keeping good black umpires was a constant battle, not so much because of funds but owing to a lack of qualified individuals. Booking games and leasing stadiums was an endless juggling act. Negro League teams had to book their games around the home games of white teams, which meant they often did not get the best days to play and they had to pay a fee even if the games were canceled for any reason. Both Foster for the NNL and Nat Strong for the ECL worked as booking agents trying to complete league schedules, find stadiums to play in, and make money for their leagues.

By the time Foster became ill in 1926 the NNL had also lost Taylor, the league's vice-president, and was barely staying afloat. Without Foster's leadership teams struggled to pay their membership fees, play their league schedule, and find stadiums to lease regularly as the Depression hit. The ECL had similar difficulties and even offered associate memberships to make money, a practice they had previously not engaged in as frequently as the NNL had. As the economic situation worsened the NNL and the ECL folded, leaving only one league, the East–West League, in operation in 1932.

The East–West League under sports promoter Syd Pollock kept black baseball alive until new leadership came forward to revive the leagues. The East–West League ran with six teams while other teams such as the Kansas City Monarchs returned to independent play because they could make more money. Not having to pay league fees and guarantees required by the league meant clubs kept more of their own money.

Pittsburgh sports promoters and businessmen Gus Greenlee and Cum Posey got involved in reforming the Negro Leagues in 1933, creating the second NNL. The second NNL began with the Homestead Grays, the Pittsburgh Crawfords, and six other franchises from as far south as

Baltimore and as far west as Detroit. The league still struggled with franchises changing hands and players jumping their contracts, but it survived through 1948 before folding, owing in part to the integration of the majors but also because of television and the growth of minor league baseball. For example, the Bluebirds did not complete the first season, being replaced by the Cleveland Giants at mid-season.

Greenlee brought his Pittsburgh Crawfords into the league as one of the new powerhouse teams who would be challenged by their cross-town rival, Posey's Homestead Grays. The Grays and Crawfords took advantage of the continuing migration of blacks from the South to the industrial North. Greenlee built his own stadium, bought his team a bus, and started the East–West Classic, an All-Star game that was played annually at Chicago's Comiskey Park. Black baseball flourished during the 1930s and 1940s, as audiences grew and black newspapers covered these teams extensively. By the early 1940s, Newark Eagles owner Effa Manley claimed the Negro Leagues were a million-dollar business for African Americans.

The NNL was joined in 1937 by a second league, the Negro American League (NAL), which lasted through 1959. Entrants into the NAL included southern teams like the Kansas City Monarchs and the Memphis Red Sox, as well as other clubs from the industrial Midwest. Teams like the Monarchs decided to rejoin league play after playing independently because public interest in organized professional baseball continued to grow, and because they wanted to play in big events such as the newly restarted Negro World Series and the immensely popular East–West Classic.

The East–West Classic became the biggest drawing card for the Negro Leagues starting in 1933, as everyone – including large numbers of white fans – came out to see the stars of the various leagues. The Negro League All-Star Game outdrew the white major league contest regularly, with crowds as high as 55,000. The money helped many teams survive from one year to the next and fueled the growing argument for the integration of baseball. Major league scouts and managers got to see the talent in the Negro Leagues, and white and black fans proved they could get together and watch without incident. From Mule Suttles' home run in the first All-Star game to the record thirteen appearances by Alec Radcliffe, the East–West Classic showcased the best the Negro Leagues had to offer.[8] Fans came from all over to watch these great players, with major league scouts present from the first game. Photos from these contests reveal that the audiences were fully integrated, and that the event required one to dress to be seen. Even with the gentlemen's agreement still in place, white scouts attended the Classic to see the level of talent – and because they sensed that the day might soon come when things would change.

Figure 4. The Pittsburgh Crawfords, owned by Gus Greenlee, were champions
of the Negro National League in 1935. Greenlee also had a stable of boxers
that included light-heavyweight champion John Henry Lewis, pictured here
wearing a suit. With Lewis are, from left to right, an unidentified player,
Oscar Charleston, Satchel Paige, and Josh Gibson. Noirtech Research.

The NNL and NAL flourished in the 1930s and 1940s under new leadership.
The owners of the Newark Eagles, the New York Black Yankees, the Pittsburgh
Crawfords, and others were part of a new breed of businessman known as the
numbers kings. Gus Greenlee financed his team by owning a grill and running
a numbers business (an illegal lottery of sorts). Greenlee's Crawfords and the
Crawford Grill served as his legitimate businesses. In this way he could and
did give back to the community. Greenlee earned great respect from those in
his neighborhood because he helped so many with their financial difficulties
when no one else did. Abe Manley of the Newark Eagles was also involved in
the numbers game, which financed his purchase in 1936 of the Newark Eagles,
who went on to win the Negro League World Series in 1946.

Star players brought out the fans and kept the Negro Leagues alive during
the Depression. There was no greater star than Hall-of-Famer Satchel Paige,
who pitched primarily for the Kansas City Monarchs, though owner J. L.
Wilkinson also contracted with other teams for Paige to pitch for them

Figure 5. Satchel Paige. NoirTech Research.

in order to increase fan attendance. Having Paige on the advertising flyer guaranteed a higher attendance for any game. Paige entertained fans with his variety of pitches and deliveries as well as his outstanding control. Pitching for the Baltimore Giants against a team of white major and minor leaguers in 1943, Paige struck out nine and gave up no hits in five innings. The Giants won by a score of 5–1 before 5,000 fans.[9]

Paige was not the only star to draw in the crowds. Fans swarmed to see the catcher for the Crawfords and Homestead Grays, Josh Gibson. Gibson was an excellent defensive catcher but was better known for the monstrous home runs he hit. Statistics are not complete for the Negro Leagues, but some estimate that Gibson hit over 900 home runs in his career. He was often referred to as the "Black Babe Ruth," and was wildly popular south of the border, where children and adult fans swarmed all over him.

Fans also got the chance to watch future Hall-of-Famers Cool Papa Bell, who flew around the bases for the St. Louis Stars, and Ray Dandridge, who scooped up everything hit his way at third base. Negro National League President Rube Foster's half-brother Willie was a southpaw (i.e. left-handed) pitcher and "Double Duty" Radcliffe earned his nickname pitching and catching doubleheaders. Oscar Charleston played every position on the field and Martin Dihigo earned induction into halls of fame in four different countries because of his outstanding play. Buck Leonard anchored the infield at first base while Turkey Stearnes, Cristobal Torriente, and Jud Wilson patrolled the outfield grass. All of these players were admitted to the Baseball Hall of Fame in Cooperstown, New York once it opened its doors to Negro Leaguers beginning in 1971. Few lived to witness their own enshrinement.[10]

With Negro League teams in cities from New York to Kansas City and Newark to Birmingham, there were plenty of weekly opportunities for fans to come out and see the stars. Local boys also got their chance to play against the Negro Leaguers when the Homestead Grays, the Baltimore Elite Giants, or the Kansas City Monarchs came through town on their way to another league contest. It was a chance for the local hero to play against the best talent in the game, and fans loved to watch these contests. Kansas City had their own booster club for the Monarchs that organized parades and bands when the Monarchs were in town. Negro League teams played about 160 league games a season, but barnstorming brought their totals closer to 300 games a year. Teams would play any competition they could find as they traveled across the country. Barnstorming helped players and teams (both black and white) make extra money. The Baltimore Black Sox could find themselves playing the Washington Potomacs one day, then the Jacksonville Red Caps followed by the Winston-Salem Pond Fence Giants. Barnstorming also included white competition, although the organized leagues were still segregated. Satchel Paige created an all-star team that barnstormed against white teams headlined by Dizzy Dean and Bob Feller. Black teams played in semi-pro tournaments in Denver and in a West Coast league during the off-season.

Many Negro League players found it necessary to work during the off-season because they did not make enough money during the season. (The same was true for most white players in the years before free agency.[a]) Some

---

[a] Andrew Zimbalist presents an economic history of white baseball, including the players' struggles under the reserve clause that bound them to their teams and limited their salaries, in "Baseball's economic development" in this volume, 201–215.

worked as waiters, as janitors, or in factories, and many played baseball out west or south of the border. Paige, Gibson, Willie Wells, Roy Wellmaker, and many other players went to Cuba or Venezuela or Mexico to continue to play. In the Caribbean and Latin America, players found enthusiastic fans who accepted them as ballplayers, without regard to their race. They also discovered the money was good, and that sometimes made it hard to return to the United States. Looking through the record books of Latin American leagues, one finds them full of names from the Negro Leagues as well as those of major and minor league players. This integrated style of play contributed to the growing push for integrating the major leagues that really began in earnest in the mid 1930s.

Odd entertainment also played a big role in keeping teams afloat. For example, Olympic champion sprinter Jesse Owens was often hired to come in and race against a horse between innings. Or King Tut and the Indianapolis Clowns might perform their shadow ball routine prior to a game. Abe Saperstein, owner of basketball's Harlem Globetrotters, also owned a baseball team of the same name. Then there were the Zulu Cannibal Giants and the House of David clubs that fans came out to see partly owing to curiosity, even though they played excellent baseball as well. The Zulus dressed in grass skirts and the House of David never cut their hair. There were ladies' days, special days for military servicemen, and other such promotions to encourage attendance.[11] Some argued that the signing of three female ballplayers between 1954 and 1956 was solely a publicity stunt. While it certainly did not hurt attendance, the play of Toni Stone, Connie Morgan, and Mamie "Peanut" Johnson for the Kansas City and Indianapolis clubs proved these women were also baseball players.

As World War II neared in the late 1930s, the call for integrating major league baseball continued to grow. Sportswriters such as Sam Lacy, Wendell Smith, Dan Burley, and Lester Rodney called for change in the pages of the *Courier, Defender,* and *Village Voice.*[12] In the 1930s they were joined by the Communist Party, which saw a political opportunity in supporting integration when few others did, and by the black community, whose cultural self-awareness was spurred by the Harlem Renaissance in the 1920s. The New Negro, so named by Alain Locke in 1925, would no longer tolerate waiting for things to get better, and so these groups pushed for change. The black community sponsored boycotts of white businesses, picketed outside the ballparks, held anti-lynching days, and more, in an effort to force integration. Newark Eagles co-owner Effa Manley used her club to support many of these early civil rights efforts. Effa and Abe Manley ran the Newark Eagles together with Effa running most of the day-to-day affairs, paying salaries, booking games, and the like. Her name can be found on contracts and pay checks in the league records housed at the Newark Public Library.[13]

In the end World War II became the deciding factor, as it became harder to argue that both black and white young men could fight and die for their country, but not play baseball together.[b] This double victory campaign helped the push for integration as blacks felt they were literally fighting two wars – one at home and one overseas. World War II took on a wider significance for blacks, who saw it as offering an opportunity for social change at home. Many believed baseball could help lead the way because of its unofficial status as America's national pastime. In 1942, for example, the Red Sox held a symbolic tryout for three black ballplayers, though it led nowhere at the time. This push led to the involvement of Brooklyn Dodgers general manager Branch Rickey in the new United States League (USL) in 1945. Rickey wanted to create a league where he could scout black players as part of his search for the right athlete to integrate the Dodgers. Rickey's team in the USL was known as the Brown Dodgers. The league survived two seasons during which Rickey put his scouts to work.

Rickey's efforts paid off in October, 1945 when he announced that Brooklyn had signed Jack Roosevelt Robinson, the first African American player since Moses Fleetwood Walker back in 1884. Robinson's signing with the Dodgers broke baseball's gentlemen's agreement after sixty years. Robinson played for the minor league Montreal Royals in 1946 before joining Brooklyn in 1947. Johnny Wright, who had played ball in the Navy before his discharge, was signed to join Robinson in Canada, providing him with a roommate and someone to travel with.[14] Robinson played in Canada for his first season because the country had less racial tension and Rickey thought this would make the transition easier. It also allowed Rickey time to send people to the major league cities to help prepare the communities for Robinson's visits. Black leaders met to encourage the best behavior in their neighborhoods so that this experiment would be a success. Rickey and Robinson both knew that if Jackie failed, the door would close again – and who knew when it might reopen.

It was for this reason that Rickey had worked hard to find just the right player to sign. He was not necessarily looking for the best player but the right one. Robinson had experience in integrated play already, was educated, and a family man. He had experience in integrated play, including during his collegiate career at UCLA, and had served in the military. Robinson

---

[b] For more on the link between World War II and the integration of major league baseball, see "Baseball and war" in this volume, 88–89.

was also older than the usual rookie, nearly twenty-seven at the time of his signing. Robinson had been court-martialed in the military for refusing to give up his seat on a bus, showing his resolve and his ability to take whatever was thrown at him. Rickey sought a man who could take all the abuse and name-calling that was sure to occur, and who would also agree not to answer back. Rickey insisted on this latter condition because, influenced by his deep Christian beliefs, he felt that the experiment could succeed only if Robinson turned the other cheek, and he convinced Robinson to conduct himself in this way.

When he joined Brooklyn in 1947, Robinson played well enough to earn Rookie of the Year honors, thus sealing the success of the experiment. Robinson's play and Rickey's bold move opened the door for others to follow, and they quickly did so. Larry Doby followed Robinson and integrated the American League. Satchel Paige got a chance to pitch for the Cleveland Indians as a 42-year-old rookie, and youngsters such as Willie Mays, Hank Aaron, and Ernie Banks became stars.

The doors to the majors did not open wide immediately. It took until 1959 for all major league clubs to integrate, with Boston being the last when the Red Sox signed Pumpsie Green. As a result, there were many Negro Leaguers who never got the chance to play in the majors, but did get to play in the minors. The Mandak League in Canada provided opportunities for many Negro Leaguers to finish out their careers in the minors.[15] For others such as Josh Gibson, Cool Papa Bell, Mule Suttles, and Buck Leonard the move came too late. Their Hall of Fame careers were played entirely in the Negro Leagues.

While Robinson, Doby, Monte Irvin, Roy Campanella, Banks, Joe Black, and many others began to play in the majors, the Negro Leagues continued to operate through the 1960 season, when the Birmingham Black Barons finally called it quits. The last Negro League World Series was played in 1954 and the East–West game also faded away. The Negro Leagues began a slow decline after Robinson signed with the Dodgers, as each year saw teams folding or moving their franchises to new cities. For example, the Cleveland Buckeyes moved to Louisville in 1949 in the hope of reviving their team's finances but the team folded at the end of the season. Negro League owners had mixed feelings about what they saw happening. On the one hand, they all wanted their players to get the chance to play at the highest level of the game – but as businesspeople, they also knew that integration removed the need for their own leagues and sealed their eventual demise. News reports in the 1940s warned that the collapse of the Negro Leagues would mean a big loss for black communities. Owners foresaw that it was not just the teams that would shut down, but also associated jobs and industries, from ticket takers to umpires and restaurants and hotels that would be hurt.[16]

Effa Manley felt that if the major leagues wanted her players, then they should pay for them as they would pay the Brooklyn Dodgers or the New York Yankees. One of the reasons given for not paying the Negro League owners for their players was because according to the major leagues, the Negro Leagues were not organized and had no contracts. Manley argued against this misstatement and eventually achieved her goal when the New York Giants paid $5,000 for the right to sign Monte Irvin in 1949. Some thought this money would not only lend legitimacy to the Negro Leagues but also help them survive a little longer.

The major league play of the great stars from the NNL, ECL, and other Negro Leagues paved the way for the players of today. Their efforts made it possible for athletes such as Bob Gibson, Curt Flood, Barry Bonds, and Prince Fielder to play in the major leagues. These later players did not have to toil in obscurity with little press coverage, on fields that sometimes had no fences, or travel in cars that often served as their hotel rooms. As Matthew Jacobson details in the succeeding interchapter, Curt Flood not only distinguished himself on the field but also put his name in the history books when he famously challenged the reserve clause in baseball. His efforts helped to move the game to where it is today. But none of it would have happened if Rube Foster had not started the NNL, or Gus Greenlee not pushed to create the East–West Classic, or the NSL not existed for over forty years.

NOTES

1. Maurice Mander, "The Cuban Giants: Baseball Heroes and Second Class Citizens, 1865–1890," MA thesis, Morgan State University, 1996.
2. Sol White, *Sol White's Official Baseball Guide* (Philadelphia: Camden House Library of Baseball Classics, 1984). There are many excellent works on the history of black baseball that readers can consult to learn more about this important history. One usually begins with the groundbreaking work by Robert Peterson, *Only the Ball Was White* (Oxford: Oxford University Press, 1992). John Holway and James Riley have written numerous works over the years that are important resources, especially Riley's *Biographical Dictionary of the Negro Leagues* (New York: Carroll and Graf, 1994), which continued the rosters, short bios and the like begun by Dick Clark and Larry Lester in *The Negro Leagues Book* (Cleveland: Society for American Baseball Research, 1994). David Zang's *Fleet Walker's Divided Heart* (Lincoln: University of Nebraska Press, 1995) provides an excellent understanding of the importance of Moses Walker in black baseball history.
3. "Dell Mathews, Old Settler and Widely Known Barber Dies," *Metropolitan Post*, December 17, 1938, 3.
4. Jim Kaplan, "Bittersweet Barnstorming," *Sports Illustrated*, February 16, 1981, 45ff.

5. Leslie Heaphy, *The Negro Leagues, 1869–1960* (Jefferson, NC: McFarland, 2003), 25–26.
6. Art Rust, *Get That Nigger off the Field* (New York: Delacorte Press, 1976); Donn Rogosin, *Invisible Men: Life in Baseball's Negro Leagues* (New York: Athenaeum Press, 1983).
7. Neil Lanctot, *Fair Dealing and Clean Playing: The Hilldale Club and the Development of Black Professional Baseball, 1910–1932* (Jefferson, NC: McFarland, 1994).
8. Larry Lester, *Black Baseball's National Showcase: The East–West All-Star Game, 1933–1953* (Lincoln: University of Nebraska Press, 2002).
9. "Satchel Paige Pitches Brilliantly," *Los Angeles Tribune*, December 6, 1943, 9.
10. John Holway, "Black Baseball Greats Belong in Hall of Fame," *New York Daily World Sports*, August 6, 1975.
11. "Jesse Owens Will Race in Wichita," *Negro Star*, September 22, 1939, 3.
12. Jack Epstein, "Lester Rodney Dies, Helped Break Color Barrier," *San Francisco Chronicle*, December 25, 2009. To learn more about the process of integration one can consult Jules Tygiel, *Baseball's Great Experiment: Jackie Robinson and His Legacy* (New York: Oxford University Press, 1983).
13. Effa Manley with Leon Hardwick, *Negro Baseball ... before Integration* (Evanston, IL: Adams Press, 1976).
14. "Wright Reports to Royals with Jackie in March," *Los Angeles Tribune*, February 16, 1946, 14.
15. "The Negro Leagues/Cuban Connection," www.attheplate.com/wcbl/negro.htm; Barry Swanton, *The Mandak League* (Jefferson, NC: McFarland, 2006).
16. Effa Manley, "Negro Leagues Spend Half a Million," *Afro American Journal*, July 26, 1941.

MATTHEW FRYE JACOBSON

Interchapter: Jackie Robinson and Curt Flood

Jackie Robinson is most famous for joining a team; Curt Flood, who sued Major League Baseball when he was traded from St. Louis to Philadelphia twenty-two years later, is most famous for refusing to join one. But the two represent distinct chapters in a single story: Flood's late-1960s challenge to the reserve clause that bound players to their teams is not merely the preface to baseball's era of free agency, but also a coda to the saga of desegregation.

Robinson has rightly become an icon of the modern civil rights era. Though there was plenty of ugliness when he joined the Brooklyn Dodgers – epithets hurled by fans and players, deliberate spikings by opposing baserunners, and constant death threats – in hindsight his has become a triumphal narrative of fortitude and acceptance. Robinson himself wrote that he began that historic season "a lonely man," "a black Don Quixote tilting at a lot of white windmills." But by season's end, "all of us had learned something. I had learned how to exercise self-control – to answer insults, violence, and injustice with silence – and I had learned how to earn the respect of my teammates. They had learned that it's not skin color but talent and ability that count. Maybe even the bigots had learned that, too."[1]

Baseball's desegregation evokes players like Larry Doby and Monte Irvin, a generation born in the teens and twenties, playing in the Negro Leagues, then entering the majors directly in Robinson's wake. But even players far younger spent years in a baseball environment no less white and no less hostile than Robinson's Ebbets Field. Hank Aaron calls them "second generation black players" – players like Curt Flood, Bob Gibson, Lou Brock, Willie Stargell, and Dick Allen. Though associated with the 1960s, far removed from Dodgers general manager Branch Rickey's Robinson "experiment," most came through the minors in the 1950s, and, according to Aaron, "almost all of them had their own horror stories."[2] "Playing on minor league teams in tiny southern towns meant the crowds – even the home crowds – were usually hostile," writes David Halberstam of that time. "Worse, most of their fellow players were rural country white boys, who, more often than not, seemed to accept the local mores."[3]

"I didn't know anything about racism or bigotry until I went into professional baseball in 1953," writes Frank Robinson, whose initiation in the taunts of "go back to Africa" came in minor league towns like Augusta and Macon, far from his native Oakland.[4] Such incidents punctuate the biographies of this entire generation. Bill White spent 1953 as the only black player in the Carolina League, a "beacon to local rednecks, who would come out to the ballpark and ... yell at this one young black player, who symbolized to them a world beginning to change."[a] Bob Gibson recalls that White sometimes carried a bat with him as he left the clubhouse, "to get through the hostile crowds that stood between him and the team bus."[5] Aaron and Wes Covington desegregated Eau Claire, Wisconsin (Aaron: "we didn't exactly blend in"; Covington: "I felt like a sideshow freak") before Aaron was sent to the Jacksonville Braves to break the color line in the Sally League.[6] League president Dick Butler followed Jacksonville "to keep a lookout. You were never sure what was going to happen. Those people had awfully strong feelings about what was going on."[7] In Fayette, North Carolina, Curt Flood "heard spluttering gasps, 'There's a goddamned nigger son-of-a-bitch playing ball with those white boys! I'm leaving'"; and in Greensboro Leon Wagner faced a gunman by the outfield fence who issued a warning, "Nigger, I'm going to fill you with shot if you catch one ball out there."[8] Even after they reached the majors, most had to negotiate the southern racial climate and segregated facilities of spring training sites like Bradenton or Clearwater. Most also experienced some element of segregation in their team's travel, lodging, rooming, or eating arrangements in cities like Washington during the regular season; many had objects hurled at them, even by the "fans" in their home ballparks. To protect himself from thrown coins, screws, and similarly dangerous objects, Dick Allen took to wearing a batting helmet in the field.

Allen had drawn a cruel hand: in 1963 he landed with the Arkansas Travelers, the Phillies' all-white farm team, whose field was two miles from Little Rock's Central High. "When I arrived at the park," Allen recalls, "... there were people marching around with signs. One said, DON'T NEGRO-IZE BASEBALL. Another, NIGGER GO HOME ... Here, in my mind, I thought Jackie Robinson had Negro-ized baseball sixteen years earlier." As if to underscore the militant whiteness of this world, the ceremonial first pitch

---

[a] White would go on to integrate the corps of announcers after his playing days were over. See "Baseball and mass media" in this volume, 235.

of the team's season was thrown by the state's notoriously segregationist governor, Orval Faubus.

Allen's deliverance from Arkansas to the Philadelphia Phillies was less than joyous: Philadelphia baseball had itself a spectacular history of racism. Philadelphia's stadium – like the Phillies line-up – remained the most stubbornly anti-integrationist in the National League. The Phillies were in fact the very last team in the National League to desegregate and, according to historian Bruce Kuklick, when Robinson joined the Dodgers "the cruelest taunts he received at Ebbets Field came from the visiting Phillies." Phillies general manager Herb Pennock pleaded with Rickey not to bring Robinson on Dodger road trips to play the Phillies: "Branch, you can't bring the nigger here. Philadelphia's not ready for that yet." When Robinson did come, pitchers threw at him, infielders spiked him, and Phillies players lined up on the dugout steps, leveling their bats like shotguns. By the mid 1950s, the Phillies were the only remaining all-white team in the National League; and even after the team did integrate, it remained among the last to end segregated housing during spring training.[9] In 1964, when days of rioting engulfed Lower North Philadelphia, one black resident lamented, "The only thing I regret about the riot … was that we didn't burn down that goddamn stadium … They had it surrounded by cops, and we couldn't get to it. I just wish we could've burned it down and wiped away its history that tells me I'm nothing but a nigger."[10]

Allen's big Afro landed him on the cover for *Sports Illustrated*'s story on "Baseball in Turmoil" in the spring of 1970, in the wake of the Allen-for-Curt Flood trade. The "turmoil" had less to do with Allen – "I'll play anywhere," he said, "third, short, anywhere but Philadelphia" – than with Flood, who refused to report to the Phillies. Flood was reluctant to go to America's "northernmost southern city," as he said, "… to succeed Richie Allen in the affections of that organization, its press and its catcalling missile-hurling audience."[11]

"After twelve years in the major leagues," Flood wrote to Baseball Commissioner Bowie Kuhn, "I do not feel I am a piece of property to be bought and sold irrespective of my wishes. I believe that any system which produces that result violates my basic rights as a citizen and is inconsistent with the laws of the United States …"[12] When Kuhn denied his entreaty to remain in St. Louis, Flood filed a million-dollar lawsuit against Major League Baseball for violation of the Sherman Antitrust Act. In the entire cosmos of American business, argued Flood and his allies among the players' union, Major League Baseball alone enjoyed such a grip over its employees. *Flood* v. *Kuhn* worked its way through the courts until 1972, when the Supreme Court ruled against Flood and upheld baseball's exception to antitrust law. (Three years later, as detailed in the interchapter following

Chapter 14 of this volume, pitchers Andy Messersmith and Dave McNally won a similar suit against Major League Baseball, ushering in the era of modern free agency.)

Given the bondage-and-emancipation motifs of the legalities involved, it was perhaps inevitable that a black ballplayer would be the first to challenge baseball's reserve clause and seek free agency. Noting that "the word *slavery* has arisen in connection with my lawsuit" (and conceding sardonically, "the condition of the major-league baseball player is closer to peonage than to slavery"), Flood appealed to the language of a 1949 court decision, when Giants left-fielder Danny Gardella had similarly sought free agency: "Only the totalitarian-minded will believe that high pay excuses virtual slavery."[13] The slavery analogy was neither casual nor incidental, in Flood's view. As he wrote in *The Way It Is*:

> Frederick Douglass was a Maryland slave who taught himself to read. "If there is no struggle," he once said, "there is no progress. Those who profess to love freedom, and yet deprecate agitation, are men who want crops without plowing up the ground ... Power concedes nothing without a demand. It never did and never will." To see the Curt Flood case in that light is to see its entire meaning.[14]

Flood's erstwhile teammate Bob Gibson was clearly referencing slavery when, with the Flood–Allen trade in mind, in dark jest he hung a sign above his locker, "Another happy family sold."[15] Allen, for his part, drew from the same lexicon: "They treat you like cattle. It was like a form of slavery." "[Phillies Manager Bob] Skinner once said he could handle me," Allen later remarked, "... Well you don't handle human beings, you treat them. You handle horses."[16]

Curt Flood might have said that; so might Frederick Douglass.

So might Jackie Robinson. "As I write this," he reflected in his 1972 autobiography, "... I cannot stand and sing the anthem. I cannot salute the flag; I know that I am a black man in a white world. In 1972, in 1947, at my birth in 1919, I know I never had it made."[17] Desegregation did not come off as advertised.

NOTES

1. Jackie Robinson, *I Never Had It Made* [1972] (New York: HarperCollins, 1995), 68.
2. Hank Aaron, with Lonnie Wheeler, *I Had a Hammer: The Hank Aaron Story* (New York: Harper Torch, 1992), 209. See also Jules Tygiel, "Black Ball: The Integrated Game," in *Extra Bases: Reflections on Jackie Robinson, Race, and Baseball History* (Lincoln: University of Nebraska Press, 2002), 104–117; and *Baseball's Great Experiment: Jackie Robinson and His Legacy* [1983] (New York: Oxford University Press, 1997).

3. David Halberstam, *October '64* (New York: Fawcett, 1994), 113.

4. Frank Robinson and Barry Stanback, *Extra Innings* (New York: McGraw-Hill, 1988), 23, 26.

5. Halberstam, *October '64*, 203; Bob Gibson, with Lonnie Wheeler, *Stranger to the Game: The Autobiography of Bob Gibson* (New York: Penguin 1996), 58.

6. Aaron and Wheeler, *I Had a Hammer*, 55, 56.

7. *Ibid.*, 79.

8. Curt Flood with Richard Carter, *The Way It Is* (New York: Trident, 1971), 38; Samuel Regalado, *Viva Baseball! Latin Major Leaguers and Their Special Hunger* (Urbana: University of Illinois Press, 1998), 66, 67.

9. Bruce Kuklick, *To Everything a Season: Shibe Park and Urban Philadelphia, 1909–1976* (Princeton: Princeton University Press, 1991), 145–148; William Kashatus, *September Swoon: Richie Allen, the '64 Phillies, and Racial Integration* (College Station: Penn State University Press, 2005), 9–37; Howard Bryant, *Shut Out: A Story of Race and Baseball in Boston* (Boston, MA: Beacon, 2003), 5; David Faulkner, *Great Time Coming: The Life of Jackie Robinson from Baseball to Birmingham* (New York: Simon and Schuster, 1995), 163–164; Tom McGrath, "Color Me Badd," *The Fan*, September, 1996, 39.

10. Kuklick, *To Everything a Season*, 155–156; Gerald L. Early, *This Is Where I Came In: Black America in the 1960s* (Lincoln: University of Nebraska Press, 2003), 75–89; Kashatus, *September Swoon*, 76–80, 111–113.

11. Flood and Carter, *The Way It Is*, 188.

12. *Ibid.*, 236.

13. *Ibid.*, 139.

14. *Ibid.*, 206; see also Halberstam, *October '64*, 364.

15. Gibson and Wheeler, *Stranger to the Game*, 219; *Sports Illustrated*, March 23, 1970, 22.

16. See "Oppositional Identity," in William Kashatus, "Dick Allen, the Phillies, and Racism"; *Newsweek*, August 21, 1972, 84.

17. Robinson, *I Never Had It Made*, xxiv.

6

RICHARD CREPEAU

Baseball and war

As the self-proclaimed and generally acknowledged national pastime, baseball has generally tried its best to maintain an intimate relationship with American culture and the American nation. Major events affecting the country had an impact on the game, and in every major national crisis, the high priests and acolytes of the major league establishment sought to identify baseball as a patriotic institution of pure Americanism. At times this has proved difficult and at times it has provoked excess, but it has always been somehow possible. National crises of any kind had an impact on the game. War was one such crisis. Before the twentieth century, there was no necessary connection between baseball and war because baseball had not yet gained a high profile in the mass media.[a] But once baseball became enmeshed in the same news-making machinery that covered wars, its own response to the nation's wars became more explicit.

In times of war the baseball establishment has sought first to protect its investment – including its players – and at the same time to maintain its claims to the title "national pastime" by supporting war with expressions of patriotism. These two goals have not always been compatible, and have sometimes resulted in conflicting public and private policies. Moreover, public reaction to policies in earlier wars has affected the policies pursued by baseball in later ones. Through the decades and with the growing awareness of public relations, the baseball establishment has become more sophisticated in its manipulation of its public image, while simultaneously protecting its investment in players.

The first major war of the twentieth century came to Europe in 1914 but Americans did not join the fray until April of 1917. Europeans saw unprecedented casualty totals mount before them; for good reason they would call this the Great War. But for most Americans the tragedy of war and

---

[a] For a history of baseball in the mass media, see "Baseball and mass media" in this volume, 221–240.

the devastating carnage "over there" did not strike home. Instead the war seemed a great and noble crusade in which an abstract American fought to make the "world safe for democracy." After all, nothing could be nobler than a "War to End All Wars."

The enthusiasm for World War 1 was calculatedly whipped to a frenzied level by the Woodrow Wilson administration. The Creel Committee – officially the Committee on Public Information – developed programs to create and sustain an atmosphere of super-patriotism. At times crude and at times emulating high art, the propaganda effort was highly effective. Everyone was expected to support the war enthusiastically, and those who were less than enthusiastic, or who expressed doubt, were identified as "slackers," "traitors," or simply "un-American."

Like most others in the wartime society, baseball's executives and its players were caught up in the fervor for war and found every opportunity to express their patriotism. Nothing less would be expected from the national pastime. At the ballparks there were war bond sales, and players went through military drills carrying their bats like rifles over their shoulders.

The war had little impact during the 1917 baseball season. A number of players were rejected for the draft as physically unfit (a common enough draft classification during that year), and rosters remained largely unaffected.[1] As the 1918 season came to a close the story was different. There were growing demands for expressions of patriotism. Baseball was hurt by the fact that few players were volunteering for service in the war. Those who did volunteer hoped to serve as physical trainers and play baseball for service teams. Others were taking jobs in defense-related industries where many of them "worked" primarily as players for the factory baseball team.[2]

In May of 1918 the Provost Marshall of the United States classified baseball with other games, sports, and amusements as nonessential to the war effort, much to the chagrin of baseball's leadership. The 1918 season was cut short and the World Series was contested in early September. A young Babe Ruth was the star of the Series for Boston, pitching them to wins in two games as the Red Sox rolled over the Cubs. The World Series was held early because Secretary of War Newton Baker declared that after September 2, players would be drafted and inducted into the service under his "Work or Fight" order. A two-week extension was given to those players in the World Series.

In total 227 major league players joined the armed forces. Some died in action and others sustained career-ending or career-shortening injuries. Retired pitching-great Christy Mathewson's gassing during military training led to an early death from tuberculosis in 1925 at age 45. Established stars such as Ty Cobb, George Sisler, and Grover Cleveland Alexander served honorably, as did administrators such as Branch Rickey, Colonel T. L. Houston, and Larry MacPhail. Among those accused of being slackers were stars such as Shoeless Joe Jackson and Babe Ruth.[3]

Sensitive to the charges that there were slackers and draft dodgers in baseball, some sportswriters suggested that baseball try to improve its image by canceling the 1919 season and turning over ballparks for military use. Little support developed for this position among owners or players. Facing the uncertainties of the postwar economy and the influenza epidemic, the owners shortened the 1919 season to 140 games, an action they came to regret as attendance rebounded strongly in the first postwar season.

In February of 1919 American League president Ban Johnson announced that copies of *The Sporting News*, "the Bible of baseball," were being sent to the soldiers still "over there" to lift their morale and give them something "real American" to read on their way back to "home and mother."[4] Clark Griffith's Bat and Ball Fund provided the YMCA with baseball equipment to distribute on American military bases overseas.

Back on the home front Hank Gowdy, the first baseball player to volunteer for the service, was paid $1,500 a week for a thirty-week swing around the vaudeville circuit relating tales of how he helped to beat the Hun. Johnny Evers of the Chicago Cubs went on a lecture tour relating his experiences working for the Knights of Columbus in France. Tom Herbert, an usher at the Cleveland ballpark, was given a hero's welcome when he returned from a London hospital after having his plane shot down.

War memorials remained a part of the major league baseball scene long after the war ended. One of these was erected at the Polo Grounds in memory of Eddie Grant, who died in combat in the Argonne Forest in 1918. In 1919 Major Branch Rickey, president of the St. Louis Cardinals, spoke for all of baseball when he said: "I don't think there is a more patriotic, virile or enthusiastic body of men anywhere than the baseball players in the service. And they're coming back to help the game, too."[5] In 1921 the American League held "Hospital Day" to honor war veterans under the theme "lest we forget." *The Sporting News* took this occasion to remind its readers how important baseball was to the national defense as it proved to be "a very essential thing" during the dark days of the war. Quickly the criticism of players as slackers was forgotten, and baseball made its contribution to the quest for a return to normalcy.[6]

After the disturbances of the Black Sox gambling scandal, baseball settled in to bask in the prosperity of the new decade. Baseball's golden age would be undisturbed by war, with the interventions in Latin America and the Caribbean hardly noticed as the big guns settled in at Yankee Stadium. There was overseas contact with the occasional Japanese team, usually a college team coming to the USA or playing US teams in Japan. Following the 1922 season a group of players toured Japan, China, and the Philippines. Another major tour of the Far East was led by Lou Gehrig in 1931.

The biggest international event of all came in 1934 when Babe Ruth joined Lou Gehrig for another Far East tour. The Japanese had been trying for years to get Babe Ruth to come to Japan, and when he did, the reception rivaled those given to the most celebrated foreign visitors in the nation's history.[b] Obviously this tour did not prevent war between the USA and Japan, but it did have some significance for that war when it came.[7]

Moe Berg, a journeyman catcher, was a member of the 1934 tour. Berg was a linguist, spoke fluent Japanese, and was steeped in Japanese culture. Overshadowed in baseball terms by the likes of Ruth and Gehrig, Berg made a welcoming speech in Japanese and addressed the Japanese legislature. Berg was on his second baseball tour to the country. Two years earlier he had been a member of a delegation with Lefty O'Doul and Ted Lyons sent to offer baseball seminars at several Japanese universities. During the 1934 tour Berg was often absent from the delegation as he was taking pictures and motion pictures, some from the rooftops in the city of Tokyo and in other locations across the country. In fact, Berg was working as a spy and his work proved of some use in planning the bombing campaigns of Tokyo and Japan when the war came.[8]

By the mid thirties, with tensions rising between the nations of Europe, baseball people and sportswriters expressed their anxiety over these developments. The names of Hitler and Mussolini occasionally made their way on to the sports pages and the feeling that America was lucky to be separated from Europe both geographically and spiritually grew in direct proportion to the growth of international tension.

After the war in Europe began, baseball became more war-conscious and patriotic. In 1940 the American Flag Day Association called for a fitting observation of Flag Day, and *The Sporting News* endorsed the call for Flag Day observances at ballparks. There was growing sentiment for the playing of the national anthem before each game. The president of one of baseball's larger minor leagues, the International League, called for the practice in the United States in June of 1940, pointing out that the Canadian anthem was already being played in ballparks across Canada. By the 1941 season the playing of "The Star-Spangled Banner" before each baseball game was firmly established in America.

---

[b] For another view of Ruth's tour and its impact on Japanese baseball, see "Global baseball: Japan and East Asia" in this volume, 159–160.

In 1940 the United States took a step toward war preparedness when Congress approved conscription. In October it made headlines when ball-players joined their fellow countrymen and registered for the draft. Fully cognizant of the bad reputation of baseball players as slackers in World War 1 and the foot-dragging by baseball executives in acknowledging that war, baseball moved deliberately to position the game as patriotic while simultaneously arguing against the disruption of the 1941 season. One suggestion from a correspondent of *The Sporting News* was that players do six months of training after the end of the 1940 season and then be given a year's leave to participate in the 1941 season.[9]

Again and again baseball publications, executives, and players expressed their patriotism and support for the draft, in spite of any qualifications or exceptions they may privately have favored. *Baseball Magazine* joined the national patriotic chorus, noting that fighting to preserve the democratic way of life was consistent with the philosophy of baseball. The national pastime was the bulwark of democracy, a "common leveler," and would do "its full share to preserve the democratic way of living. War or no war."[10]

During the winter between the 1940 and 1941 seasons the Commissioner weighed in on the subject of war and baseball. He warned that war disrupts the social order and so all involved should make a special effort to guard the integrity of the game. The War Department announced that it would be purchasing a million dollars' worth of sports equipment, and called on professional baseball teams to play exhibitions at army camps. Speculation began over who would be the first major league player to be drafted. It appeared that it would be Hank Greenberg of the Tigers because of his low lottery number. Greenberg let it be known that he would ask for no special treatment from his draft board.

There were increasing references being made by baseball writers to Abner Doubleday, the Civil War general and mythical founder of baseball. Even President Roosevelt joined in the evocation of Doubleday, saying that the country should be more grateful than ever that the general invented this game that would play an important role in maintaining national morale.[11]

The issue of the draft was sensitive. On April 24, 1941, Washington Senators team owner Clark Griffith was quoted as saying that the War Department was aware of baseball's particular needs and was willing to help. He went on to emphasize that baseball had not gone to the War Department for special treatment. But Griffith had earlier sent a letter to General Edwin Wilson, secretary to the President, asking for just such special treatment. He made two proposals: first, he called for an army sergeant to be assigned to each team to drill the players, with the cost being paid by the teams; and second, he asked that the War Department restrict the draft to one player per season from any one team. These proposals were rejected, and a note on the letter sent by Griffith indicated that General Wilson had discussed the matter personally with Griffith.[12] As it turned out, baseball people need not have been so concerned about being perceived as unpatriotic. A Gallup poll in May indicated that 84 percent of the public favored deferments for players, while those who followed baseball regularly offered a 79 percent approval rate for deferments.

By Opening Day in 1941 the spirit of patriotism was widespread. Dan Daniel and other baseball correspondents suggested that the 1941 All-Star Game be a festival of Americanism and patriotism. In May, "I Am an American Day" was held at Yankee Stadium, where 30,000 fans heard the Seventh Regiment Band play "martial tunes" and the national anthem while the American flag was raised in center field.[13] In June the American League president, Will Harridge, announced that all servicemen would be admitted free to all his league's games. The National League followed suit shortly thereafter. Then in August, baseball participated in "Defense Bond Day."[14]

The first major league player to be inducted into military service was 27-year-old Philadelphia Phillies pitcher Hugh Mulcahy, who reported on March 8, 1941. Greenberg, the 1940 American League Most Valuable Player, was the most notable of the early draftees. He got his draft call on May 7, 1941, and readily gave up his $55,000-a-year job for one that paid $21 per month. Greenberg served until December 5, 1941 when he was given an honorable discharge under a new provision of the law that released all men over the age of 28 from service. The attack on Pearl Harbor came two days later, and on February 1, 1942, Greenberg volunteered for the Army Air Corps. Bob Feller, star pitcher for the Cleveland Indians, was the first major league player to enlist after the Japanese attack, as he volunteered for the Navy. By the start of the 1942 season there were 61 major league players in the service, and by the end of that season the number had increased to 243 out of approximately 400 in total (assuming 16 teams with a roster size of 25). Within a short time 90 percent of those on rosters at the time of Pearl Harbor were in the military.[15]

Baseball made much of the enlistment numbers and proclaimed its patriotism from the housetops. Behind the scenes, though, each team had an employee charged with keeping its players out of the draft, and baseball lobbied heavily to get a draft exemption for players, or at least a guarantee that any one major league team would lose only two players during the 1942 season. All of these clandestine efforts failed.

Baseball made much of the so-called "Green light" letter from President Roosevelt to Commissioner Landis on January 15 of 1942, saying that play should go forward as the game was necessary to the maintenance of civilian morale. "I honestly feel that it would be best for the country to keep base-ball going," wrote the President, and he indicated that he thought there should be more night games so that working people could attend.[16]

Major League Baseball tried to show its patriotism in many ways. The leagues donated $25,000 to the military to purchase baseball equipment. Foul balls that went into the stands during games were returned by fans and sent to the armed forces. All-Star Game receipts in 1942, 1943, and 1944 were given to Armed Forces baseball equipment funds, while seven interleague games replaced the 1945 All-Star Game, with proceeds going to the Army–Navy relief fund. Receipts from other games and exhibition games contributed substantially to Armed Forces baseball. War bond drives and scrap metal drives were conducted at the ballparks.[17] Meanwhile, mili-tary personnel in uniform were given free admission, and more night games were scheduled as suggested by the President. To accommodate the havoc that wartime transportation restrictions wreaked on travel during the war, baseball games started anywhere from 9.30 am to 9.30 pm. Players were used within the military to raise funds for the war effort.[18]

The impact of war was greatest on the minor leagues, which were deci-mated. There were forty-one minor leagues in 1941 and only nine in 1943, a drop explained primarily by the large number of young men being drafted. In Florida all minor leagues had shut down by 1943. Florida was also severely hit economically by the termination of spring training in the South in 1943 and for the remainder of the war.

In addition, baseball became part of the armed forces' effort.[c] Military baseball emerged as a major entertainment, as service rivalries developed in baseball. The Great Lakes Naval Training Center in Illinois became the baseball powerhouse of all the service teams. Captain Robert Emmet, the base commander, was known as the number-one man in baseball. Big-time baseball was played on the base two to three times a week, and crowds of 10,000 to 12,000 men came to watch. Games were scheduled with rival bases and with major league teams. Emmet had access to excellent talent, as 35 percent of all incoming naval recruits came through Great Lakes. Between 1942 and 1944, forty-three major leaguers, including six All-Stars and two future Hall-of-Famers, played for Great Lakes. In 1944 the team was 48–2 overall and 7–1 against major league teams. Only the Norfolk Naval Training Station rivaled the Great Lakes, as Norfolk had Bob Feller and Fred Hutchinson leading their pitching staff in 1942.[19]

---

[c] The US occupying force also used baseball as a diplomatic tool in Japan after the war. See "Global Baseball: Japan and East Asia," 160–161.

Two major leaguers and 128 minor league players lost their lives in World War II. The low casualty rate for major leaguers is due in part to the fact that many were assigned to morale-building positions out of the line of fire. Yet several players had their careers ended and many others had theirs shortened by war injury.

The quality of professional baseball suffered considerably as a result of the labor shortage, and the 1944 season (including the World Series) is generally considered the historical low point in major league play. By 1945, 260 players classified by Selective Service as 4Fs, (that is, medically unfit for military service) were on major league rosters, including the one-armed Pete Gray. Players came out of retirement, and managers and coaches returned to play; the young were rushed to the majors, including 15-year-old pitcher Joe Nuxhall, still the youngest player ever to play in the major leagues. Red Barber recalled that "it got so that anyone who could breathe could play."[20]

Not surprisingly, fewer fans turned out to watch major league games. By 1939 attendance had finally recovered from the Depression and reached 18.5 million, but by 1943 it had fallen back to 8 million, and in 1945 had risen only to 11.5 million. Teams were still able to turn a profit because there was a salary freeze. Adjusted for inflation, player salaries fell by 30 percent ($900) while revenues continued to climb.[21] Despite this desperate need for players, major league baseball did not turn to the obvious labor pool of African Americans, or to women.

Women instead found employment in the new All-American Girls Professional Baseball League (AAGPBL), created by Cubs owner Phil Wrigley in 1943. Female players helped to fill the quality gap left by the major leagues, and the quantity gap created by the diminishing minor leagues. Women had been playing baseball for over a half-century, and women's leagues had been in existence for decades. The war offered an opportunity for women to display their considerable baseball skills to a larger public. They offered good baseball and entertainment, and new role models for the generation of women who left their homes and moved into the workplace during the war. This league continued into the mid 1950s, after which the AAGPBL faded away.[22] Their story was resurrected in the 1992 film, *A League of Their Own.*[d]

The war also affected the debate over the integration of baseball. Occasional competitions in the military that involved both whites and African Americans, and the discussion of Nazi racial policies along with the tremendous emphasis on the war as a struggle of democracy against

[d] See "Baseball at the movies" in this volume, 112.

racist and totalitarian forces, led to an increase in the questions raised about racism in American society. African American leadership pressed the government on these issues, and sports commentators expressed impatience with the continuing segregation of baseball. Shortly after the war, the sporting world came to take a closer look at baseball. Having practiced segregation since the late nineteenth century, baseball came under increased pressure to change its racial policies. One theme in this discussion was that if African Americans could fight for democracy abroad, then certainly they should be eligible to play baseball at home. The resulting change, discussed in more detail elsewhere in this volume,[e] was important not just for baseball, but also for American society generally. Known as Baseball's Great Experiment, the desegregation of baseball was one of those public acts that symbolize a shift in public life

It would be only five years before baseball once again faced the issues raised by war. The Korean War, which began in June, 1950, failed to generate an impact even remotely comparable to Pearl Harbor. The draft did not seriously alter major league rosters, although military call-ups did result in a higher number of older players on major league rosters. Between 1953 and 1955 the number of ten-year veterans on major league rosters doubled. There were several players who had served in World War II who, as reserves, were recalled to Korea. By far the highest-profile player recalled was Ted Williams. Williams received his notice to report in 1952, and before long he was in Korea flying combat missions and adding to his legend. Of his thirty-seven missions, the most famous occurred when Williams successfully crash-landed his burning aircraft.

To bolster troop morale and show support for the war, the baseball establishment sponsored visits to Korea by star players like Joe DiMaggio. For the most part, however, Korea was not prominent on baseball's radar. The fact that the loss of players to military service was minimal, coupled with a growing public unhappiness over the war, meant that baseball did not come under the kind of public scrutiny that it experienced in previous conflicts.

The Korean War was generally believed to have contributed to a decline in major league baseball attendance, although attendance drops in the first half of the 1950s are more often explained by other factors relating to economics, demographics, and aging stadiums located in deteriorating urban locations. At the same time, baseball played its expected role in the Cold War, with officials arguing that the sport symbolized the democratic values of the United States in contrast with the totalitarian Soviet Union.[23]

[e] See "Baseball and the color line" in this volume, 71–73.

In the mid fifties in a fit of Cold War paranoia the Cincinnati Reds changed their name to the Cincinnati Redlegs, while the patriots running Little League baseball adopted a Little League Pledge:

> I trust in God
> I love my country
> And will respect its laws.

Baseball Commissioner Ford Frick added to the Cold War rhetoric when he claimed that America would be safe "as long as boys went to bed with catcher's mitts under their pillows."[24]

Baseball ownership did not welcome the interference of the Vietnam War with its business, but continued publicly to express its patriotism with its endorsement of the war. Tours by players and club executives to Vietnam, as well as visits to hospitals treating wounded service personnel, were frequent and highly publicized, but the players were not encouraged to volunteer for active duty. Players were able to avoid the draft and Vietnam service by joining the National Guard and the Reserves, maneuvers accomplished with the assistance of club owners and executives. This was such a common occurrence that the first general agreement between the Major League Baseball Players Association (MLBPA) and owners included a clause requiring a continuation of full pay for those serving in the National Guard and the Reserves.

In an extension of its Cold War stance, baseball continued to present an image of strong anti-Communism and support for the Vietnam War. The image of major league baseball emphasized its patriotism in the face of growing dissent against the war. Players who were selected for the goodwill tours to the war zone and hospitals treating wounded soldiers praised the troops for their courage and determination, even though these players were not prepared to volunteer for active duty themselves. Vietnam was not World War II.[25] Commissioner Bowie Kuhn encouraged visits to military personnel in Southeast Asia. A 1968 delegation was led by Ernie Banks of the Chicago Cubs, and in 1969 Kuhn joined a delegation led by Tug McGraw, Reggie Jackson, and Denny McLain. In 1970 four groups were sent to the war zone, with one led by Bob Feller.

On the home front, *The Sporting News* encouraged readers to purchase a subscription to the paper for a serviceman in Vietnam. The Official Baseball Guide was offered free to servicemen. General William Eckert, known as baseball's Unknown Soldier for his brief and undistinguished tenure as Commissioner from November of 1965 to the end of the 1968 season, was given an award for supporting the morale of the troops. His successor, Kuhn, aligned baseball with the policies of President Richard Nixon, who fancied himself a genuine baseball fan. During the 1969 All-Star week in Washington, Nixon invited to the White House over 400 baseball dignitaries, including those named by fans in a poll as the "greatest living players."

According to the Armed Forces Committee of the Society for American Baseball Research (SABR), fifty-two major league players served in Vietnam. Most of these athletes gained their major league experience following their tour of duty in Vietnam, and they were not always considered top prospects by their organizations. Among the players who did serve in Vietnam and went on to careers in the majors were Al Bumbry, Jerry Koosman, and Dave Goltz. No major league player died in action in the Vietnam War, although at least half-a-dozen players signed to minor league contracts did.[26] It should be noted, though, that many players missed parts of seasons while doing their six months of active service before entering reserve units, and many teams lost key players for two weeks, sometimes at critical times during the season, as they fulfilled their military Guard and Reserve obligations. By the mid 1960s it was becoming increasingly difficult to secure positions in National Guard and Reserve units. A Michigan congressman charged that athletes were getting preferential treatment to avoid the draft, and Pentagon figures seemed to confirm the charges. In 1967 there were 360 professional athletes serving in these draft-proof military units. Of this number, 145 were baseball players.[27]

Support for the Vietnam War in baseball was primarily a public-relations effort. Neither players nor their owners believed enough in the war to sacrifice baseball for it. And in the end there was little direct impact of the Vietnam War on baseball. It could be said, however, that baseball and its players were affected by the shifting cultural values of the 1960s produced by the counterculture, the civil rights movement, and the antiwar movement.[28] Certainly the successful organization of the MLBPA and the growing assertiveness of players owed something to this atmosphere. Less profound but still noticeable were the changes in length of hair and the appearance of facial hair around the ballparks, including on the field.

The next few decades saw little effect of war on baseball. Not until September 11, 2001 would the game again be drawn into the center of a national crisis. The immediate question following the attacks was when to resume playing baseball. There was some indication that the schedule would begin again on Friday following the Tuesday attack, but when the National Football League (NFL) canceled its Sunday games, and college and high school football games were also canceled for the weekend, it was clear that baseball would not start play again until after the weekend. Ever cautious on matters of policy and public relations, baseball let the NFL take the lead.

When the games did resume, the ceremonies were appropriately impressive. When the first game was played in New York on September 21 by the Mets, police bagpipers played "Amazing Grace," Diana Ross sang "God Bless America," and Marc Anthony sang the national anthem. Liza Minnelli did a rendition of "New York, New York" at the seventh inning stretch, backed by a chorus line of New York firemen and policemen. Mayor Giuliani, a Yankee fan, was at Shea Stadium as he participated in this communal act of mourning and gratitude, and Mets players donated their salaries for the night (totalling $4.5 million) to the families of city workers who had died during the rescue operations at the Twin Towers.[29]

The World Series at Yankee Stadium the next month was the scene of another patriotic explosion, with President George W. Bush on hand to throw out the first ball while wearing a New York Fire Department fleece over his bullet-proof vest. Bush gave the thumbs-up sign to the roaring crowd and fired a strike to the plate, illustrating what he meant when he said Americans should continue with their normal routines, like going shopping and going to sporting events. He added, "It helps keep the fabric of our country strong."[30]

The singing of "God Bless America" during the seventh inning stretch subsequently became universal at major league ballparks, and American flags were sewn on team uniforms. A year later ceremonies marked by moments of silence and special honors for 9/11 victims were held in major league stadiums across the country. Five years on, baseball held similar ceremonies in all the ballparks under the theme "We Shall Not Forget."[31] The playing of "God Bless America" has since diminished in frequency and is now played primarily on Sundays and holidays – except at Yankee Stadium, where it continues unabated, and where it caused a legal problem when fans were prohibited from leaving their seats during its playing.

With the invasion of Iraq came pressure on baseball to express not just faith in America but also either enthusiasm for the war or the more palatable alternative, support for the troops. The latter sentiment of course came to the fore as the public's negative feelings toward the war increased. The troops received assistance in a number of ways: the traditional sending of baseball equipment to American forces, the free admission to men in uniform to games (although often in low-priced seats), blood drives at the ballparks, and visits by players to wounded soldiers in hospitals and to troops in war zones. One of the most interesting and successful support programs was "Strikeouts for Troops," which was started in 2005 by Oakland A's pitcher Barry Zito. Pitchers donated a fixed-dollar amount for every strikeout, and position players made donations for base hits. Slowly, corporate sponsors came forward and pledged matching funds, which were used to support wounded soldiers in hospitals and to help meet the needs of their families. By 2009 over sixty players were participating and over two million dollars had been raised. Other players sponsored similar programs at their home ballparks.[32]

Two controversies emerged in connection with the Iraq war. One was New York Met Carlos Delgado's refusal to stand for the singing of "God Bless America." Some fans were upset with his actions, while others seemed to tolerate his position, which he said resulted from the fact that the invasion of Iraq was "the stupidest war ever."[33] Another controversy developed in April of 2003 when Dale Petroskey, the president of the Baseball Hall of Fame, cancelled a fifteenth-anniversary celebration of the film *Bull Durham* at the Hall. He said he feared that Susan Sarandon and Tim Robbins, who had starred in the 1988 film and were actively opposed to the Iraq war, might use the occasion to make an antiwar statement. Petroskey took a beating in the mainstream press over his decision.[34]

In conclusion, it seems as if the baseball establishment responded to the wars of the twentieth and early twenty-first century with ad hoc policies designed for each particular time and place. Within these variations there seem to have been two guiding principles: protect the business from immediate intrusion and protect the image of baseball as the dutifully patriotic national pastime. It was only in World War II that the business enterprise could not be protected, as the primacy of war engulfed all of American life. In the postwar world and the environment of the Cold War the executives who led baseball became increasingly adept at the black arts of public relations. Wrapping itself in the flag, the national pastime was able to achieve both objectives, protecting its investment and its image.

NOTES

1. One-third of all World War I draftees were found to be physically unfit; among members of the working class and farm families the rate was higher.
2. Richard C. Crepeau, *Baseball: America's Diamond Mind, 1919–1941* (Lincoln: University of Nebraska Press, 2004), 1–2.
3. "Category: World War I Veterans", www.baseball-reference.com/bullpen/Category:World_War_I_Veterans.
4. "To the Boys Coming Home," *The Sporting News*, February 13, 1919, 4.
5. Crepeau, *Baseball*, 3.
6. *Ibid.*
7. *Ibid.*, 198–200.
8. There are many sources on Berg, and among the best is Nicholas Dawidoff, *The Catcher Was a Spy: The Mysterious Life of Moe Berg* (New York: Pantheon Books, 1994), 87–96.
9. "Baseball's Role in Preparedness Plans," *The Sporting News*, August 1, 1940, 4.

10. Crepeau, *Baseball*, 207.
11. *Ibid.*, 209. Roosevelt's exhortation was in a letter to the New York Chapter of the Baseball Writers' Association on the occasion of their Annual Dinner.
12. *Ibid.*, 210–211.
13. *Ibid.*, 214.
14. *Ibid.*, 203–212.
15. *Gary Bedingfield's Baseball in Wartime*, www.baseballinwartime.com.
16. David Voigt, *American Baseball*, 3 vols., Vol. II (University Park: Pennsylvania State University Press, 1983), 146.
17. Stephen R. Bullock, *Playing for Their Nation: Baseball and the American Military during World War II* (Lincoln: University of Nebraska Press, 2004), 28–39.
18. Crepeau, *Baseball*, 215.
19. *Ibid.*, pp. 76–85.
20. Red Barber, *1947: The Year All Hell Broke Loose in Baseball* (New York: Da Capo Press, 1982), 30.
21. Voigt, *American Baseball*, 255–265; *Baseball in Wartime*, www.baseballinwartime.com.
22. Benjamin G. Rader, *Baseball: A History of America's Game*, 3rd edn. (Urbana and Chicago: University of Illinois Press), 173–175.
23. Ron Briley, *Class at Bat, Gender on Deck, and Race in the Hole* (Jefferson, NC: McFarland, 2003), 59–62.
24. Robert Elias, *The Empire Strikes Out: How Baseball Sold US Foreign Policy and Promoted the American Way Abroad* (New York: The New Press, 2010), 187–190.
25. *Ibid.*, 179–180, 189–190.
26. www.baseball-reference.com.
27. Ron Briley, "Baseball and Dissent: The Vietnam Experience," *NINE: A Journal of Baseball History and Culture* 17.1 (Fall, 2008), 63–66.
28. *Ibid.*
29. Tyler Kepner, "Baseball: Mets' Magic Heralds Homecoming," *New York Times*, September 22, 2001.
30. Buster Olney, "World Series: President Warms Up, then Throws Strike," *ibid.*, October 31, 2001.
31. "September 11, One Year Later: A Day of Remembrance," http://mlb.mlb.com/mlb/official_info/mlb_remember_911.jsp; "September 11, Five Years Later: We Shall Not Forget," http://mlb.mlb.com/mlb/official_info/anniversary_911.jsp.
32. www.strikeoutsfortroops.org.
33. Quoted in multiple newspaper and magazine sources including *The Nation*, December 7, 2005.
34. "Carlos Delgado," www.baseball-reference.com; Ira Berkow, "Sports of the Times: The Hall of Fame Will Tolerate No Dissent," *New York Times*, April 11, 2003.

7

DAVID FINOLI

Baseball and the American city

August 19 and October 8, 1957 are days that will live in baseball infamy. Those are the dates that the Giants and Dodgers announced they were leaving New York City for the greener pastures of California, moves that forever changed the landscape of the game. For the Dodgers in particular, it was the beginning of a phenomenon that saw baseball teams hold their clubs for ransom, pitting one city versus another in the hopes of getting a new stadium. The Dodgers' Brooklyn–Los Angeles move provoked a landmark controversy that set the terms for the stadium battles that go on today between government and professional franchises. Cities now had to assess not only the economic impact of losing a major league franchise, but also the emotional impact of losing a team on their loyal citizens.

Baseball franchise shifting began a few years earlier when the Braves, a poor stepchild to the Red Sox in Boston, packed up and left for Milwaukee. After drawing only 281,278 fans to Braves Field in 1952 (an average of fewer than 4,000 a game), majority team owner Lou Perini and his brothers began buying up the shares of the various other franchise stockholders in an attempt to become the team's sole owners. The Boston Braves already owned the baseball territorial rights to Milwaukee since they owned the minor league team there, and they had the right of refusal should the city pursue a major league franchise, which it was already aggressively doing. Perini promised the city he would not try and block their attempt to secure a club. With this assurance, Milwaukee's taxpayers invested $6.6 million (about $53.4 million in today's dollars) to build a modern facility in County Stadium capable of showcasing the national pastime at its highest level. City officials then began negotiating with the two St. Louis major league baseball teams, the Browns and Cardinals, to occupy the new stadium.

But Perini wanted his own team to be the tenants of the fabulous new stadium in Milwaukee. When Perini declared his intention to move on March 13, 1953, National League owners acted quickly, taking only five days to approve the first major league baseball franchise shift since the Baltimore

Orioles of the American League moved to New York in 1903. (That move occurred when New York businessman Frank Farrell purchased shares in the club after a dismal 1902 campaign and moved them to the Big Apple in 1903, giving American League president Ban Johnson a much-needed club in that very important market.)[1]

While no one shed tears for Boston – since most New Englanders acknowledged only the Red Sox as their home team – Perini's move opened the eyes of the baseball establishment to new options. The first thirteen home games the Braves played in 1953 brought in more people than the team had drawn during the entire year before. By the end of the season they had drawn more than 1.8 million patrons to County Stadium, averaging almost 24,000 per game.

Seeing the remarkable success of the Braves, the St. Louis Browns and Philadelphia Athletics both followed suit, moving to Baltimore and Kansas City, respectively, in 1954 and 1955. These too were shifts of second-rate franchises from cities that already had more successful major league clubs. It wasn't until the 1957 announcements by the Giants and Dodgers that established and successful franchises rocked baseball by moving their clubs. None of the three previous moves had occasioned any tense negotiations of one city against another for the best deal possible. The Dodger and Giant moves certainly did.

First to announce his move was Horace Stoneham, the penny-pinching owner of New York baseball's third wheel, the New York Giants. But the idea to migrate to the West Coast did not originate with Stoneham; he acted under the persuasive force of the domineering Walter O'Malley, owner of the Dodgers.[a] Only three years removed from their upset victory over the Cleveland Indians in the 1954 World Series, the Giants were financially hemorrhaging in the dilapidated Polo Grounds. The club had also slipped on the diamond, turning in consecutive sixth-place finishes in 1956 and 1957. As play suffered on the field, attendance decreased accordingly, lagging behind the local competition, the Yankees and Dodgers. Only 824,112 paying customers showed up to watch the Giants in 1955, the year after the team's championship, and 629,179 a year later. A New York team needed to sell more seats than that.

New York City officials proposed to Stoneham that the Giants relocate from Manhattan to the Bronx, becoming co-tenants in Yankee Stadium. There were also suggestions that they move into a facility in Manhattan where Madison Square Garden is now located, as well as proposals to build

[a] For more on O'Malley's forceful personality and the significance of the Dodgers' move from Brooklyn, see the interchapter on O'Malley immediately following, 107–110.

a domed stadium for the Giants and Yankees to share. Meanwhile, attendance nudged up only slightly in 1957.

A shift to the West Coast, on the other hand, would make the Giants baseball pioneers, for no major league team had until then ventured west of St. Louis. San Francisco outbid Minneapolis, and Stoneham got the deal New York couldn't (or wouldn't) give him. In return for his buying the San Francisco Seals of the Pacific Coast League and moving them to Salt Lake City, he got quite a gift from the Bay Area. San Francisco agreed to build a 45,000-seat, $5 million stadium, Candlestick Park, with 10,000 to 12,000 parking spaces. As tenants, the Giants agreed to pay just $125,000 per year (or 5 percent of their gross revenues, if that figure proved higher), a saving of more than 25 percent over their New York rent. Not only would they get a brand new stadium then, but with the Northern California market to themselves, they would not have to share the headlines with two other teams in New York. The team's Board of Directors voted by an eight-to-one margin to move to San Francisco. The only dissenter was M. Donald Grant, who four years later became the Chairman of the Board of the New York Mets, the National League replacement for the Giants.

Some experts doubted that the Giants would see the same boom in attendance enjoyed by the other recently relocated franchises. (Milwaukee's attendance increased more than sixfold compared to its last year in Boston, while Baltimore's attendance more than tripled the Browns' final-season mark of 297,238, and the Kansas City Athletics drew nearly 1.4 million, a huge increase over the 304,666 patrons that came to Philadelphia's Shibe Park during the team's last year there.) But the trend held. Despite having to play in a minor league facility while Candlestick Park was being completed, the Giants still almost doubled their attendance their first year in California.

While the Giants and Yankees shared the downtown New York headlines, the Dodgers were the kings of Brooklyn. It was an intimate relationship with a community that began in 1884 and was rarely seen in the annals of sports. Win or lose, the Dodgers were affectionately known to the borough as "Dem Bums," lovable also-rans who had often tantalized their fans before falling short of victory. After years of being thwarted time and time again by the Yankees, the club finally captured its first championship in 1955, defeating the Yankees in a tie-breaking seventh game. Attendance regularly topped a million a year. The future looked bright for the loyal Dodgers fans. But unbeknownst to them, the team's owner, Walter O'Malley, was looking for a different kind of future in Southern California.

O'Malley well knew of the success that other teams were having with their new stadiums, and he wanted to move the Dodgers from antiquated Ebbets Field. His symbolic gesture of scheduling eight Dodgers games a year in New Jersey during the 1956 and 1957 seasons helped make his wishes clear. O'Malley first sought to build a new stadium for the Dodgers in Brooklyn. He was repeatedly rebuffed by New York Parks Commissioner Robert Moses, who was so powerful that nothing could be built in New York without his permission. Years later many blame the Dodgers' move on Moses. Moses' biographer Robert Caro states that Moses "killed, over the efforts of Brooklyn Dodgers owner Walter O'Malley, plans for a city sports authority that might have kept the Dodgers and Giants in New York."[2] Michael Shapiro, author of an account of the Dodgers' last season in Brooklyn and the negotiations that led to their move to California, also claims Moses, not the Dodger owner, as the lead scoundrel in this saga.[3]

It would be simplistic to blame one or the other, for the reality is that while O'Malley had his economic reasons for moving, Moses certainly had some plausible objections. Historian Henry D. Fetter points out that Moses was against O'Malley's stadium plans from the outset, not because he wanted the Dodgers to leave but because he doubted that O'Malley's plans were realistic. Fetter points out that the city could have got more for the property O'Malley wanted than the price the Dodgers owner wanted to pay for it.[4]

Most important, there was no significant political support for funding a stadium that would be run by "a profit-making enterprise." New York councilman Stan Isaacs stated that he was against a project that was nothing more than "an effort to take care of the Dodgers." Congressman Emanuel Cellar, a Brooklyn resident who was the House Judiciary Committee chair, asked O'Malley at an antitrust hearing, "Do you think that a baseball club which has made the profits that your club has should be benefited by acquisition of land by eminent domain?" New York City Council president Abe Stark, who was best known in the baseball world for his sign on the Ebbets Field wall that offered a free suit to a player if he hit the sign with a batted ball, criticized the way O'Malley was conducting his business. "Dodger management has maintained a cold war of silence and evasion toward the people of New York while engaging in a warm flirtation with the mayors of the Pacific coast," said Stark.

With many men, both political and within team management, at odds with each other, O'Malley offered himself up for courtship by other cities. In February of 1957, Los Angeles Mayor Norris Poulson and LA County Supervisor Kenneth Hahn decided to visit the club during preseason spring training in Florida to pitch O'Malley on the benefits of taking the franchise to the West Coast. New York Mayor Robert Wagner countered in a letter to O'Malley, stating that "The Dodgers are uniquely identified with this city ... All possible efforts to arrive at a satisfactory solution in the best interest of the community will be made."[5] Wagner's statement cheered O'Malley, who believed that he would be able to secure the stadium he wanted.

But O'Malley did not anticipate the opposition he would receive from the politically powerful Moses. In an April 11, 1957 memo, O'Malley detailed his frustration with Moses in trying to obtain land in Brooklyn to build his stadium: "We frankly discussed the general political apathy toward the new stadium in Brooklyn. Bob said there was not a chance of the Atlantic & Flatbush site [in Brooklyn] being approved." Moses was trying to offer a Queens site to the Dodgers, at Flushing Meadow (the eventual site of Shea Stadium, the first permanent home of the New York Mets). This angered O'Malley, who went on to say, "I told him that if the Dodgers would have to go out of Brooklyn any site would have to be weighed against such available locations such as Los Angeles."[6]

Los Angeles offered 400 acres of land in a section of the city called Chavez Ravine, with an additional 40 acres to be developed for recreational purposes. The city also gave O'Malley $4.7 million to begin construction on what would turn out to be the premier facility in baseball, Dodger Stadium. With Moses refusing to help O'Malley stay in Brooklyn, the Dodgers owner shifted the team to Los Angeles. On October 7, 1957, the Los Angeles City Council approved the deal by a ten-to-one vote, and a day later O'Malley agreed to it.

O'Malley claimed financial hardship, but he was predictably made out as an outlaw by the New York media. *New York Post* scribe Milton Gross accused O'Malley of "hiding behind statements that seemed to have substance but really were only shadows." "'Damn the fans,'" Gross imagined O'Malley saying, "'California, here we come' ... The only word that fits the Dodgers is greed."[7] Loyal fans of the Dodgers also disdained O'Malley. When Dodgers devotees Pete Hamill and Jack Newfield got together to compose a list of their ten worst human beings of the twentieth century, the two journalists came up with the same top three: Hitler, Stalin, and Walter O'Malley.[8] Newfield later commented that "you're not really from Brooklyn unless you hate the man who broke our teenage hearts ... O'Malley killed a generation's innocence."[9]

Shapiro says that:

> When the Dodgers left, it didn't rip the heart out of the borough ... That's too much. I think people said that because they couldn't quite put into words the sense of what was lost. The departure of the Dodgers denied Brooklyn, for half the year, this common conversation – the idle chitchat you have with people on the subway or waiting for the elevator or going to the butcher. Baseball informed so much of that. "Can you believe that Furillo last night? Snider's a bum! Is Hodges gonna get a hit?" It created a relationship between

strangers – you felt close to them, if only for a minute or two. What was lost was each other.[10]

That "each other" included the the Dodger players themselves, for many of the players were actually part of the community. Brooklynites might spy shortstop Pee Wee Reese and his family at the local store, or first baseman Gil Hodges and his family about town. There is a famous, perhaps apocryphal, story about a priest asking his parishioners to pray for Hodges when he was in a career-threatening slump. When Reese died in 1999, a memorial service was held for him in Brooklyn as well as in his home town of Louisville, Kentucky.

O'Malley's move proved financially successful right away, as the Dodgers almost doubled their 1957 attendance. Nearly two million fans passed through the turnstiles at the Memorial Coliseum in 1958. But not all of the citizens of Los Angeles were enamored of the city's new acquisition from Brooklyn.

O'Malley had hoped to open Dodger Stadium by 1959. His attempts were delayed by a taxpayers' lawsuit claiming the Dodgers received the land for the stadium illegally, because the land was earmarked for a public purpose. The plaintiffs argued that a baseball stadium, as a private enterprise, didn't meet this criterion. The city argued that major league baseball filled a civic need.

This assertion of civic need may lie at the heart of the controversy, for it inflects virtually all arguments for or against professional sports franchise movement. In Brooklyn, where the majority of residents were crushed by the loss of their beloved team, many blamed the loss of the Dodgers for the eventual decline of the borough itself, though it seems unlikely that the migration of the Dodgers caused the later downturn of population and economic status in the borough. Writer Sam Anderson points out that:

> The Dodgers weren't the only ones who left – a whole generation followed O'Malley's lead. The white middle classes – a couple of centuries' worth of Europe's persecuted poor – fled in new cars on even newer roads to the freshly minted suburbs of Long Island ... A whole generation of Brooklyn kids lost the mythic homeland right on the brink of adulthood ... The Dodgers, of course, didn't cause any of this, [but] ... they became powerful shorthand for it.[11]

The team may have been a civic enhancement, but it's far less clear that it served a civic *need*.

The Los Angeles side of the civic-need argument played out in the lower courts, where the taxpayers first won their suit. The city appealed to the state's Supreme Court, and emerged victorious.[12] By the time that the case reached the state's high court, the cost of construction had gone up, leading O'Malley to strike a deal with the Union Oil Company to sponsor the club's broadcasts. Finally in 1962, after years of fighting with opponents and four years in Southern California, O'Malley opened Dodger Stadium.

The Dodgers' Brooklyn–Los Angeles ordeal ushered in an era of endless cases that would pit baseball franchises in search of lucrative stadium deals against the cities competing for them. Cities now had to factor in the economic impact of losing their teams if they did not build the facilities for them.

Team relocations, taboo for many years in sport, now happened with alarming regularity. The Washington Senators, proud inhabitants of the nation's capital for sixty years, left for Minnesota in 1961. The American League gave Washington, DC an expansion club that season to replace them, but the replacement Senators again showed that Washington was not a profitable baseball market. They moved to Arlington, Texas in 1972. Milwaukee, which took the Braves from Boston, lost the club in turn following the 1965 season, as the owners moved it south to Atlanta.

Even the expansion of 1969, when San Diego, Seattle, Kansas City, and Montreal were awarded franchises, led to relocation, for one team immediately and another decades later, in both instances replacing franchises for the cities that lost them. The Seattle Pilots played just one season in the Emerald City before moving to Milwaukee, where they remain today as the Brewers. The Montreal Expos lasted thirty-five years in Canada before becoming Washington, DC's third major league team since 1901.

The business climate had changed drastically for the national pastime. Relocation was now a real fear for those cities that could not offer baseball clubs modern facilities. After a half-century of stability, richly storied teams and expansion clubs alike – and the governments of the cities they played in – faced new issues.

Beginning with Milwaukee County Stadium in 1950, nearly all the new (and refurbished) baseballparks were municipally funded.[13] In this era of relocation and then expansion, city leaders discovered that owners would settle their franchises only if cities, in the pursuit of "major league" status and (sometimes elusive) economic growth, built, subsidized, and maintained stadiums. Not that mayors, council members, business people, journalists, and boosters objected: how else, as economist Andrew Zimbalist has noted, could one's city attract a team, since antitrust laws did not apply to organized baseball and major league owners jealously restricted the number of franchises?[14] Costs to the public rapidly escalated; after Milwaukee had spent $6.6 million to build County Stadium in the early 1950s, and Kansas City $3 million to refurbish its minor league park for the arriving Athletics, New York paid $28.5 million for Shea Stadium in the early 1960s, Pittsburgh $35 million for Three Rivers Stadium a few years after that, and Cincinnati $41 million for Riverfront (whose rental and upkeep it then subsidized). The renovation of Yankee Stadium, estimated at $24 million in 1971, came in at approximately $100 million in 1976.[15] In 2009 the Yankees and Mets secured financing in the neighborhood of $2.3 billion altogether from New York City to build the new Yankee Stadium and the Mets' Citi Field (which ironically was modeled after Ebbets Field).[16] The best seats in the new Yankee Stadium were priced at an astronomical $2,625 per seat. This caused some irritation among the fans as many of the prime seats went unsold. Despite fans' discontent at the inflated prices to see a game, however, the teams combined to seat over 6.9 million fans in 2009.

Major league baseball's first foray into the Sunshine State presents a complex contemporary case. While Major League Baseball had been openly interested in bringing its product to Florida for years, it was thought that Tampa Bay would be the place they would choose to go. Instead, Miami was granted a franchise in 1993. Blockbuster Video owner Wayne Huizenga thwarted conventional wisdom when he purchased half of Joe Robbie Stadium (home of the National Football League's Miami Dolphins), and put on an intense public-relations campaign that included staging two exhibition games there that drew 113,000 fans. (It didn't hurt either that Blockbuster was in charge of the video productions for the league.)

In the first five years of the franchise, Florida finished in the top six among National League team attendance three times, drawing over three million fans in their inaugural season. The following twelve campaigns were anything but successful. Six times the Marlins finished fifteenth out of sixteen teams in total attendance, and the last four of those they finished dead last. They registered these low attendance figures despite winning records in five of the last seven of those seasons, and the team even won a World Series championship in 2003. Club ownership announced that the team needed a new baseball-only facility, and demanded help from the local and state governments to build a stadium. The team commissioned reports to show what such an investment could do for the local economies.

A 2005 report on the impact of sports and recreation on the state of Florida paints a very rosy picture. During 2004, sports produced $32 billion in statewide revenue while employing about 434,000 people. Professional franchises alone generated $2.1 billion that year, along with 18,200 jobs.[17] A closer look shows that the nine sports franchises located in Florida in 2004 generated a combined attendance of 7.4 million fans, 361,000 of whom traveled from outside the state, bringing their disposable income into Florida. Most impressive – but also anomalous – is the economic impact of baseball's preseason spring training, which many teams conduct in Florida during February and March. Over a half million fans attended spring training games in Florida in 2004, with about half coming from outside the state, bringing 129 million of their dollars with them. That spring training bonanza is an economic circumstance unique to Florida and Arizona, which between them host all thirty-two major league teams as they prepare for each season.

After years of being rebuffed in their attempts to build a baseball-only facility, the club threatened to relocate. Ownership visited San Antonio in 2005 and formally petitioned Major League Baseball for permission to relocate. The threat apparently worked, as the county and city agreed to a $515 million financing plan to construct a state-of-the-art stadium on the site where the Orange Bowl once stood.

So does a city have a "civic need" for major league baseball? It's hard to say, though economic desire clearly figures in the equation on both sides. But it's much more difficult to calculate what a major league team may be worth to a city against the obvious costs.

What if a team fails financially despite a new subsidized facility? They may still relocate, leaving the city with a stadium without a team to play in it. Consider the plight of the Pittsburgh Pirates. Several times over the past twenty years, the Pirates have been in danger of moving. To keep the team in the city (even though it was failing on the field soon after a period of success in the early 1990s), a new facility named PNC Park was constructed in 2001 to replace Three Rivers Stadium, which dates from 1970. Ironically, the city of Pittsburgh had originally defeated a financing proposal for a new stadium for the Pirates and football's Pittsburgh Steelers in 1997, by a significant margin. This defeat raised a real possibility of Pittsburgh losing the Steelers to nearby Washington County and the Pirates from the area all together.

Local Pittsburgh politicians, led by Mayor Tom Murphy, believed that losing the team would be an economic black eye for the city. They came up with an alternative financing plan that took money from a tax already being collected, which would be diverted into construction of both stadiums and an upgrade to the convention center. Plan B, as it was called, was controversial among those who voted public financing down, but nonetheless an agreement with the club was finalized, keeping the Pirates in Pittsburgh until at least 2031.

An important reason that cities don't freely hand out money to baseball franchises is the growing belief that the economic impact of a team and new facility on a city is nothing more than a mirage. A 2005 study by economists Victor A. Matheson and Robert A. Baade found that baseball franchises and the sparkling new stadiums that cities build to house them may not really be economic winners after all. Matheson and Baade note that "Public finance economists … are in general agreement that the figures produced by sports boosters are wildly inflated." They cite many studies that suggest that "new stadiums provide little or no net economic stimulus to the communities in which they are located."[18]

Matheson and Baade emphasize two points. First, they say that it is a mistake to assume that a person who spends money at a baseball game won't spend money anywhere else if there is no team to see. Speaking about the 2000 World Series between the Yankees and Mets, Andrew Zimbalist argues that, "If you buy a $100 ticket to the Series, that's money you might have spent on a Broadway show or food."[19] "Indigenous" fans may simply reallocate their spending. Matheson and Baade conclude that the "distinction between gross and net spending has been cited by economists as a chief reason why professional sports in general do not seem to contribute as much to metropolitan economies as boosters claim."[20]

Their second assessment follows from the first: that one can't necessarily judge the economic impact of a franchise on a city by looking at the spending of local fans, but instead must look at only those who come in from out of town. Certainly that is an important factor but, as stated before, one that might be more impressive in the spring training areas of Arizona and Florida. While consumer money would surely go into other activities if a sports franchise did leave an area, it's not realistic to assume that all the money would necessarily be spent in other local endeavors.

There is a huge disparity between Matheson's and Baade's conclusions and the economic impact reports commissioned by the teams. Perhaps the reality falls somewhere in between. With so much money being generated by these teams, there certainly is a benefit to the economy of a city – maybe not to the extent that the teams claim, but certainly something. Major league franchises also might add to the quality of life and help attract businesses, as the Florida report suggests.

This chapter has dealt primarily with the economic impact of professional baseball franchises on a community, but let's not forget the emotional impact a team has on a city. One need only look to the faces of Chicago Cubs fans lamenting their years of futility together. Or look to the celebrations of "Red Sox Nation" celebrating the banishment of the "Curse of the Bambino" in 2004, their first championship season since Sox owner Harry Frazee sold Babe Ruth to the Yankees in 1919. That emotion can even be found in the eyes of the almost two million Pirate fans who descend upon PNC Park every year looking for a new version of Roberto Clemente to help them end nearly two decades of ongoing futility.

A major league franchise offers more than economic gain. It can bind a community like nothing else a city can offer. A small percentage of citizens may enjoy a world-class orchestra or museum, but win a World Series and half-a-million fans will dance through the streets in pride for their team and city. Does that mean Walter O'Malley was wrong to move the Dodgers and Pittsburgh Mayor Tom Murphy wrong to keep the Pirates? To answer those questions one must ask: should community governments consider the emotional impact of a sports franchise on a city as well as the economic impact? The answer, I would suggest, is that emotion should weigh in the balance, but it cannot supersede economics as the main reason a city and a team should form a partnership. Sports is finally a business, and if both parties are not making out financially, it makes no sense to continue the relationship – even though it may crush the fans of the particular team, as it did those loyal Brooklynites over fifty years ago.

NOTES

1. Donald Dewey and Nicholas Acocella, *Total Ballclubs* (Toronto: Sports Classic Books, 2005), 333–334.
2. Robert Caro, *The Power Broker: Robert Moses and the Fall of New York* (New York: Alfred A. Knopf, 1974), 1018.
3. Michael Shapiro, *The Last Good Season* (New York: Doubleday, 2003). Dave Anderson, a sportswriter who covered the Brooklyn Dodgers, argued recently that O'Malley, not Moses, was the culprit, in "Time Doesn't Relieve the Pain, or Change the Facts," *New York Times*, September 30, 2007. Available online at www.nytimes.com/2007/09/30/sports/baseball/30anderson.html?scp=1&sq=walter%200%27malley&st=cse.
4. Henry D. Fetter, "Revising the Revisionists: Walter O'Malley, Robert Moses, and the End of the Brooklyn Dodgers," *New York History* 89.1 (Winter, 2008), 55–76. Available online at www.historycooperative.org/journals/nyh/89.1/fetter.html#FOOT3. Quotations in the following paragraph are also drawn from the online source.
5. www.walteromalley.com.
6. *Ibid.*
7. Fetter, "Revising the Revisionists."
8. *Ibid.*
9. Jack Newfield, "O'Malleys Can't Dodge Their Shame," *New York Daily News*, January 29, 1990.
10. Sam Anderson, "Exorcising the Dodgers," *New York Magazine*, September 16, 2007. Available online at http://nymag.com/news/sports/37643/.
11. Anderson, "Exorcising the Dodgers."
12. Andy McCue, "Walter O'Malley," *Baseball Biography Project*, http://bioproj.sabr.org/bioproj.cfm?a=v&v=l&bid=790&pid=16919.
13. Thanks to David F. Venturo for the material on stadium costs in this paragraph.
14. Andrew Zimbalist, *In the Best Interests of Baseball? The Revolutionary Reign of Bud Selig* (Hoboken: John Wiley, 2006), 171.
15. Steven A. Riess, *City Games: The Evolution of American Urban Society and the Rise of Sports* (Urbana: University of Illinois Press, 1989), 234–245.

16. David Samuels, "Before the Fall," *The National*, October 30, 2009. Available online at www.thenational.ae/apps/pbcs.dll/article?AID=/20091030/REVIEW/710299996/1008.

17. The Washington Economics Group Inc., *The Economic Impact of Sports and Recreation Activities in Florida* (Coral Gables, FL: The Washington Economics Group Inc., 2004).

18. Victor A Matheson and Robert A Baade, "Striking Out? The Economic Impact of Major League Baseball Work Stoppages on Host Communities" (April, 2005), http://ideas.repec.org/p/hcx/wpaper/0507.html.

19. Andrew Zimbalist, quoted in *Forbes* magazine, October 21, 2000. Available online at www.forbes.com/2000/10/21/1021series.html.

20. Matheson and Baade, "Striking Out?"

LEONARD CASSUTO

Interchapter: Walter O'Malley

During the late 1950s a joke circulated widely among Brooklyn residents: if you were to find yourself in a room with Hitler, Stalin, and Walter O'Malley and you had a gun with only two bullets, you'd have to shoot O'Malley twice.

Over fifty years have passed since Walter O'Malley announced his plans to move the Brooklyn Dodgers to Los Angeles, but there are still Brooklynites who recognize that joke. Some have inherited it, being too young to have seen a Brooklyn Dodger in the flesh themselves. Branch Rickey, general manager of the Dodgers starting in 1942 and part-owner of the team from 1944 until O'Malley bought him out in 1950, described Brooklyn as a "proud, hurt, jealous" community "seeking geographical and emotional status as a city" – which it had been until 1898. "One could not live for eight years in Brooklyn," said Rickey, "and not catch its spirit of devotion to its baseball club."[1]

Baseball owners were vilified before Walter O'Malley and they've certainly been vilified since, but the vitriol hurled at O'Malley set a standard for acidity that has never been approached. What made O'Malley so easy to hate?

Walter O'Malley was hated because of his honesty. I don't mean to suggest that O'Malley was open in his baseball dealings. He said he wanted to keep the Dodgers in Brooklyn, but it's hard to test the extent of his devotion to that goal, and the record is murky. History, as recounted in the previous chapter and elsewhere, suggests that O'Malley did make an effort to find a new Brooklyn home for the Dodgers, and there's no question that Parks Commissioner Robert Moses opposed him. But O'Malley also wanted to get as much profit out of his baseball franchise as possible, and he saw the economic potential that lay in the West. The outcome of O'Malley's dealings shows that he wanted to make money more than he wanted to keep his team in its historic home.

Of his desire for gain O'Malley made no secret. He didn't portray himself as a guardian of a sacred compact between fans and their team, but rather as

Figure 6. Los Angeles Dodgers owner Walter O'Malley looks over a drawing
of his proposed Dodger Stadium in Chavez Ravine in July, 1958, during the
team's first season in California. AP Photo/Ellis R. Bosworth.

a businessman out to make the best deal for himself. In this respect O'Malley
differed from previous baseball owners, most of whom had been content to
stay out of the spotlight and cash their checks while doing their best to
maintain the notion that major league baseball barely involved money at all.
Baseball's pastoral legend has always conflicted with its economic reality in
this way, and O'Malley did little to varnish that reality. "It had always been
recognized that baseball was a business," wrote columnist Red Smith, "but
if you enjoyed the game you could tell yourself that it was also a sport."
Smith fingered O'Malley as "the first to say out loud that it was all business – a business that he owned and could operate as he chose."[2]

O'Malley was a dominating personality who molded the business of
the Dodgers according to his own vision. Bill Giles, part-owner of the

Philadelphia Phillies and son of former National League president Warren Giles, said that in his father's time O'Malley "was by far the strongest and most outspoken owner, and he kind of led things."[3] His peers considered him to be something of a business genius. Bowie Kuhn, Baseball Commissioner from 1969 to 1984, suggested that if O'Malley "had decided to be king of Ireland, the Emerald Isle would be a monarchy today – and a profitable one at that."[4]

Now that the Los Angeles Dodgers are a longstanding fact of life, the results of their move west bear out what Roger Kahn, elegist for the Brooklyn Dodgers, called O'Malley's "dispassionate brilliance."[5] Baseball scholar John Thorn says in retrospect that O'Malley may be seen as "the Johnny Appleseed of the game," the man who planted it in the country's great western expanse.[6]

The Dodgers set attendance records in Los Angeles. In their first year there, playing in cavernous Los Angeles Memorial Coliseum while waiting for court permission to build their own stadium, the Dodgers recorded over 1.8 million paid fan admissions, against a National League average of 1.3 million. During their first year in Dodgers Stadium in 1962, the Dodgers drew 2.8 million, more than twice the league average of 1.1 million. In 1978 the Dodgers became the first major league baseball team to reach the 3 million mark in paid attendance. There has not been a year since they moved to Los Angeles that the Dodgers' attendance has not exceeded the league average.

Walter O'Malley died in 1979. His son, Peter O'Malley, sold the team to Fox Group (part of Rupert Murdoch's communications empire) in 1998 for about $350 million, a record for a sports franchise at the time. In 2008 the team, since sold to real-estate mogul Frank McCourt, was valued by *Forbes* at $694 million, of which $294 million was attributable to the Los Angeles market, and another $104 million to "brand management."[7]

In 2008, Walter O'Malley was elected to baseball's Hall of Fame.

NOTES

1. Branch Rickey, quoted in Geoffrey C. Ward and Ken Burns, *Baseball: An Illustrated History* (New York: Alfred A. Knopf, 1994), 348.
2. Red Smith, quoted in John Helyar, *Lords of the Realm: The Real History of Baseball* (New York: Ballantine Books, 1994), 62.
3. Richard Sandomir, "O'Malley and Kuhn Enter Hall, Forever Linked by Bold Moves," *New York Times*, July 27, 2008. Available online at www. nytimes.com/2008/07/27/sports/baseball/27hall.html?scp=7&sq=walter%20 o%27malley&st=cse.
4. Bowie Kuhn, *Hardball: The Education of a Baseball Commissioner* (New York: Times Books, 1987), 23.

5. Roger Kahn, "Walter O'Malley in the Sunshine," *New York Times*, February 5, 1978, 8C.

6. Sewell Chan, "Executive who Moved 'Dem Bums' Out of Brooklyn Is Hall of Famer," *New York Times*, December 3, 2007. Available online at http://cityroom. blogs.nytimes.com/2007/12/03/exec-who-moved-dem-bums-out-of-brooklyn-to-join-hall-of-fame/?scp=5&sq=walter%20o%27malley%20dies&st=cse.

7. "The Business of Baseball," *Forbes* magazine. Available online at www.forbes. com/lists/2008/33/biz_baseball08_Los-Angeles-Dodgers_338671.html.

8

GEORGE GRELLA

Baseball at the movies

Whatever the facts of history, geography, government, or law – as if facts really mattered in any discussion of baseball – the national mythology we call the American Dream dwells in two capitals: those very different but equally magical municipalities, Cooperstown and Hollywood. Growing out of a rich mixture of rumor and reality, lore and legend, history and sheer fantasy, and permanently associated with those two places, over their separate lifetimes the twin arts of baseball and the cinema follow parallel courses that, oddly, only occasionally intersect. Despite a potential for fruitful development, the two endeavors, so closely identified with American culture, enjoy a loose, irregular, and complicated relationship, in which they often exhibit a disappointing failure to communicate and collaborate. Because they share a sporadic allegiance to some major strains in the national discourse, by rights baseball really should be a major subject of film and the baseball film itself really should be a major genre. As most students of either or both arts know, however, those rights count for little. The baseball movie remains, for the most part, something like an important, populous, but minor form compared to the great genres of American popular cinema.

Initially baseball seems an entirely appropriate subject, the perfect inspiration for what blurb writers invariably call major motion pictures. Its special place in the history and culture of the country, its appeal as the national pastime, and its practice as an everyday American activity certainly account for its innumerable incidental appearances in hundreds of non-baseball motion pictures, as a characterizing touch, a thematic statement, even a kind of cinematic wallpaper.[1] In addition, despite its spotty history, the baseball movie itself boasts its own traditions, some peculiar to its particular temporal context. Since the 1980s, a good decade for the form, the success of a handful of works, and a subsequent proliferation of baseball films of all kinds and levels of merit suggest that the category may be undergoing a minor renaissance. After many years of mediocre performance at the box office, the baseball movie, though hardly thriving, currently enjoys a modicum of popularity and, occasionally, a dash of genuine quality.

Both film and baseball actually share origins in the dark backward and abysm of time, in events shrouded in the mists of racial memory. Baseball begins somewhere in the stick-and-ball games played for religious reasons in prehistoric societies – to herald (or guarantee) the death of winter, the advent of spring, the renewal of the community. Although dependent on an immensely complicated, labor-intensive process involving chemistry and technology, motion pictures, surprisingly, also grow from roots in the distant past, eons before photography ostensibly gave birth to the cinema. The art of cinema, like the sport of baseball, then, exhibits a sufficiently venerable history to justify a union of the two.

The lackluster box-office performance and the tepid critical response to so many early baseball films, though much exaggerated by the usual "experts" in and out of Hollywood, contradict some of that history and the inherent appeal of the combination of the sport and the art. The sheer visual enchantment of the game, for example, should provide sufficient support for its presence in the cinema. The familiar paeans to the beauty of its stadiums, those lyrical effusions over the great green cathedrals that annually irrigate and fertilize the barren wastes of Opening Day sports-writer prose, suggest something of the cinematic possibilities of its admittedly lovely space. In the sheer grandeur of its distances, the sport's arena presents rich possibilities for the motion-picture camera.

Curiously, however, few baseball films fully exploit the visual potential of the ballpark, another reason for the long stretch of generally unsatisfying movies. Among contemporary films, the only one that suggests the thrill any fan feels ascending a stadium ramp to that first glimpse of the vista of green fields, deals not with the major leagues but with the All American Girls Professional Baseball League. In *A League of Their Own* (1992), director Penny Marshall allows her two major characters one brief moment when they regard the beauty of Wrigley Field as it opens up for their first breathtaking sight of a major league stadium. The other important motion picture that most eloquently celebrates the sheer look of the playing ground is *Field of Dreams* (1989), which shows a homemade ballpark in the middle of an Iowa cornfield, an amateur's singlehanded creation born of visions and fantasies, appropriate to the bucolic setting and the work's themes of nostalgia, loss, death, and rebirth.

On the other hand, in fairness, the special nature of the game itself also apparently defies many attempts to translate it entirely successfully to the screen. Of all the movies about sports, the most prolific and successful subgenre is the boxing film, which demonstrates by its diametric difference some of the challenges baseball presents for the film director. The prize fight offers a great deal in technique and substance to the filmmaker: a constricted arena; simple and obvious conflict; rapid, violent action; gritty surroundings; the contrasting glamor and melodrama of many typically shady stories; a cast of interestingly sinister characters outside the ring. No wonder the boxing film occupies a solidly identifiable genre with its own history and conventions and seems never to go out of style or fade in popularity. Inversely, the very spaciousness and complexity of baseball, the sources of so much of its appeal, which initially seem to recommend it, paradoxically create some of the major obstacles to the filmmaker; those grand green fields rarely inspire more powerful movies than that small roped rectangle.

Another challenge for baseball filmmakers derives from the nature of the game, which requires outstanding athletic ability, and the reality of another difficult endeavor, acting. Although a number of big stars and accomplished actors (not always the same thing) appear in baseball movies, only a few, whatever their talents, demonstrate much athleticism once they don the uniform and step onto the field. Gary Cooper, who looked a little like Lou Gehrig, impersonated him in *The Pride of the Yankees* (1942), delivering Gehrig's immortal speech at the end with the dignity and restraint the historic occasion deserved. His play at first base in several scenes, however, if not absolutely disgraceful, did little to burnish the legend of the Iron Horse. Since Cooper couldn't convincingly swing left-handed, the director shot him batting from the right side of the plate, then running around the bases clockwise; he then reversed the film. Establishing but perhaps also limiting his career by playing a series of mentally unbalanced characters, Anthony Perkins took on the role of Jimmy Piersall in *Fear Strikes Out* (1957), where in the Hollywood tradition he displayed both excellent acting skills and inferior athletic ability; in *Psycho* he wielded that chef's knife, the real Tony Perkins autograph model, far more adroitly than the bat he swung at Fenway Park. One of the most honored actors to play a player, Robert De Niro as the doomed Bruce Pearson in *Bang the Drum Slowly* (1973) appears slight and frail in a baseball uniform, nobody's idea of an athlete, let alone a major league catcher. Those few examples suggest that a movie buff/baseball fan could probably make up a whole nonstar team, with a solid bench, of good actors/bad ballplayers.

In recent years, perhaps responding to a demand for greater verisimilitude or simply through the happy accidents of casting, a new generation of actors plays the game far more convincingly on the screen. Robert Redford in *The Natural* (1984), for example, despite his short stature, *looks*, as they say, like a ballplayer; a physically graceful performer in many films, he knows how to move and how to stand still, abilities that carried over successfully into his impersonation of Roy Hobbs. Tall, muscular, and athletic, Tom Selleck convincingly plays an over-the-hill major leaguer in *Mr. Baseball* (1992). In *Major League* (1989) several actors behave appropriately on the field – Tom Berenger, Charlie Sheen, and the diminutive Wesley Snipes, among an ensemble cast, appear comfortable swinging bats, throwing balls (usually the major problem), and running the bases. Perhaps most important, they all look comfortable in their uniforms, not like actors dressed in costumes, but like ballplayers wearing their usual working clothes.

Of all the contemporary stars who appear as ballplayers in film, however, the one who stands out as the best athlete is Kevin Costner, who has played baseball on the screen more often than any of his contemporaries. Costner displays his talents most fully in one of the best baseball films, *Bull Durham* (1988), as the washed-up minor league catcher Crash Davis. He spends a good deal of screen time on the field, calling the pitches of the wild, headstrong young phenom, Nuke LaLoosh (Tim Robbins) and compiling a not entirely desirable career record for home runs in the minor leagues. He displays his hitting prowess best in a batting cage – while bantering with Annie Savoy (Susan Sarandon) he swings a bat easily left-handed, right-handed, and even one-handed, striking the ball with the casual authority of a genuine professional. He also ends *Field of Dreams* by playing catch, with a certain purposeful clumsiness, with his dead father on the field that he constructed in accordance with instructions from a disembodied voice.

In *For Love of the Game* (1999), as Danny Chapel, a veteran pitcher for the Detroit Tigers, Costner pitches a perfect game, which also structures the whole movie, then gracefully retires. Costner plays essentially the same character in *The Upside of Anger* (2005), where he is a retired Tigers pitcher named Denny Davies, now a Detroit radio talk show host who supplements his income with personal appearances at supermarket openings and the sale of autographed baseballs. (The character, incidentally, seems closely based on the former Tigers pitcher Denny McLain, who also hosts a radio show in Detroit.) Costner's obvious physical skills separate him from the many actors who put on spikes, but in addition, his career in film, unusually, parallels his fictional career as a baseball player, so that he becomes the rare actor who follows a familiar trajectory in both the sport and the art, aging with some dignity and plausibility in both endeavors.

If the geography and geometry of the game present difficulties for the cinema, and if the problematic athleticism of the players in film often subverts credibility, baseball's simple human stories remain a constant and probably unending source of appeal. Whatever the challenges of the visual and the athletic, the human dimension remains the actual subject of any baseball film, and a constant that no writer or director can ignore. For the necessary elements of drama and narrative, both the sport's history and its contemporary reality furnish plenty of substance for a screenwriter or director. Aside from the familiar, often sentimental stories, both true and fictional, of sports-related movies – those uplifting tales of aspiration, the conquest of adversity, victory and defeat, tragedy and triumph – baseball positively abounds with colorful and charismatic characters. Life itself, which, as Mark Twain pointed out, has no obligation to be probable, provides an abundance of memorable people, strange occurrences, and eccentric stories, more than enough to inspire any artist. Neither fiction nor film could invent many of the actual characters and events that enliven the saga of the American game, which in its fecundity has yielded such varied and distinctive personalities as Babe Ruth, Ty Cobb, Lou Gehrig, Satchel Paige, Casey Stengel, Yogi Berra, Jackie Robinson, and a half-a-dozen players nicknamed, for good reason, Dizzy, Daffy, and Dazzy.

Those characters inspire a number of movies, some fictional, others based to various degrees on fact. A whole class of baseball films, for example, constitute what are known in the business as biopics – biographies of actual ballplayers whose stories provide the sort of material that Hollywood loves to put on the screen. Most of the early ones often fit more comfortably in the genre of hagiography. Undoubtedly the most famous of these is *The Pride of the Yankees*, in which Gehrig's brilliant career and brief life form a tragic but perfect combination of trajectories for the filmmaker, with emotional echoes of A. E. Housman's 1896 poem "To an Athlete Dying Young." Whatever its fidelity to fact, the movie, which appeared only a year after Gehrig's death from amyotrophic lateral sclerosis, not only exploited the genuine tragedy of a great ballplayer's crippling illness and untimely death, but also reflected some of the currents of its time in specifically mentioning the sacrifices of brave young men in the war that in 1942 had just begun, and begun badly, for the United States. Gary Cooper had already played American heroes in westerns, and as the title character in *Sergeant York* (1941) displayed those qualities that led peace-loving Americans to join World War I and, once in that war, to fight bravely and honorably. In its account of Alvin York's conversion from pacifism to a heroism that won him the Medal of Honor, the movie prepares Americans, many of them dubious about the situation, for entry into another European conflict. *The Pride of the Yankees*, not coincidentally, serves the same purpose, with a prose crawl suggesting that the American endeavor of baseball and its sacrificial hero parallel the need to sacrifice brave young men once again in the war that has finally engaged the nation.

The greatest hero the sport has ever known remains George Herman Ruth, the eternal Babe, who like the figures of myth emerged from an obscure background to perform his remarkable feats as if by some supernatural gift that made him greater in degree, if not in kind, than his fellow athletes. Not surprisingly then, the Babe appears in a great many movies, playing himself or a version of himself in some silent comedies, but more important, being impersonated by a series of actors in several visions and revisions of the man and the career. Although much scorned, the first Ruth biopic, *The Babe Ruth Story* (1948), features William Bendix as a sanitized version of the real-life character. The movie skates over his numerous excesses, ignoring his mammoth appetites for food, drink, and women, and transforms him into a kind of saint, truly the savior of baseball. In the movie he not only hits his home runs but also heals the sick, causes the lame to walk, and even saves the life of a pet dog before succumbing to an unspoken illness (the cancer that was sapping the real Babe's life at the time). Several later pictures show some of the less attractive sides of Ruth's character, depicting him as a boorish boozer with understandable internal conflicts. The number of times his character, however interpreted, appears in major or minor roles in other baseball-related films testifies to the continuing power of his heroic deeds and Rabelaisian appetites, and the immortality of his legend.[a]

As *The Pride of the Yankees* suggests, the baseball movie not only belongs to itself – that is, to its own genre – but also connects with other films of its time and emerges from a particular temporal context. *The Jackie Robinson Story* (1950), for example, loosely based on the struggle of its subject (who played himself in the movie) to succeed in the major leagues, also naturally addresses racial prejudice, a rarely treated issue in American cinema of its era. At the same time, its final sequence shows a truncated version of Robinson's testimony before the House Un-American Activities Committee, which dissolves into the patriotic image of the Statue of Liberty while "America the Beautiful" plays on the sound track. Functioning as a counter to the public statements of the leftist African American singer-actor Paul Robeson, the sequence underlines the Cold War fear of Soviet Russia, and hints at the guilty suspicion that centuries of oppression might drive African Americans to embrace Communism. Despite its earnest attempts to show the success of its protagonist in overcoming enormous obstacles, *The Jackie Robinson Story* also exploits the athlete and the national game to advance a political agenda, linking it with such other 1950s anti-Communist films as *I Was a Communist for the FBI* (1951) and *My Son John* (1952), or even all those science-fiction flicks that warn of the menace from somewhere Out

[a] For more on the Ruthian legend, see the interchapter on Babe Ruth in this volume, 45–48.

There, in which Mars the Red Planet becomes an easy metaphor for Russia the Red Menace.

In addition to reflecting its context, the baseball movie also exhibits connections with a wide variety of popular genres. Its predominantly male ensemble cast recalls the scores of institutional movies – especially those dealing with the military, most notably the Hollywood bomber crew or infantry platoon – creating a microcosm of the larger society within an enclosed, sometimes isolated group of men in uniforms engaged in a common, often exciting endeavor. The use of the sport for comedy, on the other hand, a subject that emerges back in the silent era and continues through the films of the 1920s and 1930s, remains a constant to the present day, allowing for a somewhat different vision of the baseball microcosm. Movies like *Major League* (1989), *Rookie of the Year* (1993), *The Bingo Long Traveling All-Stars & Motor Kings* (1976), and *The Bad News Bears* (1976), which features a Little League version of the baseball comedy, derive a good deal of their humor and meaning from the diversity of the cast of players. The "serious" baseball movies use that diversity to demonstrate connections to the myths and legends of the past, with characters who recall some of the archetypal figures of those ancient narratives. The wounded hero, the athlete dying young, the raging warrior, the superb champion with one fatal flaw all echo the stories of other legendary figures from the past. The comedies, on the other hand, probably best represented by *Major League*, often provide a dugout full of classic baseball archetypes, like the Rookie, the Flake, the Delinquent, the Goofball, the Hot Dog, the Religious Nut, and the Spoiled Brat, characters who frequently blend and merge into one.

Despite all its rich possibilities of history, biography, action, and character, the cinema still frequently fails to comprehend baseball fully and satisfyingly. Even the best baseball movies – and the truly outstanding ones can be counted on the fingers of an outfielder's glove – fall somewhat short of excellence, and appear in the view of the passionate and knowledgeable fan as somehow inadequate to the essence of the sport and the cinema. Ultimately, two somewhat contradictory truths govern the making, meaning, and success of baseball in film. The first suggests that the most significant and eloquent, possibly even the purest and truest depictions of the sport occur casually, incidentally, incompletely, organically, and by accident, as occasions embedded in a context essentially outside the direct representation of the game itself – baseball sequences, scenes, moments in motion pictures dealing with other subjects and themes. Baseball shows up in westerns, war movies, family dramas, even horror flicks, reflecting its place as an ordinary American activity, a thread in the fabric of daily life. Some memorable baseball scenes and sequences enliven moments in westerns as different as *The*

Great Northfield, Minnesota Raid (1972), *Heaven's Gate* (1980), and *Son of the Morning Star* (1989); in war movies like *Battleground* (1949), *Memphis Belle* (1990), and *Pearl Harbor* (2001); even in the science-fiction film *The Day the Earth Stood Still* (1951) and the recent horror film *Twilight* (2008). It also naturally and meaningfully appears in such movies as *Big* (1988), *Save the Tiger* (1973), and *The Pope of Greenwich Village* (1984).[2]

The real success of the baseball film derives from the combination of the magic of the game with the magic of the art. The ordinary and the real collide with the mystical and the supernatural, creating the two essential possibilities in baseball on film, so that the genre constantly struggles between the authentic and the fantastic. In Barry Levinson's adaptation of Bernard Malamud's *The Natural*, for example, the director took great pains to duplicate the stitching on the balls, the gloves, the uniforms of the past, but combined that attention to verisimilitude with such elements as the special bat carved from the lightning-struck tree, Roy obeying his manager's urging and literally knocking the cover off a ball, and of course the famous climactic home run. In *Field of Dreams* the director, Phil Alden Robinson, used W. P. Kinsella's account of an actual ballplayer, Moonlight Graham, a saintly doctor in a small Minnesota town, then reincarnated him as the young rookie who finally got his chance to bat on his own field of dreams with the ghosts of the game's dark and complicated history; and of course, the resurrection of the 1919 Chicago White Sox, followed by other players from other eras, demonstrates the magic of the movie within the realm of the sport.

The zany quality of baseball, its unpredictability, its susceptibility to the vicissitudes of chance, its remarkable dependence on sheer luck, account for the fact that so many games display some new or at least unusual event within their familiar structure – the weird bounce of a batted ball, the inexplicable error of a talented fielder, the baserunning mistake that lands three men on third, some bizarre sequence that leads to a putout. Other, stranger phenomena occur throughout the course of any season: some examples in living memory suggest the game's potential for craziness. In a game at Fenway Park in 1974 Detroit slugger Willie Horton popped up a pitch that killed a passing pigeon; the poor creature landed dead at home plate. Similarly, a decade or so later, the Mets left-fielder Kevin McReynolds trotted in to catch a line drive, which hit a bird in flight and enabled the batter to end up on second base. In a Dodgers game Davey Lopes missed stepping on home plate; after reaching the dugout, he learned of his mistake and ran out to slide in just ahead of the relay from the outfield. Larry Walker of the Colorado Rockies once caught a fly ball for what he thought was the third out and generously flipped it into the stands; when he realized his mistake, he begged a fan to return the ball so he could try to throw a runner out. Managing the Chicago Cubs, Charlie Metro, evidently misunderstanding ventriloquism, thought he could learn to "throw" his voice and thus mislead opposing baserunners; apparently gifted with a penchant for oddball notions, he also considered studying graphology so that he could read his opposing managers' strategies based on their handwriting. In a discussion of the sloppiness of record keeping in the infancy and juvenility of the game, Alan Schwarz, in *The Numbers Game*, quotes a statistician/researcher named Jordan Deutsch, who reported that "a rabbit once ran around the bases and was credited with a run."[3] Even in the major leagues every season will demonstrate the game's infinite capacity for the unexpected, for some unusual, possibly even unique occurrence. The craziness of the comic baseball films and the goofiness of many of their characters result quite naturally from the essential irrationality of the game.

Perhaps because it permeates the sport, then, the merely improbable appears throughout the baseball film. Beyond the entirely comic movies – full of silliness and slapstick, featuring the cereal box of nuts and flakes who play for so many Hollywood teams – the importance of luck, the strangely oddball nature of the game, allow a number of works to stray from the realm of reality. Even *The Jackie Robinson Story*, for instance, which focuses on the serious struggles of its title character to break the sport's color barrier, features a character named Shorty who keeps failing at the plate until he dons some sort of elevator spikes that enable him to reach the high pitches and hit the ball safely, a blatant absurdity that acknowledges the comical nature of the game. In *It Happens Every Spring* (1949), Ray Milland plays a college chemistry professor and baseball fan who accidentally invents a substance that repels wood; he applies it to baseballs, which then always jump over a bat, and quickly becomes a successful pitcher for the St. Louis Cardinals. *Roogie's Bump* (1954) and its more entertaining and successful imitation, *Rookie of the Year* (1993) both employ a freak incident that allows a 12-year-old boy to throw a baseball at phenomenal speeds and therefore pitch in the major leagues, in the earlier movie for the Brooklyn Dodgers and in the later for the Chicago Cubs. A child manages a team in *The Kid from Left Field* (1953) and in *Little Big League* (1999); a cat becomes the owner of a baseball club in *Rhubarb* (1951) and, continuing the animal motif, a chimpanzee plays third base and accomplishes an unassisted triple play in *Ed* (1996). Hey, it's baseball and it's always a little crazy.

More important, because the game begins in the prehistoric past as a ritual endeavor and a religious practice and occupies a sacred space, and again because of the omnipresence of chance, it proceeds in an atmosphere of magic; it retains from its beginnings a hint of the supernatural that accompanies and perhaps also explains some of its eccentric possibilities. The very best baseball novels, for example, all depend upon some degree of the mysterious and the miraculous to represent the essence of the sport, telling their tales through the mode known as magical realism, a kind of oxymoron that perfectly describes the conduct of the game. For most students of literature and sport, Bernard Malamud's *The Natural* (1952), Robert Coover's *The Universal Baseball Association, Inc., J. Henry Waugh, Prop.* (1968), Eric Rolfe Greenberg's *The Celebrant* (1983), and W. P. Kinsella's *Shoeless Joe* (1982) constitute something like the gold standard for baseball fiction – "literary" novels that also reflect both the reality and the fantasy of the game.[b] All of them, significantly, include various events, people, and devices that, in the great tradition of American literature, follow the patterns of the fictional romance, which, as Hawthorne points out, allow a "certain latitude" to the writer.[4]

The mode provides an opportunity to transcend the boundaries of the probable, to mingle the factual and the fanciful, and thus serves as a perfect medium for baseball fiction. Malamud's Roy Hobbs's bat Wonderboy, carved from a tree struck by lightning; the harpy Harriet Bird shooting him with a silver bullet; J. Henry Waugh's characters from his invented baseball game assuming their own reality in Coover's story; the ghostly speaker in *Shoeless Joe* instructing Ray Kinsella to build a baseball field and kidnap a famous author – along with all the other supernatural events of the novels in which they appear, these derive from the same impulse that made romance the dominant mode of prose fiction in America. They also respond to the inherent magic of baseball. No wonder, then, that so many baseball movies, even those concerned with more or less authentic, truthful representations of the game, often in some way employ both the eccentric and the fantastic, serving quite easily and naturally as motion-picture versions of the American romance.

If magical realism may provide the best way to represent the sport in fiction, then the cinema, that most magical of our arts, provides its natural and appropriate visual medium. Aside from the sport's characteristic quirkiness, a great many baseball movies exploit the supernatural in one form or another; the marvelous, after all, constitutes the essence of film itself. Almost all the important examples of the genre, along with many minor works, include some element of the irrational, the fantastic, the miraculous, an appropriate translation of the approach of those distinguished baseball novels. In *The Babe Ruth Story*, the hero's healing ability initially emerges when he hits a

---

[b] For further discussion of these important baseball novels, see "Baseball in literature, baseball as literature" in this volume, 21–32.

home run in a spring training game, inspiring a crippled boy to stand on his own for the first time, a miraculous incident that will recur later in the film when the slugger hits another homer to save a dying child: the eternal Babe becomes not only the savior of the game but also the first saint of baseball.[5] He shows up again as a ghost to encourage the young boy in *The Sandlot* (1993), which confirms and continues his power to instruct and uplift the young. He even appears in a hallucinatory sequence in *Cobb* (1994), as part of an otherwise gritty portrait of Ty Cobb's last days.

Innumerable instances of extraordinary, even otherworldly intervention in the play of the game appear throughout the history of the modern baseball film. The most obvious examples appear in two directly contrasting moral and theological visions, the two versions of *Angels in the Outfield* (1951, remade in 1994) and *Damn Yankees* (1958). In both *Angels* movies, the title characters, initially visible only to an innocent orphan, help a struggling team of perennial losers win ball games and, eventually, the pennant. The first version, charming, understated, thoroughly enjoyable, deals with the Pittsburgh Pirates, whose manager (Paul Douglas) finds himself conversing with spirits who exact a vow from him to moderate his temper and clean up his foul language (difficult in baseball for anyone) in exchange for their help. The angels only appear in the form of a stern voice speaking from above, a few booms of thunder when Douglas misbehaves, and a single feather floating from the heavens. The remake, which follows roughly the same plot, exaggerates the special effects and the comedy, showing the angels, who naturally help the Los Angeles Angels, swooping down to lift outfielders to impossible catches, speed up the pitched ball, and turn weak hits into home runs.

Pitching for the other team, so to speak, Douglass Wallop's novel *The Year the Yankees Lost the Pennant* (1954), retitled *Damn Yankees* and transformed first into a hit Broadway musical, then a successful motion picture (1958), presents a different sort of supernatural intervention. The movie adds yet another chapter to the Faust legend, as Joe Boyd, a middle-aged real-estate salesman and avid Washington Senators fan, accepts an offer from the devil, and exchanges his soul for the chance to become Joe Hardy, a sensational star for the Senators. After some complications, Joe fulfills his dream and helps his team win the pennant over the perennial winners of the 1950s, the New York Yankees. Directed by two accomplished musical-comedy veterans, George Abbott and Stanley Donen, with choreography by Bob Fosse and some memorable songs, the film achieved considerable success. No critic pointed out, however, that any baseball fan would gladly sell his soul to the devil for a chance to star in the major leagues, and many would also delight in the added bonus of defeating the detested Yankees.

Probably the most obvious and important examples of magical realism in the baseball film occur in the movies based on two of the best-known "literary" baseball novels of the twentieth century, Malamud's *The Natural* and Kinsella's *Shoeless Joe* (brilliantly retitled *Field of Dreams*). Malamud's novel wonderfully combines the imagined semiliterate vernacular of traditional, old-fashioned baseball fiction, most evident in Ring Lardner's works and Mark Harris's Henry Wiggen narratives, with the familiar stilted sports-writer prose of a thousand newspaper stories. At the same time, the action and characters depend upon the rich history of Arthurian romance and ancient myth, with a strong infusion of the supernatural. Those elements undergo significant changes in the film adaptation, which concentrates mostly on a depiction of the sport in some vague time recalling the 1930s. Benefiting from a stellar cast, skillful cinematography, and an evocative score, the 1984 movie captured the hearts of many viewers, not all of them – the true test of a motion picture – particularly fans of the game. The adaptation limited the magic mostly to obscure hints, retaining the notion of the bat carved from a tree struck by lightning, for example, but oddly focusing on the actual process of the young Roy Hobbs creating his powerful weapon, his own sword from a stone, the enchanted bat Wonderboy. Reversing the novel's resounding note of regret and despair, the film settles for a Hollywood happy ending, culminating in Roy's mythic home run – surely the most spectacular in the history of the baseball movie – a blow that shatters the rooftop light towers, which pour a torrent of giant sparks on the field while Robert Redford circles the bases in graceful, triumphant, oh-so-slow motion through showers of stars.

Field of Dreams (1989), a kind of companion piece to *The Natural* as the most honored baseball film, exploits more fully, and oddly at the same time more matter-of-factly, the supernatural essence of its source and of literary baseball fiction in general. Reflecting and in a sense comprehending the history of the genre, the movie mingles the historically accurate with the outrageously unreal. In keeping with the notion that the Black Sox Scandal of 1919 remains the most important and influential event for baseball fiction, the film quite literally resurrects the players on the Chicago White Sox team who threw the World Series of 1919, most notably Shoeless Joe Jackson. Other old-time players join the Sox on the field that Ray Kinsella, obeying instructions from a disembodied, unidentified voice, carves out of his Iowa cornfield. The spectral ballplayers, the fusion of cornfield and ballfield that recalls the vegetation rituals in the sport's primitive origins, the subsequent confusion of Heaven and Iowa, the strange eschatology that somehow allows for posthumous play on the homemade diamond, the familiar baseball theme of fathers and sons, and the mawkish emotionalism combined to make *Field of Dreams* the most successful baseball film of them all: a hit with audiences and critics, an instant classic, a favorite with many serious students of the game, a generally susceptible bunch anyway, pushovers for sentimentality.

Whatever the quality of its achievement and the value of its vision, *Field of Dreams* thus serves very nicely as a nearly perfect example of the baseball movie, a kind of culminating work. Epitomizing that familiar conflict between the authentic and the fantastic, it combines a variety of the subjects and themes that appear in so many of the films that precede it, providing something like a compendium and index of the form of the baseball film. Its confusion of myth, mysticism, and mystery somehow works for audiences of all kinds (many knowledgeable fans objected to the fact that Ray Liotta, who played the left-handed Shoeless Joe Jackson, batted right-handed, but for some reason none of them questioned the appearance of ghosts playing baseball in Iowa). Its frequent allusions to real people and events may anchor its fantasy in some area of fact, and its implicit gesture of redemption for the Chicago White Sox of 1919 may provide a kind of moral basis for its essentially preposterous premise. The concluding encounter between the protagonist, Ray Kinsella, and the ghost of his father, John – suited up in the Sox uniform and now younger than his son – in their final game of catch, underlines the theme of reconciliation, clarifying at last the words of the mysterious voice that whispers to Ray, "If you build it, he will come."

Finally, *Field of Dreams* also includes a plangent rhetorical flourish in James Earl Jones's valedictory speech on the significance of baseball for America, an eloquent set piece often quoted in film and print discussions of the game, and an appropriate coda to the motion picture and to the meanings of the baseball movie. *Field of Dreams* is the baseball film Hollywood has always aspired toward, the fantasy of a forever game played by a company of immortals on the magical terrain of rural America, possibly the last major cinematic representation of the truly mythological possibilities in the sport, a fitting climax to any examination of baseball at the movies. The picture assures us that somewhere out there, in the great green spaces of America, in Iowa or anywhere, the game goes on and on.

NOTES

1. For an immensely detailed filmography that separates baseball in film into three categories, see Stephen Wood and J. David Pincus, eds., *Reel Baseball: Essays and Interviews on the National Pastime, Hollywood and American Culture* (Jefferson, NC and London: McFarland, 2003).
2. See George Grella, "The Baseball Moment in American Film," reprinted in Wood and Pincus, *Reel Baseball*, 208–221.

3. Alan Schwarz, *The Numbers Game* (New York: St. Martin's Press, 2004), 97.
4. Nathaniel Hawthorne, Preface to *The House of the Seven Gables* (1852; New York: Signet, 1961), vii.
5. For a fuller discussion of Ruth's appearance in film, see Frank Ardolino, "From Christ-Like Folk Hero to Bumbling Bacchus: Filmic Images of Babe Ruth, 1920–1992," in Wood and Pinucus, *Reel Baseball*, pp. 102–119.

9

AL FILREIS

The baseball fan

Fred Stein's *A History of the Baseball Fan* begins by describing the fan as "the least publicized or recognized figure in baseball." Stein's next sentence, however, is an unintentional capitulation: "Baseball essentially is about the player …"[1] Here we will ask: *Is it?*

The proposition that baseball is essentially about spectatorship, not participation, would seem to present merely a philosophical question in a particular world that revels only in the instance. Keith Hernandez, one of the game's most cerebral players, is for example entirely uninterested in philosophical or abstract thought in any form. Contemplation – "thinking" is the favored term – is deemed by Hernandez a matter of conclusions derived from details. "I can't think about baseball other than in … specifics," Hernandez writes in the preamble to *Pure Baseball: Pitch by Pitch for the Advanced Fan.*[2] A moment-by-moment analysis of every move and motion made in two games played in June, 1993, Hernandez's book never once breaks out of the particular. Rarely has the term "pure" been used so completely to mean *focused* – untainted by rather than made lucid by theory. Hernandez will give us several pages about guessing a pitch on a favorable hitter's count, only, seemingly in the midst of writing the scene, to recall that his narrative is supposed to be for the fan. He had been addressing and instructing the batter (try such a guess late in a game, do not attempt this gambit too often, etc.), but then pulls up to urge: "So, as a fan, don't hold your breath waiting to see this trick."[3] Though admirable, Hernandez's book is not about the fan, nor "for" the fan. The former player's strength is pedagogical. He narrates authentic ("pure") not ideal participation. The baseball fan in *Pure Baseball* is a marketing afterthought.

Instruction marketed as spectatorship – let us call it the Hernandez Fallacy – plagues most histories of the baseball fan. Even the most perspicacious of these, Donald Dewey's *The 10th Man*, evinces the tendency at times; a chapter on "The New York Game" is only superficially about the "awakening community" of Giant, Dodger, and Yankee rooters.[4]

Instead, it recapitulates the teams' increasing accomplishments between 1945 and 1956. An exceptional work is William Freedman's *More than a Pastime*: pure subjectivity in the critically selfless mode of Studs Terkel, Freedman's assemblage is, after all, an oral history – its *only* voices being literally those of fans.[5] J. David Pincus, Stephen Wood, and Fritz Cropp have studied the overall effects of the game-first/fans-second milieu. Fans' "love of the game seems to transcend whatever worsening business and structural problems" confront baseball. The "fan-as-customer philosophy" pervades baseball economics, in which spectators are defined as "'fan-nies' to fill seats" (though the term "fan" actually derives from "fanatic").[6] This economic view parallels the ascendancy of hyper-rational, economics-driven notions of improving a team's output. The fad of *Moneyball* coincides with the demise of qualitative – one might say humanistic – studies affirming the centrality of spectatorship.[7] The tail of productive performance is said to wag the dog of fan involvement, in spite of many persuasive "voices" bespeaking the inverse: the so-called "New Breed"[8] of New York Mets fans setting attendance records between 1962 and 1968 to see tenth- and ninth-place teams; Cub rooters' quasi-sacramental, multigenerational narratives of curse, loss, and sell-outs; Brooklyn Dodgers fans who reckoned winning to be fairly memorable but loved losers (their "Bums") equally well and described integration as totally life-changing; mythic regionalist accounts of the birth, rise, and decline of Red Sox Nation long preceding their first modern World Series victory. Each is a mode of witness that made the witnessed teams profitable. In this particular sense, Buzz Bissinger's *3 Nights in August* (2005), although not explicitly about fans, is a breathless prose-poem written from the dark inside of a fan's heart: it is a long implicit disputation against *Moneyball* epistemology, an ode to the manager (Tony LaRussa) whose every move is a "rational" or strategic act repressing psychopathological back-story.[9] Bissinger's narrative voice is the fan's on the verge of realizing the dream of violating the fan–player divide by hanging out near the white-lime line – and of crossing, through sentimentalist journalism, into participation. For Pincus, Wood, and Cropp, fans are the "cultural or moral owners" of most teams, though this "has not been recognized by either owners or fans" themselves, and thus fans have "no role in the decision-making process."[10] Their subtitle, "A Voice Too Long Silent?" is a rhetorical question. Similarly, Bob Costas gives his *Fair Ball* the subtitle *A Fan's Case for Baseball* and presents a series of reformist legislative proposals, but Costas realizes that his argument depends entirely on the rhetoric of subject position. He cannot write as a commentator, even though he's a well-known one, and he is desperate to avoid the Hernandez Fallacy. He must write as a spectator: "This isn't a commentator's diatribe against the sport, but rather a fan's case *for* baseball. What do I want? I think the same thing most baseball fans want: To see the game worthy of our devotion."[11] The move out of the clubhouse or TV network box is indiscernible in these bland, self-vindicating words. Presented in empty lyricism (phrases like "worthy of our devotion"), Costas's presumption will likely strike the reader as protesting too much. Yet Costas is also capable of this powerful sentence about memory: "I rode the subways to Yankee Stadium, and saw and heard many things."[12] A focus on "things" not in the game makes possible a perfect Hemingwayesque paradox: ambiguous precision that nonetheless perfectly captures the problem of describing the game. Costas's understanding of baseball derives its authority from attention to what he has seen and heard in the ambience *around* and *beyond* it.

Dewey's *The 10th Man* celebrates this generative *around* and *beyond* of baseball, noting, for instance, the ironically positive effect of Charlie Finley's otherwise usually destructive mania for marketing his Athletics.[a] When the team resided in Kansas City, he deemed it a good stunt to hire the first woman to be part of a baseball radio team. Her name was Betty Caywood, and she spent most of her on-air time talking about happenings in the grandstands. For Finley it was "another way of keeping attention away from what was happening on the diamond" – in other words, drawing attention away from poorly played baseball.[13] The diversionary stunt had the ironic effect of focusing listeners ever more on the whole game. By permitting Caywood's narrative peregrinations away from the game being played on the field, Finley was not, to be sure, promoting equality of gendered perspective, nor was he expressing any kind of belief in the voice of the fan. But he was exploring the (actually quite profitable) world of words emanating directly from the fan-centered game, the convergence of baseball and language that "generate[s] excitement – / a fever in the victim," as Marianne Moore described it in a poem called "Baseball and Writing."[14] Moore was a fanatical Brooklyn Dodgers devotee, and her poem, which begins "Writing is exciting / and baseball is like writing," was written not in response to a game but to "post-game broadcasts." To whom, she asks, does the victimhood of generated excitement apply? "*Who* is excited?" "[P]itcher, catcher, fielder, batter"? On the contrary: "Might it be I?" This is the poetic "I" – the speaker, but, more generally, the voice teaching us to see what should be seen. This is the "I" that *observes* "Carl Furillo's ... big gun" (which drove in four of the team's six runs on a day remembered in

---

[a] For more on Finley and his unusual legacy, see the interchapter on Andy Messersmith, Charlie Finley, and George Steinbrenner in this volume, 216–220.

another poem) but *celebrates* "fans dancing in delight" in response.[15] Moore was devoted to the game but the lens of her devotion was a wandering eye that spots, for example, "the Dodger Band in [Section] 8, row 1." That motley ensemble was famously capable of improvising – for example, playing "All of Me?," which asks in its second phrase "Why not take all of me?" when the local tax collector happened to walk by.[16] As a *form of expression* analogous to Don Zimmer's surprising infield dexterity (which produced feats Moore elsewhere extolled), such extemporaneity was the whole poetry of the Dodgers.

At the heart of Marianne Moore's modern art is an orientation to process and a mania for the precise details of mediated language. She savored the language of the hackneyed newspaper account and the clichéd post-game broadcast, preferring it to first-hand observation of the game, and she maintained this preference even when – as was often the case – she had been in the stands herself. She was a real fan, to be sure, and her baseball poems also look to the players; her verse is filled with direct encomia to the play of Ralph Branca, Pee Wee Reese, Gil Hodges, Preacher Roe, and the big gun-toting Furillo. William Carlos Williams, Moore's modernist colleague, was not nearly the fan she was. His brilliant poem "The crowd at the ball game," from the famous 1923 *Spring and All* sequence, bothers not at all to observe the game. Its dynamism derives from watching fans watching the game, "the power of their faces," and the "beautiful" and special form of precision with which they spectate.

> The crowd at the ball game
> is moved uniformly
>
> by a spirit of uselessness
> which delights them –

There is no meaning or purpose to "the exciting detail / of the chase / and the escape, the error / the flash of genius." These are

> all to no end save beauty
> the eternal –
>
> So in detail they, the crowd,
> are beautiful[17]

Williams both fears and cherishes the convergence of unity and diversity in the crowd at a baseball game. The potential classlessness of the fans makes his crowd far more progressive than the game itself, thus justifying a poem about baseball that only glancingly mentions what happens on the field. Williams dwells on aspects of democratic culture that suggest fragmentation, cultural breakdown, and a reversal of traditional subject–object relations. He likes to observe the seers seeing rather than simply reporting the seen. The ballpark serves this goal ideally; there people form an alluring visual and aural *mélange*. Fans are "so fused together," Jane Addams wrote in 1920, "that a man cannot tell whether it is his own shout or another's that fills his ears."[18] William Carlos Williams's fan-centered game bore out Addams's more overtly political question: Did not baseball belong to "the undoubted power of public recreation to bring together all classes of a community in the modern city unhappily so full of devices for keeping men apart?"[19]

For American progressives like Addams and her sociological descendants such as Kenneth H. Marcus (who wrote "Baseball Stadiums and American Audiences"), baseball's civic space brings discordant citizenries together. The commensurate writerly device is the democratic list or catalogue, and most great fan-chroniclers engage it in the lineage of Walt Whitman. Whitman, our first literary baseball fan, invented the catalogue's naturally ecstatic association with the convergence of democracy and baseball. To him, the game "belongs as much to our institutions, fits into them as significantly, as our constitutions, laws: is just as important in the sum total of our historic life."[20] The key paradox here lies in the phrase "sum total": Whitman's eye was always on the whole dwelling in the part, but the parts also needed to be seen as great in number and diverse in kind. Whitman was by nature immune to the Hernandez Fallacy. He always addressed himself directly to the nonplayers, and always identified with the nonparticipant who dreams of participation. Everyone was either a fan or a prospective fan. But Whitman shared in – one might say invented – *Pure Baseball*'s epistemology of the enumerated detail. So the connection between Williams's ecstatic sense of the crowd's beautiful yet useless uniformity and, let us say, Roger Angell's long list of New England places where fans celebrate Carlton Fisk's miraculous home run to end game six of the 1975 World Series[b] is an insight these two writer-fans and others share: a key moment in the development of democratic culture is the point "when it no longer matters so much what the caring is about, how frail or foolish the object of that concern, as long as the feeling itself can be saved."[21] Content is secondary. Caring is primary, and lies entirely in the domain of the observer.

This engagement becomes most democratic when the observers are not even at first hand. The citizen celebrants in Angell's classic catalogue are, in his words, "absent and distant." As Fisk waves his arms wildly, willing the near-foul shot fair with body English, Angell contemplates

> all my old absent and distant Sox-afflicted friends (and all the other Red Sox fans, all over New England), and I thought of them – in Brookline, Mass., and

---

[b] Fisk's hit changed the history of baseball television coverage; see "Baseball and mass media" in this volume, 232.

Brooklin, Maine; in Beverly Farms and Mashpee and Presque Isle and North
Conway and Damariscotta; in Pomfret, Connecticut, and Pomfret, Vermont;
in Wayland and Providence and Revere and Nashua, and in both the Concords
and all five Manchesters; and in Raymond, New Hampshire (where Carlton
Fisk lives), and Bellows Falls, Vermont (where Carlton Fisk was *born*), and I
saw all of them dancing and shouting and kissing and leaping about like the
fans at Fenway – jumping up and down in their bedrooms and kitchens and
living rooms, in bars and trailers, and even in some boats here and there, I
suppose, and on back-country roads (a lone driver getting the news over the
radio and blowing his horn over and over, and finally pulling up and getting
out and leaping up and down on the cold macadam, yelling into the night),
and all of them, for once at least utterly joyful and believing in that joy – alight
with it.[22]

His impulse essentially poetic, Angell transposes American social geography into a homophony. His list-poem consists of a series of plain rhymes
(*Wayland/Raymond*), near rhymes (*Brookline/Brooklin*), assonance and syl-
labic rhymes (*Mashpee/Presque*), parallelism (*where Fisk lives/where Fisk
was born*), and total rhymes (*Pomfret/Pomfret; all five Manchesters*). Yet at
the same time he seeks to preserve class difference and regional variety, and
to respect New England's stubborn normative sense of dislocation as fundamental to the way their team actually plays the game. Absence and distance
are overcome not by Carlton Fisk's miraculous swing, but by the partisan
observer's choice of rhetorical device and language to convey it – or, to be
more precise, to convey the conveying of it (Angell telling us how others
got "the news over the radio"). Rather than disqualifying participation, distance from Fisk's feat is a proportionate measure of closeness. Watching and
listening, not action, presuppose caring.

That fans remember such a moment more precisely than Fisk does is further evidence of the significance of the reversal just described.[23] (Fisk has
famously blocked the memory: "I remember certain things that happened
leading up to that. I don't remember much afterward, like it was in a time
warp.") Yet players can also care, can also be fans. After retiring early from
the game, Doug Glanville discovered a talent for written observation, a revelation precipitated therapeutically by the need to describe the death of his
father. Glanville began his new career by composing personal columns with
a baseball slant for the *New York Times*. This work culminated in *The Game
from Where I Stand*, a book that is almost entirely about perspective, seeing
the game from a particular personal point of view. The particularities of that
view form a dedicatory (and specifically elegiac) version of the fan-centered
game. "I was a center fielder," Glanville begins proudly, "I never wanted
to play any other position." Why? Because center field offers "uninhibited

sight lines." The writer-fan was born when Glanville perceived the way in which his position on the field reproduced the qualitative experience of a fan watching fans. His book is a portrait of the artist as a young son: from center field you can see the catcher setting up, a pickoff play developing at second base, and – most crucially for him – "you can even see what is happening in the stands and note that your dad just got back to his seat after buying a big bag of popcorn."[24]

Through his writing Doug Glanville becomes spectator to the presence of a memory of his psycho-emotional formation. His father is a spectral figure here but so, in the writing, is the son standing in center field. Nonparticipation secures the future of memory. Among fans who never played, life is marked by years of greater and lesser involvement. The decisive moment in Doris Kearns Goodwin's *Wait till Next Year* comes not at the height of her twinned girlhood infatuations with Jackie Robinson and her old-school Catholic father, but during her time as a doctoral student, a phase of her life when she at first – in the 1960s at Harvard, during an era of feminist, theoretical, and leftist involvements – seemed to repress the daddy's girl/tomboy-fan.[25] She actively forgot her working-class ethnicity and its manifestations in the world of (male) sports, misremembering temporarily the profound American story inherent in the double desire (not quite sexual for this adolescent) for beloved Catholic father and beloved African American breaker of social barriers. Accidentally, she then rediscovered baseball through the team beloved of her adopted hometown, reckoned the parallel between these Red Sox and her old Dodgers (Ebbets Field and Fenway Park as sites of social convergence and experiment), and began only then to "reenact ... many of the rituals I had shared with my father."[26] The fundamental image in Goodwin's memoir is of her father's death – which came as he watched a Mets game on television in 1972[27] – and thus the recognition, after disengagement and embarrassing rebuke, that the man who taught the historian how to see the world by instructing her in the art of seeing baseball leaves her this final image of himself watching the game. The adult Goodwin, the "I" of the memoir and an Ivy League educator now, has internalized this lesson. She learns again to "watch ... the knowledgeable fans"[28] – to watch the watchers who are adept at watching. It becomes a basic method of history.

Angell, too, is a methodologist. Assigned to write about the indecipherable start to the New York Mets 2002 season, he knows he must exit the clubhouse and press box. Thinking that the team's usual strategic and personnel "assumptions have turned out to be wrong," he procures day-game tickets and sits "jam-packed in the stands" along the left-field line, and exactly halfway through what turns out to be a long essay discovers his real subject: the familial meaning of the retirement of longtime relief pitcher John Franco. Franco unexpectedly "broke down in tears" when he told reporters he would retire; he had spoken with his family the night before, and his 10-year-old son had asked if his father's now-dead arm was caused by the father–son catch they'd played the day before.

The scene follows from that afternoon game, where Angell, surrounded by "pale sunshine and mild booing ... and the shrilling of kiddie fans," finds himself more "cheerful" than the Mets' poor play warranted. And then Angell turns to watch the watchers. He discovers a "busy dad" both present and absent, unable to watch. This man "missed Alomar's first-inning homer while on forage, and then blew Robbie's next dinger, in the third, when he'd gone down again for ice cream." In part presumably because he felt the urge to mind the children while their father was away getting ice cream, Angell begins to describe precisely the "fractional glimpse of the batter" the children themselves could catch: the

> mini-minors near me had to stand on their seats, teetering and peering – and sometimes grabbing my shirt or ear to keep balance – to catch fractional glimpses of the batter, way off to our right ... Now and then one of the standees would step on the wrong part of his seat and disappear from view, like a wader taken down by a shark, but then resurface smiling, with peanut dust and bits of popcorn in his hair.[29]

This antic manner somewhat masks the depth of linguistic control and constructedness: the "busy dad" is said to have "gone down again" for treats and become absent; the child, as if learning to watch the game through fits and starts of presence, is "like a wader taken down by a shark" – both fathoming the bottom and emerging happy. For Angell, the quality that causes the observer's happiness is nothing less than *heroism*. Thus John Franco's sentimental familial tale, told at the very moment of his transition to spectatorship, is hardly cause for lament. Indeed, Franco "looked more human than triumphant: a Met like the rest of us." In Angell's parlance – he has made this claim several times in earlier writings – being "a Met like the rest of us" refers to the state of *not* being a player but rather a savior of the game's capacity to teach us to see each other.[30]

Angell, Moore, Goodwin, Bissinger, Jim Brosnan, George Plimpton, Roger Kahn, and others believe that baseball's meaning is produced by its observers, not by the game's rules. (Whenever Angell writes about baseball's rules, it is invariably a satire.) The website eHow.com, which offers simple, highly organized "instructions" for "how to" learn nearly anything, suggests "learn[ing] the rules of baseball" as *fourth* on a list of five ranked baseball recommendations. The first is to attend a game and watch knowledgeable fans watching it – "to experience the excitement of other fans and to learn from those around you."[31] If such a novice is lucky – so George Plimpton contended in a famous *Sports Illustrated* article – these guides would include a person of precisely Marianne Moore's ilk, who during a game "is talkative, and often apparently randomly so, *to the point of distraction*, though clearly 'lively' and possessed of outré bits of abstruse information."[32] Replicating and affirming the cubist view of the batter as what a "kiddie fan" can see (only "fractional glimpses"), Angell fully ironizes what "distraction" might mean, and Williams's digressive, fragmented, apparently off-topic poem is a radically modernist version of precisely the same perspective.

Because baseball is typically unrushed, Richard Skolnik writes, "spectators need not always be paying attention; other activities may intrude."[33] Chief among those "other activities" is the work of making meaning of the game. Stadium announcements warn against inattention, but these admonitions arise from insurers' liability requirements. In fact, it is absolutely in the teams' interest – financially, and also culturally – that fans be permitted their antic, expressive, and counterproductive digressions. The least example is Angell's intermittently absent dad's missing home runs while "foraging" for snacks. The greatest example, sitting nearby, is Angell, almost unable to see the batter, instead minutely observing and describing bits of peanut dust in the hair of a young fan. The game thus constantly sends a game-sustaining double message. The title of Skolnik's book, *Baseball and the Pursuit of Innocence*, suggests what he's after. He shuns triteness as the opposite of innocence. That is a high standard, and Skolnik does not always reach it. But he comes closest when exploring the fan as "exceptionally comfortable and playful at the ballpark."[34] He tells of rites of synchronous performativity (for instance, "The Wave") and of the grandstand beach ball, whose bouncing is perpetuated by strangers acting halfheartedly in concert – communal yet anarchic gestures that might remind us of Williams's moodily democratic attraction to the beautiful crowd.

Skolnik also follows fans' launchings of paper airplanes, sometimes onto the field – and there, rather suddenly, the line is drawn and innocence is lost. The innocence Skolnik means – and Angell, too, with his special definition of caring – conceptually depends on the maintenance of the separation of spectator and participant. Once fans run on the field, or interfere with the ball in play, the fan culture that has developed as the alternative to fear and loathing collapses. When Steve Bartman, a Cubs fan seeking no harm to their chances of proceeding to the World Series, leaned over a Wrigley Field rail along the left-field line during a playoff game and grabbed a ball Moises Alou probably would have caught for a crucial out (after which the Cubs lost the lead and went home for another winter), he was so completely reviled that his status as "a lifelong Cubs fan" did not mitigate but actually escalated the indignation. Cubs players notably absolved Bartman of blame, but fans refused.[35] Bartman left the park under security escort, pelted by drinks and other debris. Rod Blagojevich, then governor of Illinois, offered the poor man a spot in the witness protection program.[36] That it was not clear whether Blagojevich was joking indicates the depth of the consternation caused by this violation of spectatorship. What is still so chilling about the moment Hank Aaron surpassed Babe Ruth's lifetime home-run record – after weeks and months of racist death threats – is the blurry televised image of frenzied white teenaged males running alongside him between second base and third. The image shows them striding with him but the remembered impression is that they are chasing him. Our awareness of racist hatred doubtless animates the fearfulness of the image (though the fans were motivated by ecstasy rather than hatred in this instance, fortunately). Yet even here, the power of fans threatens to destroy spectatorship's caring.

Such moments of convergence are transitory. Yet even after the observer–participant balance has been restored, the rupture induced by fans' penetration of the game continues to beguile the fan-chronicler especially. The physical boundary dividing spectating and playing having been secured, any erosion of the differences between writing and baseball becomes all the more alluring. Episodes of fan interference suggest that the fan's involvement properly resides in the realm of the imagination. Moore's "Baseball and Writing" operates under this spell, as does Philip Roth's "My Baseball Years," in which the "emotional atmosphere and aesthetic appeal" of baseball is said to be precisely analogous to the pleasures of writing.[37] Roth, Angell, and the poet Donald Hall stand in a tradition of those attempting experimentally to spectate and play at once in order to rediscover the writer's original motivation. Visiting the Pittsburgh Pirates in Florida, wearing a uniform and participating in spring training, poet Hall cut a ludicrous (obese and big-bearded) figure. His inability to do sprints or be socially accepted paradoxically produced a friendship (and a subsequent book) with idiosyncratic pitcher Dock Ellis, who self-destructively craved outsider status and sought out the poet as a guide to a place beyond the game. Hall's poetry had begun the moment he realized he was not athletic enough to play. From inside baseball he finally learns that writers are essentially not participants and that he has joined the Pirates not in spite of but because he hears childhood echoes of "Go home, Hall." "That's why I started to write poems," he recalls. "The humiliation. I could not be good at anything in sports."[38]

Angell's "Early Innings" (1992) first expresses his feelings of humiliation at his father's ability to play competitive baseball into his late forties, then laments that the general decline of such superannuated participation signifies that "most of American life, including baseball, no longer feels feasible."[39] But that down note is not the way to conclude, and he ends unusually with a dream and its interpretation, actually aided by his therapist. In the dream, Angell rises from his bed and feels compelled to wander out onto his suburban lawn (the ballpark sward?), whereupon he discovers a gravestone marked "1920–1955." At first he thinks he's dreaming of the monuments in Yankee Stadium's center field. With his analyst's help he realizes that the grave is his own, not Ruth's or Gehrig's, and that 1955 – the present time of the dream – marks the end of his hope, still then real, that he could play baseball.

The life of baseball ends as the life of writing begins. "Early Innings," Angell's memoir of the game's beginnings in his life, thus enlarges the concept of feasibility to include interpretation of what others do: witness. Philip Roth similarly loved baseball as a young man not just "for the fun of playing it" but for its "mythic *and aesthetic* dimension."[40] It was only when he had to give up the former that the latter developed into a "feel for the American landscape,"[41] which he knew not from classroom study of Lewis and Clark but from the minor league coverage of *The Sporting News*. Roth's transition from the Newark Bears and Brooklyn Dodgers to "first looking into Conrad's *Lord Jim*"[42] was marked by a great creative adaptation. The project of his life began at the humiliating death of participation, the moment when his "good enough imitation of a baseball player's *style*" ceased to fool the coach.[43] Thus cut from the squad, denied a uniform, he became a fan without illusions, and he now finally required an aesthetic by analogy. Like every baseball fan, he turns away from a literal form of engagement and must learn to care differently. He discovers in the "spirit of uselessness" an imaginative communal utility and humility. The witnessing is plural. As Jane Addams suggested, the voice he hears, telling of the game, might just as well be another's as his own.

NOTES

1. Fred Stein, *A History of the Baseball Fan* (Jefferson, NC: McFarland, 2005), 1.
2. Keith Hernandez, with Mike Bryan, *Pure Baseball: Pitch by Pitch for the Advanced Fan* (New York: HarperCollins, 1994), viii.
3. Hernandez, *Pure Baseball*, 119.
4. Donald Dewey, *The 10th Man: The Fan in Baseball History* (New York: Carroll and Graf Publishers, 2004), 174.
5. William Freedman, *More than a Pastime: An Oral History of Baseball Fans* (Jefferson, NC: McFarland, 1998).
6. David J. Pincus, Stephen C. Wood, and Fritz Cropp, "The Fans' Role in Shaping Baseball: A Voice Too Long Silent?" in *The Cooperstown Symposium on Baseball and American Cuture, 1999*, ed. Peter M. Rutkoff (Jefferson, NC: McFarland, 2000), 333.

7. See Michael Lewis, *Moneyball: The Art of Winning an Unfair Game* (New York: W. W. Norton, 2003).

8. Charles Einstein, "The New Breed of Baseball Fan," *Harper's* 235 (1967), 69–77 (69).

9. Buzz Bissinger, *3 Nights in August: Strategy, Heartbreak, and Joy inside the Mind of a Manager* (New York: Houghton Mifflin, 2005).

10. Pincus, Wood, and Cropp, "Fans' Role," 339.

11. Bob Costas, *Fair Ball: A Fan's Case for Baseball* (New York: Broadway Books, 2000), 13.

12. *Ibid.*, 12.

13. Dewey, *10th Man*, 212.

14. Marianne Moore, "Baseball and Writing," in *The Poems of Marianne Moore*, ed. Grace Schulman (New York: Viking, 2003), 329–331.

15. Marianne Moore, "Hometown Piece for Messrs. Alston and Reese," in *Poems*, 296–298.

16. Moore refers to this bit of improvisation in "Hometown Piece."

17. William Carlos Williams, *The Collected Poems*, Vol. 1, ed. A. Walton Litz and Christopher MacGowan (New York: New Directions, 1986), 233–234.

18. Jane Addams, *The Spirit of Youth and the City Streets* (New York: Macmillan, 1920), 96.

19. Kenneth H. Marcus, "Baseball Stadiums and American Audiences," *TELOS* 143 (2008), 165–70 (168).

20. Horace Traubel, *With Walt Whitman in Camden, January 21 to April 7, 1889*, ed. Scully Bradley (Philadelphia: University of Pennsylvania Press, 1953), 508.

21. Roger Angell, *Once More around the Park: A Baseball Reader* (Chicago: Ivan R. Dee, 1991), 83.

22. *Ibid.*, 82–83.

23. John Connolly, "Carlton Fisk Home Run Forever Frozen in Time," *Baseball Digest* 60 (2001), 42.

24. Doug Glanville, *The Game from where I Stand: A Ballplayer's Inside View* (New York: Henry Holt and Company/Times Books, 2010), xi.

25. Doris Kearns Goodwin, *Wait till Next Year* (New York: Simon and Schuster, 1997).

26. *Ibid.*, 255.

27. *Ibid.*, 255.

28. *Ibid.*, 254.

29. Roger Angell, *Game Time: A Baseball Companion* (New York: Harcourt, 2003), 103.

30. *Ibid.*, 109–110.

31. "How to Become a Baseball Fan," www.ehow.com/how_2057410_become-baseball-fan.html.

32. Charles Molesworth, *Marianne Moore: A Literary Life* (New York: Macmillan/Atheneum, 1990), 429. Emphasis added.

33. Richard Skolnik, *Baseball and the Pursuit of Innocence* (College Station: Texas A&M University Press, 1994), 173.

34. *Ibid.*, 173.

35. Jay Mariotti, "Time for Fans to Reach Out, Have Say," *Chicago Sun-Times*, October 22, 2003, p. 110.

36. Mike Lopresti, "Separating Goats from Scapegoats," *USA Today*, July 29, 2008, 3C; Matthew Phillips, "Bartman!" *Newsweek*, July 21, 2008, 12.
37. Philip Roth, "My Baseball Years," in *Reading Myself and Others* (New York: Doubleday, 1975), 182.
38. Donald Hall, *Fathers Playing Catch with Sons: Essays on Sport (Mostly Baseball)* (New York: Farrar, Straus, and Giroux, 1984), 12–13.
39. Angell, "Early Innings," in *Game Time*, 130.
40. Roth, *Reading*, 180. Emphasis added.
41. *Ibid.*, 181.
42. *Ibid.*, 182.
43. *Ibid.*, 179–180.

10

DAVID F. VENTURO

Baseball and material culture

How things are made, used, and valued (economically, morally, aesthetically, and culturally) and what they signify concern material culturists. According to Jules D. Prown, material culturists tend to fall into one of two categories – *hard* or *soft* – depending on how they read or interpret objects: the "hard material culturist focuses on the reality of the object itself, its material, configuration, [and] articulation." By contrast, "soft material culturist[s] [read] the artifact as part of a language through which culture speaks its mind." That is, the "quest is not to gather information about the object itself and the activities and practices of the society that produced it, but rather to discover underlying cultural beliefs." One might say that historians gravitate to the "hard," and anthropologists to the "soft," but both form part of a continuum.[1]

This chapter, which is more "hard" than "soft," and, given the scope of the subject, suggestive rather than definitive, enumerates the extraordinary range and diversity of baseball artifacts, as well as inventions and technologies that have influenced the game.[2] Then, it briefly examines, in order to provide insight into the development of baseball and its relation to the surrounding culture, a number of baseball's most significant objects.

Players' equipment heads the list of baseball artifacts, notably balls, bats, fielders' gloves, batting helmets and gloves, baseball shoes ("spikes"), and the "tools of ignorance," including catchers' masks, mitts, shin guards, and chest protectors. Indeed, the history of the manufacture and marketing of sporting goods, from the time of Albert G. Spalding, George H. Rawlings, and others from the 1870s and 1880s forward, also belongs to the world of material culture. Baseball apparel – caps, jerseys or uniform shirts, undershirts, pants (knickerbockers), and stirrups – affords a rich subject, and the

To the memory of Warren Susman and Jules Tygiel, extraordinary material culturists, and my mother Florence Matchett Venturo, who enjoyed baseball and died during the writing of this essay; and with thanks to my wife, Jeanne Conerly, our daughter, Katherine Venturo-Conerly, and my in-laws, Ed and June Conerly, for their love and support.

cultural meanings of insignia embroidered on caps and insignia and numerals on jerseys merit special attention: rookie Joe DiMaggio, for example, was assigned the number 18 in spring training 1936, reassigned number 9 at the start of the regular season after a strong preseason, and, in 1937, honored with number 5 when Yankee clubhouse attendant Pete Sheehy (who issued all uniform jerseys) deemed him the likely successor to Babe Ruth (number 3) and Lou Gehrig (number 4) as team leader.[3]

Baseball publications, from early guides, rulebooks, and annual reports, such as *Beadle's Dime Base-Ball Player* (first printed in 1860), to team histories, player biographies, and statistical encyclopedias, occupy another important material-culture niche. One should also consider baseball sheet music, records, tapes, CDs, videos, and films. There are, furthermore, troves of licensed and unlicensed ephemera peddled to fans, such as pennants, yearbooks and scorecards, drinking glasses, baby's outfits ("onesies"), T-shirts, and dolls, as well as "official" apparel and playing equipment, all distinguished by team logos (whose production, distribution, and marketing have grown, with the rise of mass consumerism since World War II, from minor to major industries), and distinctive ballpark foods – industrially prepared, sweet, salty, greasy, and overpriced. One should not overlook ancillary ephemera and paraphernalia – commercial and folk – from nineteenth-century metal baseball banks to twenty-first-century computerized virtual baseball games. Baseball cards and autographs take pride of place among "collectible" ephemera. Finally, baseball's landscapes – its parks, fields, and stadiums – with their evolving building materials, designs, locations, funding, and upkeep – reflect over a century and a half of American history.[4]

Material culturists also study important inventions and technologies that have transformed the game.[5] Railroads and telegraphy helped baseball, after the Civil War, expand from a regional to a national pastime. In the twentieth century, electric lighting, although adopted late and reluctantly by many major league owners (minor league and Negro League management embraced it first), increased profits by expanding hours of play into the evening. Radio and television broadcasting, which owners adopted by fits and starts, and with varying degrees of enthusiasm and understanding of their potential, made the game available over distances of hundreds, even thousands, of miles to millions of people who had never visited a ballpark.[a] (In the 1940s, Elvin "Mutt" Mantle, his son Mickey, and some of Mutt's friends occasionally drove 300 miles from their Commerce, Oklahoma, home where they listened to broadcasters France Laux or Harry Caray call

[a] For more on this transformation of the game see "Baseball and mass media" in this volume, 221–240.

Cardinals games, to St. Louis, Missouri, to attend a Saturday night game and Sunday afternoon doubleheader at Sportsman's Park.)[6] The new media made baseball seem closer and more personal, allowing fans often listening to or viewing broadcasts at home alone to discuss it later with friends and neighbors. Newsreels and newspaper (especially tabloid) reporting and photography simultaneously transformed players into celebrities and made them seem familiar and approachable. Commercial aviation helped expand major league baseball from coast to coast and into an international enterprise. The growth of the interstate highway system, suburbs, and access to automobiles changed the demography of fans and the location of stadiums (closer to highway exits and farther from public transportation).

Likewise, the Reagan-era shift in the American economy – from manufacturing to sales and financial services and toward expansive corporate wealth and power coupled with income polarization and unprecedented, disproportionate growth in executive compensation – further altered fan demographics, the cost of attending a game, and stadium design (hello, luxury boxes), which in turn prompted the selling of ballfield "naming rights" to corporate "sponsors."

Bill James's abstracts, the SABR-L listserv, and innovative baseball scouting all emerged from the information-technology revolution. Computers also encouraged the phenomenon of rotisserie, or fantasy, baseball. Talk radio, cable television, computers, and the Internet have enabled the sports-obsessed, including baseball fans, to live in a perpetual sports cocoon.

Furthermore, material culture addresses collecting, and the history of collecting, baseball memorabilia. Collectors' motives, as Marjorie Akin has observed, range from "the thrill of the chase" to the naked pursuit of investment value.[7] Beginning in the 1970s, collecting baseball memorabilia metamorphosed from a hobby for children and a coterie of adults into a major industry generating hundreds of millions, even billions, of dollars annually (and offering, as well, a significant source of fraud, counterfeiting, and tax evasion). Cards and autographs became commodities – and objects of speculation – priced in national hobby journals, mass-marketed by manufacturers, sold by tradesmen in small card shops and by dealers at huge hobby shows, and auctioned by the world's leading houses. In the 1990s, retired superstars, such as Ted Williams, Joe DiMaggio, and Mickey Mantle, could make more in a year at autograph shows or signing merchandise under contract than they had in their reserve-clause-hobbled[b] major league careers.[8]

[b] The role of the reserve clause in capping salaries and thus shaping the history of labor–management relations in baseball is explored in more detail in this volume, in "Baseball's economic development" (201–215); and the interchapter on Andy Messersmith, Charlie Finley, and George Steinbrenner (216–220).

Today, in contrast to a generation ago, baseball cards and autographs are primarily the province of prosperous middle-aged men who collect to recapture the joys of youth, and to invest and speculate. Indeed, only the high end of the memorabilia business still thrives. Children, priced out of the hobby a decade ago, now play video games, and baseball cards and artifacts have become art objects and markers of cultural history.[9]

Portions of the greatest memorabilia collections now reside in prestigious repositories, including the Metropolitan Museum of Art in New York City and the Baseball Hall of Fame and Museum in Cooperstown, New York, or have been dispersed through international auction houses such as Sotheby's and Christie's. In 1999, Mark McGwire's then record-setting seventieth home-run ball from the 1998 season sold at a Guernsey's auction for more than $3 million. In 2005, the 1919 contract that sent Babe Ruth from Boston to New York went for $996,000, and, in 2004, the ash Louisville Slugger bat he used to hit the first home run at Yankee Stadium on April 18, 1923, sold at Sotheby's for $1.26 million. Only the McGwire ball and a near-mint-condition example of the famous 1909 Honus Wagner T-206 baseball card, last auctioned, in 2007, for $2.8 million, have outsold Ruth's items.[c] The Hall of Fame itself has changed since its 1939 opening from a propagator of baseball myths (most egregiously the supposed founding of the sport by Abner Doubleday in 1839) to a museum and national research center.[10]

The evolution of baseball equipment reveals how baseball became professionalized. Since their livelihood depended on their ability to play regularly during a grueling season, players adopted equipment that facilitated individual and team success while reducing wear and tear on their bodies. These aims, however, sometimes conflicted with older, amateur, gentlemanly codes of fair play and with nineteenth-century gendered norms of manliness. (Indeed, these conflicts still exist, as the debate over steroids and other performance-enhancing drugs suggests.) Moreover, as the game's popularity grew, baseball equipment and uniforms reflected the industrial-age shift from manufacture by skilled artisans to mass production. Mass production, in turn, prompted mass distribution and advertising, including players' paid (and sometimes unpaid) endorsements. The careers of Spalding and Al Reach, who began as players in the Gilded Age and switched to management, ownership, manufacturing, distribution, and sales, remind us that baseball became a business long ago.

Efforts to enhance the dynamics and appeal of this spectator sport led to changes in equipment, rules, and styles of play. Early baseballs, before and

---

[c] For more on the Wagner baseball card, see the interchapter immediately following, 152–154.

after the first codification of the game's rules by Alexander Cartwright and the Knickerbocker Club in 1845, were handmade. The familiar two-piece, figure-eight cover, probably devised in the late 1850s or early 1860s, became standard in the 1870s. When the sport was young, most of the best baseballs used in match games were handcrafted by artisans. After the Civil War, however, as baseball's popularity skyrocketed, machine-produced balls rapidly replaced their handmade predecessors. In 1870, one manufacturer alone was reported to have produced 162,000 balls.[11] By the 1880s, as monopolism spread through American industry and distribution became part of the integrated hierarchy of business, only Spalding and Reach baseballs were sanctioned for use in National League and American Association games. In fact, A. G. Spalding and Bros. *paid* the National League for the right to supply it with balls ($1 per dozen), which it thereafter advertised as the "official" N. L. baseball.[12]

As the quality of play improved, the dimensions of the ball shrank. By 1872, three years after the founding of the first professional team and a year after the inception of the first professional league, the ball reached its current weight and size, 5 to 5.25 ounces and 9 to 9.25 inches in circumference. The reduction probably made catching and throwing easier. Moreover, as the ball became smaller, it got harder – a change that probably coincided with the elimination of *soaking, patching*, or *plugging* (putting a runner out by hitting, rather than tagging, him between bases with the ball). The smaller ball proved easier to pitch, which probably accounts for some of the growing advantage of pitchers over hitters in the game's early decades.[d]

Baseball bats also evolved. Early versions were longer, heavier, and thicker than their modern counterparts. Bat length was set at 40 inches in 1868 and increased 2 inches to the present standard a year later. Players began to use individualized bats in the 1860s. By 1878, Providence Grays batters were selecting distinctive models. In 1896, *The Sporting News* reported that "some of the crack players" had bats made to their own specifications.[13] Pittsburgh's star shortstop, Honus Wagner, in September, 1905, was the first player to have his name branded on a Louisville Slugger model.[14] When pitchers began to snap or jerk their wrists in the nineteenth century (leading to the curveball) and use deceptive motions and grips, hitters sought better control of their swings with shorter, lighter bats. Still, bats remained heavy by present-day standards. Although Babe Ruth's gracefully tapered bats look modern, they are fairly cumbersome, reportedly weighing 40 to 52 ounces. By contrast, Ruth's contemporary Rogers Hornsby recognized

---

[d] For a discussion of the evolution of the rules and equipment in relation to the balance between pitcher and hitter, see "The rules of baseball" in this volume, esp. 13–16.

the advantages of a lighter bat. Though the Cardinal second baseman wasn't the first player to grasp the physics of bat speed, his hitting achievements lent authority to his opinions. Ted Williams, who as a young player trained with Hornsby, used a 33-ounce bat – positively feathery by 1940s standards. Modern lightweight bats with very thin handles became common only in the early 1950s.[15]

Gloves first appeared, worn by catchers on both hands, when pitchers began to throw harder, in the 1860s. Soon thereafter, first basemen, whose hands next to catchers' were most punished by hard throws, followed suit. Although initially criticized by fans, journalists, and some players as unmanly, fielder's gloves (and his own fledgling sporting goods company) received a boost when Chicago White Stockings star Albert Spalding, trading on his reputation, conspicuously wore a black one in 1877.[16] By the early 1890s, most major league fielders wore a glove on their catching hand, though Bid McPhee, the Cincinnati second baseman, held out until 1896, and Detroit pitcher Joe Yeager still refused in 1902. Pitcher Bill Doak, who sold his idea to the Rawlings Company, devised the modern pocket, in 1919, by adding webbing between the glove's thumb and index finger. However, the flexed outer heel, the brainchild of Rawlings's brilliant designer, Harry "Glove Doctor" Latina, which gave rise to the opposable glove, with large, modern webbing and snug, deep pocket, was not invented until 1959.[17] Today, Major League Baseball limits glove size (despite popular incredulity about enforcement) to enhance scoring.

These modifications to bats and gloves reflect professional players' primary concerns: to maximize performance, improve comfort, limit injury, and increase the odds of winning. Gloves, like balls and bats, quickly went from artisanal to mass-produced objects – a reminder of how early baseball became big business. Moreover, with professionalism and specialization, companies designed gloves and bats for the needs of individual major league players. These specific models, designed to enhance the performance of a particular player, were then mass-marketed to admiring children and adults. Anyone could obtain a star's model equipment and indulge in major league fantasies – for a price.

Changing baseball uniform fashions and fabrics reflect broader trends in American clothing. Through the 1940s, uniforms were made of wool flannel or wool–cotton flannel, though rationing during World War II reduced the weight of the fabric. Their baggy fit allowed the heavy, scratchy, absorbent cloth to breathe, especially in summer heat. In the 1960s, as synthetics proliferated, a wool–Orlon blend became popular, replaced in the 1970s by trimmer, cooler, more comfortable, durable double knits, which remain the norm.[18] Embodying the disco era's African American and Latino influences, uniforms radiated bright colors: for example, yellow and black in Pittsburgh; orange, yellow, and navy in Houston; and gold, white, and green in Oakland. Jerseys and pants grew tighter with stirrups worn high, in reaction to the conservative, baggy uniforms (and business attire) of the 1950s. Bill Veeck's White Sox even experimented with shorts for one game in 1976. Then, beginning in the early 1990s, perhaps informed by the hip-hop craze, uniform fit relaxed and stirrups virtually disappeared, either rejected or hidden beneath pants worn to, even over, the shoe. Today, a few players tailor their uniforms so loosely that they resemble 1940s zoot suits; others have returned to the high stirrup or wear knee socks, in homage to the Negro Leagues or with a nostalgic nod to the 1950s.

Since the 1960s, caps have become perhaps the most familiar and complex baseball signifiers – fashion statements (especially when worn backward with a baggy uniform shirt or sweatshirt), professions of team loyalty, cultural or generational solidarity, even declarations of political positions. They are popular where baseball is played – North America, Latin America, the Caribbean, Japan, and Korea – and where it is not – Europe, India, even African villages. When worn abroad by people comparatively unacquainted with the game, baseball caps reflect the reach – some would say the hegemony – of American popular culture, marketing, and consumerism. Certain team logos carry international cachet; New York Yankees caps predominate, signifying success, power, and cool, as well as team identification. More than fifty years after the Dodgers moved to Los Angeles, royal-blue Brooklyn-era caps with their bold white *B* still accrue profits for manufacturers and Major League Baseball as they recall the "Bums" of Brooklyn – and also their signing of Jackie Robinson. Replica caps and jerseys of Negro League teams express support for racial justice.

Parks and stadiums anchor baseball's material culture. As Steven A. Riess and G. Edward White have demonstrated, the shift from wooden grandstands in the late nineteenth century to more stable, sophisticated structures in the early twentieth reveals baseball's tacit embrace of the Progressive Era reformers' demands for stricter building codes and safer, more durable materials for urban structures.[19] Steel and concrete, products of the newly industrialized economy, virtually eliminated the grandstand fires that preceded the ferro-concrete revolution. Moreover, these bigger parks, designed to resemble imperial Roman stadia, accommodated the growing crowds – sometimes 25,000 to 30,000 – attending games. Reinforced steel meant that stands could be double-, even triple-decked, as were Yankee Stadium, in 1923, and portions of Forbes Field, in 1909.

Ballparks tended to be located on the urban periphery in middle-class or underdeveloped neighborhoods, which could be reached by trolley or subway and where land was cheaper.[20] This trend also reflected Progressive Era urban planning. Forbes Field, whose design, location, and construction reflect City Beautiful progressivism, was built in 1909 on seven acres of land in the Oakland section of Pittsburgh, a ten-minute trolley ride from downtown. Forbes Field cost Pirates owner Barney Dreyfuss approximately $1 million to build. The park was state of the art. It seated over 25,000 people, boasted telephones, ramps rather than stairs for safer access to seats, elevators to convey wealthy patrons to their luxury roof boxes on the exclusive third level, and the latest bathing and clothes-drying equipment in the home and visiting clubhouses. Even in the dead-ball era, before Babe Ruth revolutionized baseball with the long ball, Dreyfuss demanded a roomy field to limit home runs: the center-field fence lay 462 feet from home plate. Though smaller than mammoth Yankee Stadium, which originally seated approximately 58,000, Forbes Field was admired as an architectural marvel. When completed, the ballpark was the largest in the nation.[21]

The construction of uniform, multipurpose, municipally financed and supported parks after World War II reflects further changes in American values and circumstances. Like the schools and office buildings of the era, these parks were designed for efficiency and functionality. Often built for more than just baseball, they accommodated the growing middle class that resulted from New Deal economic and social policies, and featured massive parking lots for the new suburban drivers. The contrast between Ebbets Field and Dodger Stadium epitomizes these differences. Ebbets Field opened in 1913 as the Dodgers' home in the heart of Brooklyn, and was accessible mostly by mass transit. Dodger Stadium opened in 1962 in Chavez Ravine, Los Angeles. It was built off a new highway exit on 300 acres of land provided free of charge by the city (on the site of a vibrant Mexican American community) and catered almost exclusively to automobile drivers.[e]

Beginning in the 1960s, the construction of domed stadiums and use of artificial playing surfaces reflected growing competence and confidence in science and technology. Even the heat, mosquitoes, and humidity of Houston, and the rain and damp of Seattle, it was assumed, could be overcome. That these stadiums and the space race occurred simultaneously and that the most famous of them – the eighteen-storey-tall Astrodome, the "Eighth Wonder of the World" – was constructed in Houston, home of NASA's manned spacecraft center, are no coincidence. Still, unanticipated problems occurred. When the Astrodome opened on April 9, 1965, it was outfitted with a translucent roof

---

[e] For a fuller description of the Dodgers' stadium and of the move to Los Angeles that preceded it, and of stadium funding generally, see "Baseball and the American city" in this volume, 95–106.

and planted with grass. Because, in the glare, outfielders had trouble track-
ing fly balls, the club vainly tried orange sunglasses; baseballs dyed yellow,
orange, and shades of red; and batting helmets for fielders, before the team's
flamboyant owner, Roy Hofheinz, finally ordered the ceiling painted. While
this solved the fielding problem, it reduced the sunlight by a third, killing
the grass. For the rest of the year, the Astros played on a field of dead grass
painted green. In 1966, the club installed synthetic turf manufactured by
Monsanto, but because the company didn't have enough of what it then
called "ChemTurf" available initially, only the infield was ready when the
season began. Until July, the outfield remained dead grass.[22]

Although baseball traditionalists complained of the uniformity and circular shape of these "doughnut" or "cookie-cutter" parks, the design made
sense. As construction costs exploded, cities recognized that they could not
afford separate stadiums for professional baseball and football. The circular stadiums built in the 1960s and 1970s could accommodate baseball and
football, provided sections of the stands were movable, and thus could be
used from April through December, to increase revenue.[23] Moreover, in an
age of equity that coincided with New Deal and Great Society principles,
their regular dimensions made the game fairer by limiting ground-rule,
home-team advantages.

The retro ballparks of the last twenty years reflect the same nostalgia that
gave rise to, and was fomented by, Ronald Reagan, once a Depression-era
baseball radio announcer. Both Reagan's rhetoric and recent ballpark archi-
tecture evince a longing for simplicity and authenticity. Ballparks are once
again designed not as generic, multipurpose sites, but solely for baseball.
Municipalities now shoulder the massive financial burden (often over a half-
billion dollars) of building separate facilities for different sports in grandiose
sports complexes, as in Cleveland, Detroit, and Philadelphia, or they place
the baseball facility in the city and another arena in the suburbs, as in New
York. But the nooks and crannies organic to older, urban baseballparks, as a
"function of the spatial configuration of the lots" on which they were built,
became gestures of architectural artifice in contemporary stadiums that
required no such adjustments.[24] Consequently, these ballparks indulge in
self-conscious, architecturally formalistic evocations of baseball's past. But
these allusions – such as the rising center-field slope in Houston's Minute
Maid Park that echoes similar inclines in Cincinnati's old Crosley Field – are
ornamental, not essential to the landscape, and unintelligible to children and
other casual fans, who lack the context to interpret them. Indeed, they seem
intended to trick fans into forgetting the recent past of the Astrodome with
its AstroTurf and permanently closed roof, while exploiting and masking
contemporary, retractable roof technology, in a faux-historical hybrid of

old and new. While the Astrodome and other multipurpose stadiums at least maintained their architectural and historical integrity, the current effort to resurrect the past, however laudable, has ended in mere copying and imitation. Unlike Fenway Park's abbreviated left-field corner, necessitated by the exigencies of Lansdowne Street, the irregular outfield shapes of these new ballfields are no more real, no more authentic than President Reagan's folksy, choreographed photo opportunities. Both Reagan and contemporary baseball architects, following the lead of Henry Ford's Greenfield Village museum, promoted sentimental fictions of an idealized past.[25]

Let us close by considering how baseball memorabilia collecting has evolved from humble beginnings into a vast industry that markets products of often inflated and dubious value. Changes in attitudes toward collecting – as well as changes in the acquisition and production of collectibles – are exemplified in the lives of two of the greatest baseball memorabilia collectors, Jefferson Burdick (1900–1963) and Barry Halper (1939–2005). Burdick, at the age of 10, began collecting trade cards (featuring appealing images, such as baseball players, on the front, and small printed advertisements for products, such as tobacco, on the back). He was fortunate, as Dave Jamieson has remarked, that his childhood "coincide[d] with what some collectors consider the second heyday of card production … from 1909 to 1915," when the American Tobacco Company, American Caramel, *The Sporting News*, and Cracker Jacks produced some of the finest, most beautiful cards of all time.[26] In these years, Burdick discovered his natural "love of pictures," and, in a 1950 essay, tenderly recalled the cards "given away with candy and gums about 1910 [for] … precious pennies."[27] Hobbled in adulthood by rheumatoid arthritis, Burdick attended Syracuse University and never married. Using his modest assembly-line wages, from the 1930s through the 1950s Burdick amassed in his small Syracuse apartment the most extraordinary collection of printed American ephemera: alluring advertisements for shipping companies, meat products, bread, milk, cigars (6,000 box labels), tobacco, old postcards (80,000), and paper dolls, to name a few. Among these, he accumulated over 30,000 baseball cards. In 1937, he began publishing an early hobby newsletter, *Card Collectors Bulletin*, which by 1939 he had expanded from two to seventy-two pages and renamed *US Card Collectors Bulletin*. This became the *ACC: The American Card Catalog*, whose taxonomy remains standard. In the *ACC*, Burdick distinguishes cards by type of issuer (for example, purveyors of tobacco, bread, or other baked goods, and caramels); offers brief descriptions and histories of each; and provides checklists and estimated values for cards of every known set.[28] Burdick hated the commercialism that his catalogue engendered and lamented when he heard that cards were changing hands for as much as

50 cents to a dollar. (The most expensive card in the 1960 *ACC*, the last in which Burdick had a hand, was the T-206 Honus Wagner, valued at $50.) Burdick corresponded and traded by letter with other pioneering collectors, and traveled far and wide in search of rare cards.

In 1947, Burdick persuaded the Print Curator of the Metropolitan Museum of Art to accept the donation of his collection. For the next twelve years he worked from Syracuse, organizing his materials in enormous binders he mailed to New York City. In 1959, having retired early because of his arthritis, Burdick moved to Manhattan, renting a room in a Madison Avenue hotel. Given space at the Met, he worked (with assistance from friends and staff) several days a week at a small desk, arranging his cards. Increasingly weakened by his disease and its treatment, he stoically drove himself, completing the final 200 binders in 3 years. He concluded the Herculean task at 5.00 pm on Thursday, January 10, 1963: 306,353 cards, including approximately 30,000 baseball cards, in 394 albums. (Additional material remains in over 250 boxes.) Remarking "It's finished," Burdick left and the next day checked himself into University Hospital, where he died two months later. In his lifetime, Burdick was largely unknown. Not until the card-collecting craze of the 1980s was his achievement recognized; not until 1993 was part of the collection put on permanent rotating display at the Met.[29]

By contrast, Barry Halper, for the last thirty years of his life, was the most famous baseball memorabilia collector in the world. He began at 8, when he obtained his first uniform, once worn by Detroit's Barney McCoskey, at Ruppert Stadium, in Newark, New Jersey; and the signature of Babe Ruth, by creeping under a police barrier and handing a piece of paper to the Bambino on Babe Ruth Day at Yankee Stadium in April, 1948. Later joint owner of a paper goods company, Halper started purchasing complete sets of baseball cards in the late 1960s, immersing himself in the hobby. In the consumerist world of the 1970s and 1980s, Halper achieved recognition unimaginable to Burdick. When the memorabilia craze erupted in the mid 1980s, Halper became a celebrity; he was featured in the *Wall Street Journal*, *Cigar Aficionado*, *Smithsonian Magazine*, *Sports Illustrated*, and *The Sporting News*. He also appeared on the *Today Show* and many New York radio and television sports programs. Like Burdick, he retired early for health reasons in 1991, and dedicated himself to burnishing his collection, which, by the mid 1990s, was valued by Christie's at over $42 million and included an estimated 400 bats, 1,800 balls, 30,000 cards, 1,000 uniforms (634 signed), 4,000 photos, 1,000 contracts, and 500 rings, not to mention Ty Cobb's false teeth and locks of Babe Ruth's hair. He acquired a limited partnership in the New York Yankees (estimated at between 1 and 5 percent) and became a friend and acquaintance of dozens of baseball players, including Joe DiMaggio, Ted Williams, Mickey Mantle, and Yogi Berra, who visited his house (and private museum) in Livingston, New Jersey. Players signed Halper's items when they visited, enhancing their value. DiMaggio even autographed a *Playboy* issue featuring nude photos of his former wife, Marilyn Monroe. A relentless networker and bargainer, Halper bought thousands of items from retired players and the families and friends of deceased players. When Mickey Mantle spotted Halper at a news conference after Mantle's 1995 liver transplant, he joshed, "Hey, Barry, did you get my other liver?"[30] Halper knew Richard Nixon, who signed a ball for him "Richard Milhous Nixon," but balked at adding the nickname "Tricky Dick." In 1998, the Baseball Commissioner's Office purchased about a fifth of Halper's collection for $7.5 million and donated it to the Baseball Hall of Fame, which opened its Barry Halper Gallery on September 2, 1999. The rest was auctioned by Sotheby's three weeks later, September 23–29, for $21.8 million, somewhat below the Christie's estimate, following the publication of a sumptuous three-volume catalogue. When Halper died of diabetic complications in December, 2005, his passing, unlike Burdick's, was covered in the *New York Times*. He was treated as a connoisseur and mourned publicly; Burdick is buried in an obscure grave in upstate New York.

The lives and careers of Burdick and Halper epitomize some of the enormous, dislocating, post-World War II changes in baseball and American culture. Big business since the Gilded Age, baseball and related industries (including broadcast media and publishing, sporting goods, stadium construction, and sports memorabilia) have grown exponentially, especially since the 1980s, in size and value. (Even in the 1960s, as the reminiscences of many Baby Boomers attest, the sport still had a deceptively intimate feel, which explains why they, unlike many of their children and grandchildren, are still sentimentally attached to it.) But as the widespread prosperity that began with World War II narrowed into fewer and fewer hands, and as consumerism and celebrity burgeoned, an older, puritan America and its values – embodied by Jefferson Burdick – was replaced by the Barnumesque world of Barry Halper. Both Halper and Burdick loved baseball, collected cards as children, and fervently pursued their hobbies as adults. Both contributed to the commodification of baseball ephemera: Burdick by pioneering the modern, standardized catalogue and price guide, and Halper, with his Midas touch, by turning every artifact he pursued into a "collectible." Indeed, Burdick's price guide for cards may have been the North Star by which Halper navigated his early acquisitions. But in Burdick's era, baseball memorabilia was still affordable and accessible: children and adults corresponded with him, and he regarded himself as a folklorist, similar to the Works Progress Adminstration cultural historians who combed America during the Depression for traces of a disappearing past. By contrast, Halper's wealth outpaced that of the baseball players of his time and his celebrity approached theirs. Ironically, Halper helped to undermine his childhood hobby by turning it into a rich man's pastime. In the 1980s and 1990s, Barry Halper boasted a starring role in the booming, unregulated memorabilia business – as a creator, promoter, and beneficiary of an illusory, inflationary system, not unlike the Great Recession's financial house of cards.

NOTES

1. Jules D. Prown, "Material/Culture: Can the Farmer and the Cowman Still Be Friends?" in *Learning from Things: Method and Theory of Material Culture Studies*, ed. W. David. Kingery (Washington, DC: Smithsonian Institution Press, 1996), 20–22.

2. I share reservations about the "soft" or "metaphoric" school thoughtfully addressed by Jules Tygiel, *Past Time: Baseball as History* (Oxford: Oxford University Press, 2000), 3–14, esp. 4–5, 9–11.

3. Richard Ben Cramer, *Joe DiMaggio: The Hero's Life* (New York: Simon and Schuster, 2000), 107.

4. Outstanding repositories of baseball artifacts include the National Baseball Hall of Fame, Cooperstown, NY; the Library of Congress and the Smithsonian Institution's National Museum of American History, Washington, DC; and the Metropolitan Museum of Art, New York City, home of Jefferson Burdick's great American card collection. The Library of Congress boasts an exceptional web display of 2,100 baseball cards dated 1887 to 1914 at http://memory.loc.gov/ammem/bbhtml/bbhome.html.

5. See especially Tygiel, *Past Time*; and G. Edward White, *Creating the National Pastime: Baseball Transforms Itself, 1903–1953* (Princeton: Princeton University Press, 1996).

6. Tony Castro, *Mickey Mantle: America's Prodigal Son* (Washington, DC: Brassey's, 2002), 27–28.

7. Marjorie Akin, "Passionate Possession: The Formation of Private Collections," in *Learning from Things: Method and Theory of Material Culture Studies*, ed. W. David Kingery (Washington, DC: Smithsonian Institution Press, 1996), 102–128.

8. Ben Cramer, *Joe DiMaggio*, 446–463.

9. For an excellent history of baseball cards as business, art form, and hobby from the American Civil War to the present, see Dave Jamieson, *Mint Condition: How Baseball Cards Became an American Obsession* (New York: Atlantic Monthly Press, 2010). For a glimpse of baseball artifacts owned by wealthy connoisseurs, see the beautifully illustrated coffee-table book by Stephen Wong, *Smithsonian Baseball: Inside the World's Finest Private Collections* (New York: Smithsonian Books, 2005).

10. James A. Vlasich, *A Legend for the Legendary: The Origin of the Baseball Hall of Fame* (Bowling Green: Bowling Green State University Popular Press, 1990).

11. Peter Morris, *A Game of Inches: The Stories behind the Innovations that Shaped Baseball*, 2 vols., Vol. I: *The Game on the Field* (Chicago: Ivan R. Dee, 2006ᵃ), 396–397.

12. Dan Gutman, *Banana Bats and Ding-Dong Balls: A Century of Baseball Inventions* (New York: Macmillan, 1995), 171.
13. Morris, *A Game of Inches*, Vol. 1, 413–414.
14. Dennis DeValeria and Jeanne Burke Devaleria, *Honus Wagner: A Biography* (New York: Henry Holt, 1996), 140.
15. Morris, *A Game of Inches*, Vol. 1, 416–417.
16. *Ibid.*, 419–421.
17. *Ibid.*, 425–430; and Gutman, *Banana Bats*, 203.
18. Marc Okkonen, *Baseball Uniforms of the Twentieth Century: The Official Major League Baseball Guide* (New York: Sterling, 1991), 1.
19. Steven A. Riess, *City Games: The Evolution of American Urban Society and the Rise of Sports* (Urbana: University of Illinois Press, 1989), 217.
20. White, *Creating the National Pastime*, 10–46; and Riess, *City Games*, 220.
21. David Cicotello and Angelo J. Louisa, eds., *Forbes Field: Essays and Memories of the Pirates' Historic Ballpark, 1909–1971* (Jefferson, NC: McFarland, 2007), 13–35.
22. Riess, *City Games*, 242; and Michael Gershman, *Diamonds: The Evolution of the Ballpark from Elysian Fields to Camden Yards* (Boston, MA: Houghton Mifflin, 1993), 192–195.
23. *Ibid.*, 196–198.
24. Riess, *City Games*, 219.
25. Warren Susman, *Culture as History: The Transformation of American Society in the Twentieth Century* (New York: Pantheon Books, 1984), 140.
26. Jamieson, *Mint Condition*, 72.
27. Quoted in *ibid.*, 72–73.
28. J. R. Burdick, ed., *The American Card Catalog: The Standard Guide on All Collected Cards and Their Values* [1960] (Franklin Square, NY: Nostalgia Press, 1967).
29. George Vrechek, "Jefferson Burdick's Collection and *The American Card Catalog*: The Greatest Collection that You Will Never See," *Old Baseball Cards*, www.oldbaseball.com/refs/burdick.html; Paul Cummings, "Oral History Interview with A. Hyatt Mayor, 1969 Mar. 21–1969 May 5," *Archives of American Art, Smithsonian Institution*, www.aaa.si.edu/collections/oralhistories/transcripts/mayor69.htm; and Jamieson, *Mint Condition*, 69–87.
30. Jamieson, *Mint Condition*, 202.

DAVID F. VENTURO

Interchapter: the Honus Wagner T-206 baseball card

Baseball, tobacco, advertising, and children already shared a long history in 1909, when the American Tobacco Company (ATC) printed the world's best known and most valuable baseball card, the T-206 Honus Wagner. In the late 1880s, as machinery replaced hand-rolling and boosted production, tobacco companies fiercely competed with one another to sell cigarettes. But how to entice customers with a product regarded as déclassé compared to pipe tobacco and cigars? Manufacturers began to insert trade cards – which had been around for at least a century – into cigarette boxes, with photos or lithographs of athletes, actresses, or other celebrities on the front and an advertisement for the brand on the back. The cards proved hugely popular with both boys and men. Long before Joe Camel, baseball cards were an attractive nuisance, helping to create the next generation of smokers.

In 1909, ATC began advertising at least fifteen of its brands with brightly colored baseball cards in slide-shell cigarette boxes. By 1911 this series, now known as the T-206 set (so dubbed by Jefferson Burdick, the extraordinary collector and pioneering folklorist discussed in the previous chapter), consisted of over 520 different cards with more than 20 different back styles touting such cigarettes as "Hindu," "Cycle," and "El Principe de Gales."[1]

The company had planned to feature Honus Wagner, the great Louisville and Pittsburgh shortstop, in the set. In 1909 many regarded Wagner as the finest all-around player in professional baseball. But, despite ATC's plan, Wagner had reservations. Not that he categorically disapproved of tobacco: he was known to smoke cigars and chew tobacco; he had allowed his likeness to appear on cigar boxes in Louisville and Pittsburgh; and, he endorsed Murad cigarettes in newspaper advertisements during the 1909 Series.[2] But Wagner, according to his granddaughter, Leslie Blair, "didn't want children to have to buy tobacco in order to get his card."[3]

The Piedmont Tobacco Company, an ATC brand, contacted John Gruber, a local sportswriter and the Pirates' official scorer, to solicit Wagner's permission to depict him on a tobacco card, promising Gruber $10 if Wagner

Figure 7. The Honus Wagner T-206 tobacco card. Art Resource – Wagner, Pittsburgh, 1909–1911. Photomechanical print, from "Baseball series" published for Sweet Caporal Cigarettes. © The New York Public Library/Art Resource, New York.

agreed. But the shortstop demurred. He returned Piedmont's letter to Gruber with this reply:

Dear John:

I don't want my picture in cigarettes, but I don't want you to lose $10, so I'm enclosing a check for that sum.

Gruber was reportedly so moved by Wagner's thoughtfulness and generosity that he refused to cash the check and had it framed. Production of the card, at Wagner's insistence, was stopped after a short run. Today, an estimated 50 to 100 Honus Wagner T-206 cards exist.[4]

Though not the rarest of twentieth-century baseball cards, the Honus Wagner card has achieved iconic status.[5] Jefferson Burdick priced it at $50 in the 1960 *American Card Catalog*, when most cards in the book ranged from a penny to a quarter. Today it stands as a centerpiece of the New York Metropolitan Museum of Art's rotating display of baseball cards. As Mike Gidwitz – who purchased the finest known example of the card from hockey star Wayne Gretzky and former Los Angeles Kings owner Bruce McNall for $640,500 in 1996, and then sold it to Brian Siegel for $1.27 million in 2000 – once explained:

> [I]f I went to the New York Metropolitan Museum of Art, or the Louvre, or Christie's, or Sotheby's and asked each expert … "What's the best piece of art that's ever been painted?" they'd all have different opinions … But … if we went to the National [Sports Collectors Convention] and asked the sophisticated collectors and advanced dealers set up at the show, "What's the best baseball collectible in the world?" they'd say it was the Honus Wagner card.[6]

Lavish media coverage, great popular interest, and extraordinary value at auction support Gidwitz's assertion. While some romanticize the Honus Wagner baseball card as the palimpsest on which people write their baseball fantasies, it remains, in fact, the most sought-after baseball commodity in the world: the finest known specimen of the Wagner T-206 card last changed hands in 2007, fetching $2.8 million.[7]

NOTES

1. Dave Jamieson, *Mint Condition: How Baseball Cards Became an American Obsession* (New York: Atlantic Monthly Press, 2010), 36–37; and Stephen Wong, *Smithsonian Baseball: Inside the World's Finest Private Collections* (New York: Smithsonian Books, 2005), 59–60.
2. Dennis DeValeria and Jeanne Burke DeValeria, *Honus Wagner: A Biography* (New York: Henry Holt, 1996), 239.
3. Arthur D. Hittner, *Honus Wagner: The Life of Baseball's "Flying Dutchman"* (Jefferson, NC: McFarland, 1996), 244–245. Interview with Leslie Blair in Rick Hines, "Wagner's Granddaughter Tells Real Story behind T-206 Card," *Sports Collectors Digest*, October 23, 1992, 100.
4. Hittner, *Honus Wagner*, 244, 283 n. 24; Wong, *Smithsonian Baseball*, 63–65; and Harry Grayson, *They Played the Game* (New York: A. S. Barnes, 1944), 7.
5. Jamieson, *Mint Condition*, 217–219.
6. Quoted in *ibid.*, 35.
7. *Ibid.*, 36. For the most complete history of the finest example of the T-206 Wagner card, including allegations that it was altered to enhance its value, see Michael O'Keefe and Teri Thompson, *The Card: Collectors Con Men, and the True Story of History's Most Desired Baseball Card* (New York: William Morrow, 2007).

II

MASARU IKEI

Global baseball: Japan and East Asia

The introduction of baseball to Japan

After more than 200 years of self-imposed diplomatic seclusion, the nation of Japan opened itself up to the outside world in the mid 1850s during the Meiji Period and embarked upon a state-driven modernization program. One of the ways in which the state sought to promote modernization was to introduce advanced science and technology, institutions, and academic knowledge from the Euro-American world. To serve this overarching objective, many foreign teachers were recruited by the Japanese government. School teachers formed the largest contingent of such foreign teachers, or *oyatoi*, during the Meiji Period, and one of them, the American Horace Wilson, was hired into Daigaku Nanko (later to be expanded into Tokyo University) and introduced baseball to Japanese youngsters in 1872. A few years later, Kaitakushi Gakko (later to be reorganized into Hokkaido University) hired a young American teacher named Albert Bates, who not only taught the Japanese students western knowledge but also instilled in them the love of baseball. In those early years of baseball in Japan, however, the available equipment was limited and the playing field was rudimentary at best. This lack of infrastructure kept the Japanese students from forming permanent teams or playing games on a regular schedule.

Spartan as their circumstances may have been, the fact that Japan's future elites learned this western team sport during their formative school days had enormous historical significance. For example, in the United States baseball evolved from a children's game into a professional sport; in Japan, baseball, firmly embedded in the education system, followed a very different evolutionary trajectory. Once these American teachers went home and the students who learned baseball from them first-hand graduated, it appeared that the game had no future in this newly modernizing nation.[1]

Fortunately for baseball (and its latter-day aficionados), it was reintroduced into Japan through another route, this one also having to do with the nation's modernization program. In the early Meiji Period, Japan sent a large number of students abroad to learn western ways. One of them was Hiroshi Hiraoka, a railroad engineer by training. In Boston, Massachusetts, he fell in love with baseball, which was becoming increasingly popular in the United States at the time. Hiraoka avidly played the game (he is considered to be the first Japanese pitcher to throw a curveball), and returned to Japan with a set of baseball equipment and a rule book. Once back in Japan, Hiraoka obtained gainful government employment and played baseball with those initiated into the game at Daigaku Nanko. Hiraoka was also instrumental in popularizing baseball among employees of the Ministry of Engineering and forming Japan's first baseball club, the Shinbashi Athletics. Hiraoka's contribution even went further. He wrote to an acquaintance from his days in Boston, Albert Goodwill Spalding, with a photograph of his team in full uniform. A former professional baseball player and now the successful owner of a Chicago-based sporting-goods business, Spalding forwarded Hiraoka's letter and the accompanying photograph to the *Chicago Daily News* to trumpet the fact that the game he was promoting was even gaining currency in far-off Asia. Spalding also sent a set of top-of-the-line baseball equipment to his old Japanese acquaintance. While it is not clear whether Spalding did so because he eyed the island nation as a potential market, it was an investment in the future just the same.[2]

Baseball as an imported western team sport was popularized through the network of elite institutions of higher education, such as Keio, Waseda, and Meiji Gakuin. Secondary school teachers also played a key part in diffusing baseball to students across the country. The game acquired the vernacular designation *yakyu* (literally translated "field ball") in the 1880s and became amalgamated with traditional cultural attributes and practices. This fusion produced a distinct system of play. The word *yakyudo*, or "the way of *yakyu*," was coined, signifying a highly spiritualized way of playing and training influenced by indigenous Japanese martial arts such as kendo (stick fighting), judo, and kyudo (archery), which place a premium on stoicism and spiritual uplift, not just on winning.[3] Younger Japanese playing baseball in Japan are indoctrinated into *yakyudo* through strict training, where they are commonly required to prepare the playing field and clean toilets, and they are taught absolute obedience to their coaches and their upper-classmen. The ultimate goal of *yakyudo* was and remains gaining a seeding to compete in, and then competing to win, the two annual nationwide competitions known as "Koshien" (the name of the baseball field where the championship tournaments are held).

The organization of school, college, and industrial baseball

Another agent of the nationwide dissemination of baseball in Japan was the budding newspaper industry. Newspaper companies sponsored local and regional student championship tournaments across the country, and the local champions were assembled to play in a regular national tournament. By giving these students a dream of achieving baseball glory and national fame, the newspaper companies incited public enthusiasm and boosted circulation. In 1915, the nation's premier daily, the *Asahi Shinbun*, organized the first national tournament with great success. The tournament was held during public schools' summer recess, and the teams fought for the pride of their home towns. The metaphor of players' "blood, sweat, and tears" became its hallmark. The championship team was praised as the pride of Japan and its ace pitchers and key sluggers became national heroes. Then the *Asahi Shinbun*'s rival, the *Mainichi Shinbun*, began sponsoring its own national tournament during spring school recess. For this spring tournament (seniors graduate from school in March and therefore could not compete in the spring tournaments held at the end of that month), school squads' postseason records were appraised by a committee of specialists to draw up a list of the best teams to be invited to a national meet. This second national tournament began in 1924, and became the harbinger of spring for most Japanese (a bit like professional teams' spring training in the United States).[4]

In addition, what has become known as the Tokyo Big-6 Intercollegiate Baseball League began in 1925. This high-level intercollegiate circuit included five private universities (Keio, Waseda, Meiji, Hosei, Rikkyo) plus Tokyo Imperial University. This last institution added to the general prestige of the league, which was based in the Tokyo metropolitan area. The winner of the Tokyo Big-6 tournament, which was held twice a year in the spring and fall, was awarded the prestigious Emperor's Cup trophy, making this league's play something more than a mere student sporting event. Stars of middle school baseball passionately sought admission into the Tokyo Big-6 schools. Games played between the league's two arch-rivals, Waseda and Keio, were widely reported by the newspapers and even broadcast over radio. In time, the famed Waseda–Keio matchup came to be compared to the Oxford–Cambridge boat race and the West Point–Annapolis football game.[5]

The economic prosperity generated by World War I permitted the rise of industrial (corporate) baseball in Japan. Many companies began to form their own in-house competitive baseball teams around the mid 1910s. The premier players of middle school and college baseball were recruited to these industrial teams, and this institutional arrangement permitted them to continue to play after the end of their schooling, with job security. The success of this new venue for baseball culminated in the organization in 1920 of the national corporate team tournament (*shakaijin yakyu*) and the national tournament of government-run railroad division teams in 1921. The *Mainichi Shinbun* effectively capitalized on this baseball boom in Japan's Roaring Twenties. The organizers of the new tournaments borrowed a format from the US major leagues, whose franchises were closely identified with their cities. These corporate teams and railway club teams were designated as representing the cities in which they were based, and they were assembled once a year in Tokyo to vie for national championships. Since middle school baseball tournaments, both summer and spring, were held in western Japan, the Tokyo Big-6 and the corporate and railroad inter-city tournaments were held in Tokyo. The inter-city tournaments reflected Japan's international position at the time in that they also drew teams from Manchuria, Korea, and Taiwan.[6]

After World War II, the middle school tournaments were upgraded to high school tournaments as a result of the reorganization of Japan's educational system, but they continued to be widely (and minutely) covered by newspapers and popular magazines. The semi-government-run television station NHK broadcast the two annual tournaments through its nationwide network, solidifying the game's mass appeal. Meanwhile, the inter-city Tournament of industrial baseball teams became a vehicle for corporate advertising and morale boosting among employees. Some star players looked at industrial baseball as a stepping stone to professional baseball.

Playing in the national high school baseball tournaments at the Koshien Stadium became the dream of every young player in Japan. This mass fascination created a cultural context in which a distinctly Japanese style of student baseball emerged. Bunting in early innings became the norm and many teams elected to advance their baserunners by bunting. In conjunction, there developed a strategy of deliberately walking formidable sluggers (for example, New York Yankee-turned-Anaheim Angel Hideki Matsui was walked an astounding five consecutive times at bat when he was a high school player in Japan), and top pitchers were used game after game, with little concept of pitcher rotation. An example of how *yakyudo* still exists was observed during the Koshien high school tournament held in 2006, where Waseda Jitsugyo High School's ace pitcher Saito threw 553 pitches over 4 consecutive games held on consecutive days. (By comparison, 100 pitches every 5 days is considered an ample workload for a professional pitcher in the US major leagues.) The Japanese mass media glamorize such abusive practices and players willingly put their teams' immediate success before their own long-term physical well-being. Members of losing teams in the national tournament are commonly seen collecting soil from the Koshien playing field as a memento of their youthful dedication and participation in this prestigious tournament.

Baseball thus evolved primarily as an integral part of student athletics until 1934, when Japanese professional baseball was born.

The birth of professional baseball in Japan

One might say that Japanese professional baseball was another House That Ruth Built. To trace the unlikely but enormous influence of Ruth on Japan, we must turn first to early Japanese sports journalism. Generally speaking, there are two categories of newspapers in Japan. In one group are *Asahi* and *Mainichi*: high-quality opinion-leading papers that originated as publications by government critics subscribing to the Freedom and Popular Rights Movement. In the other category are mass-circulation papers emphasizing human-interest stories, institutional descendants of popular rags dating back to the Edo Period. The *Yomiuri Shinbun*, the newspaper that would host Babe Ruth's historic 1934 Japan tour, occupied a place in between these two categories. *Yomiuri*'s editorial motto was to "read and sell" – which is what the Japanese words *yomi* (to read) and *uri* (to sell) literally mean. Since *Asahi* and *Mainichi* had established their dominance over amateur (student) baseball, the late-arriving *Yomiuri* had to carve out its own journalistic niche elsewhere. At the time that *Yomiuri* came onto the scene, American baseball was receiving very little coverage in Japan, aside from annotations about the Yankees and Babe Ruth. So *Yomiuri* fastened onto American professional baseball, focusing particularly on famous players like Ruth.

In 1931, the upstart national daily invited a team of US major league players to Japan, but Ruth was not on that roster because he demanded too much money and also had plans to shoot a movie in Hollywood after the season ended. But Lou Gehrig, Lefty Grove, and other top players toured Japan and played seventeen games against the all-star team drawn from the Tokyo Big-6. Japan lost all seventeen games, but the enterprise was a huge commercial success, producing not only oversized gate receipts but also a boost to *Yomiuri*'s circulation. Clearly, *Yomiuri*'s next big thing needed to be a tour by none other than the Sultan of Swat himself.[7]

The moment for that came in 1934, when a team of major league all-stars, this time including Ruth, toured Japan again. The only catch was that the Japanese Ministry of Education refused to permit student amateur athletes to play against American pros. *Yomiuri*'s solution to this problem was to organize Japan's own pro team, assembling a roster of former college and high school baseball stars, and a number who had left school to turn pro. This hastily assembled team became the nucleus of Japanese professional baseball.

Birthing professional baseball in Japan was not Ruth's only feat. The Bambino also helped to smooth US–Japanese relations. Following its internationally condemned invasion of Manchuria in 1931, Japan removed itself from the League of Nations, and its relationship with the United States threatened to descend into a downward spiral. The US Ambassador to Japan Joseph Grew praised Ruth as a goodwill ambassador he could never hope to be himself.[8]

After Ruth's 1934 tour, Japan's first professional team named themselves the Tokyo Giants and embarked upon a barnstorming tour of the United States. After a grueling, 5-month, 110-game tour across the USA, the Giants came home with a record of 75 wins, 34 losses, and one draw. Following the Giants' US tour, the Hanshin Tigers were formed in Osaka. Others followed. In 1936, these professional teams organized themselves as the Japanese Baseball League. There were three teams in Tokyo, two in Osaka, and two in Nagoya. Four were owned and operated by newspaper companies, and three by railway companies. Japan's professional league operated in ways very different from the majors' franchise system in the USA. Japanese team owners were more interested in using a team as the parent company's advertising tool than actually making money on the games per se. Before World War II, Japan's professional baseball was no match for student amateur baseball in popularity. Some even considered the profession demeaning.

Once World War II began, baseball was branded "the enemy sport." Star professional players were drafted into military service and many never returned from the front. After the war, baseball recovered quickly because the US occupation sought to facilitate peaceful occupation by using the Emperor and baseball as pacifying agents.[a] In this hospitable environment, not only did high school and college baseball revive, but professional baseball also became hugely popular. In 1949, the San Francisco Seals of the AAA Pacific Coast League visited Japan. The Seals tour, taking place during the Allied occupation, was dubbed a US–Japanese goodwill tour. Before the games, the Japanese national flag was allowed to be hoisted for the first time since Japan's surrender, and the national anthems of both countries were played. War orphans were invited to the games, and the visiting team contributed all the proceeds minus expenses to the promotion of Japanese

---

[a] For discussion of how baseball functioned domestically in the USA during wartime, see "Baseball and war" in this volume, 81–94.

baseball. Nothing could have signified American goodwill more effectively than these gestures.[9] Beginning in 1951, major league all-stars and teams such as the New York Giants and the Yankees began to tour Japan during the off-season every few years and showcased state-of-the-art baseball to Japanese fans.

The creation of the two-league system and the recruitment of foreign talent

Big corporations that accumulated wealth in Japan's period of postwar economic prosperity seized on the baseball boom. The three key patrons of postwar professional baseball in Japan were newspapers, movie studios, and railroad companies. *Mainichi*, *Yomiuri*'s newspaper rival, finally acquired its own professional team after World War II. The proliferation of professional teams in the early postwar period led organized baseball to split into two leagues, the Central League and Pacific League, in 1950. Player raiding – in which a team would sign its rivals' star players – was rampant in the early postwar regime owing to a talent shortage, and this practice created a lot of bad blood. Teams filled the postwar talent void with players from abroad. In 1951, Wally Yonamine, a second-generation Japanese American from Hawaii, became a sensation. Trained in football, Yonamine revolutionized Japanese baseball with his fierce baserunning. Off the playing field, he was a devoted Christian and exemplary in his ascetic lifestyle, steering clear of drinking, smoking, or gambling at mahjong.[10]

Following Yonamine was Daryl Spencer, who joined the Hankyu Braves in 1964. When he landed in Japan, Spencer declared that he would bring the pennant to his team with his bat and braininess. He became both famous and hugely influential for taking note of the strengths and weaknesses of his opponents. His probing gaze forced pitchers in the Pacific League to hide their grip behind their gloves before pitching. "Thinking baseball," as it was called, became his hallmark. In 1967, Spencer was joined by Don Blasingame (nicknamed "Blazer") and together they perfected "thinking baseball."

Over 700 foreign players have played in Japanese professional baseball since the end of World War II. Foreign players were recruited because they were regarded as prepared to play at the professional level, able to hit with power, and capable of introducing new styles of play. Foreign players did much more than bring cutting-edge baseball to Japan; they also took back to the US majors what they learned abroad. After guiding the Philadelphia Phillies to the 2008 World Series championship, manager Charlie Manuel commented in a 2008 interview that, "If I had not had those six years of experience in Japan, I would not have succeeded as a major league manager."[11] Manuel played under Tatsuro Hirooka, the most draconian field manager in Japan, and he learned how to run a team under his tutelage. Hirooka demanded that Manuel and other players pay fines for being late, shun alcohol and gambling, never smoke while in uniform, and always polish their cleats. Other American players and coaches who came to Japan, among them Davey Johnson, Ken Macha, Trey Hillman, Jim LeFebvre, and Bobby Valentine, learned Japanese playing styles, including such elements as the emphasis on the bunt. Their cosmopolitan eclecticism put them in good stead when they became major league managers with Latin American and Asian players on their rosters.[12]

Japanese professional baseball also reflected the vicissitudes of the Japanese economy. Those corporations that lost out in the postwar economic restructuring, such as movie studios and railroad companies, were forced to forgo team ownership. They were replaced by new drivers of the Japanese economy, such as food companies, supermarket chains, information technology businesses, and lease companies. The Yomiuri Giants continued to reign in the changing business environment of the 1960s. The team boasted two superstars on its roster, Sadaharu Oh and Shigeo Nagashima, who were reminiscent of the New York Yankees' Babe Ruth–Lou Gehrig juggernaut during the 1920s and 1930s. Beginning in 1965, the Yomiuri Giants won nine consecutive Central League and Japan Series championships. *Yomiuri*'s monopolistic practices turned the Giants into a national brand: the national daily *Yomiuri Shinbun* reported their games and the *Yomiuri*-affiliated TV network televised them.[13]

Japanese players in the US majors

Few observers could believe it when Masanori Murakami, who was supposedly studying baseball in the United States, was recruited to play in the 1A minor league by the San Francisco Giants. In September, 1964 Murakami was brought up to play for the major league Giants, and was given the nickname Massi. He pitched 15 innings with a fine 1.80 earned-run average and 15 strikeouts, then returned home to Japan after the 1964 season. His home team, the Nankai Hawks, and Japanese fans wanted him back, but the San Francisco Giants, who signed a contract with Massi, believed they held the right to the first Japanese major leaguer. In the interest of maintaining the friendly relationship between the Japanese leagues and the US majors, the Baseball Commissioners in the two countries reached a compromise at the end of the 1965 season. The arrangement was for Murakami to make his own decision as to where he would play. In the end, he chose to return to Japan. The Murakami imbroglio was historic, and taught some bitter lessons, such as the difference between the American and Japanese views of the sanctity of player contracts. The incident also showed that Japanese fans could not yet accept the notion of Japanese major leaguers.

It took thirty years, but Hideo Nomo changed all that. In 1995, Nomo bolted from his Japanese team and joined the Los Angeles Dodgers. Winning thirteen games, Nomo won the Rookie of the Year Award and started for the National League in the Major League All-Star Game. The Japanese sensation proved a savior of Major League Baseball, which was desperate to win back fans in the wake of the player strike of the previous year that had canceled the World Series. The *New York Times* (May 3, 1995) dubbed Nomo a "Rookie in [a] League of his Own."[14] His winning weapons were his nasty forkball and a unique twirling delivery called "the Tornado throw." His popularity and unique style of pitching led Edmon J. Rodman to publish a children's book in 1996 entitled *Nomo: The Tornado who Took America by Storm*. Nomo also appealed to American baseball fans with his Samurai-like stoic style of play. The Japanese media followed Nomo's every move and Japanese network TV began to cover Dodgers games in which Nomo pitched. In time, Japanese baseball watchers were turned on to Major League Baseball more generally.[15] In light of Nomo's success in the major leagues, the Japanese professional leagues implemented a posting system in 1999 that allowed Japanese teams to claim fees for their players signed by American teams. As a direct result of this system, significant fees were paid by the Seattle Mariners in 2001 for the signing of Ichiro Suzuki to his former team in Japan, Orix, and for Daisuke Matsuzaka by the Red Sox to his former team, Seibu in 2006.

Within a decade, Ichiro Suzuki put to rest the conventional belief that even if Japanese pitchers could make it in the US major leagues, their hitters could not. Ichiro's inaugural season with the Mariners in 2001 was studded with achievements; he had the highest batting average, he stole the most bases, he was elected American League Rookie of the Year and Most Valuable Player, and he won a Gold Glove for his fielding. Moreover, he helped lead the Mariners to a division championship. Ichiro's strengths lay in his artful precision batting, his laserlike throws from the outfield, and his aggressive yet judicious baserunning. Ichiro is smaller than many American major league players, but he has had revolutionary effects on major league play. Ichiro's style of play reminded baseball fans and the sports media of the pre-Babe Ruth era when the home run was not the only thing

Ichiro's presence is emblematic of the important place Japanese players have come to occupy in the majors. The attractions of Japanese players are: (1) their reliability; (2) their solid mastery of the fundamentals of play; (3) their sober, drug-free lifestyles; (4) their gate appeal to Japanese

fans and tourists; and (5) their related boost of the value of their teams'
television broadcasting rights.[16] As part of their training in the spirit of
yakyudo, Japanese players are taught from a young age to stay away from
various vices including drugs. As anecdotal evidence of the strong draw that
Japanese players in the majors have, several large Japanese travel agents
have planned 2010 tours designed to bring several hundred Japanese to
the USA expressly to see Ichiro Suzuki and Hideki Matsui play in games
between the Mariners and the Angels. Moreover, Japanese television networks are rumored to have paid huge sums of money for the right to air US
major league games.

Baseball in Taiwan, Korea, and China

Baseball began in Taiwan around 1905 as a result of Japanese occupation.
After the Sino-Japanese War, Japan acquired Taiwan and sent many Japanese
nationals to this colonial possession. Japanese schools in Taiwan established
baseball teams, and a team representing Taiwan began to participate in the
national middle school tournament in 1924. In 1931, a Taiwanese team,
managed by a Japanese national, advanced to the tournament's semifinal.
Baseball was used as a tool of colonial administration to break the barrier
between the Japanese colonial metropolis and the periphery. In the early
postwar period, with the end of Japanese colonial rule, baseball threatened
to disappear from Taiwan under Nationalist rule, but when a Taiwanese
team won the Little League World Series in the United States in 1969, the
indigenous Taiwanese reacted rapturously to the feat. The Nationalist government began to use baseball as a way to pacify the indigenous population, and thus promoted baseball nationwide. Some Taiwanese players made
names for themselves in Japanese professional baseball. In 1990, a four-team
pro league opened in Taiwan. Later, it was tainted by a game-fixing scandal,
but the four-team league is still going strong today. Taiwanese players are
beginning to appear on US major league rosters: most notably pitcher Wang
Chien-Ming (known in the States as Chien-Ming Wang), who was briefly
the ace of the Yankees' pitching staff in the mid 2000s.

Baseball also made its way to Japan's other colonial outpost, Korea,
around 1905. The game was introduced by an American missionary posted
in the YMCA in Seoul. After Korea's annexation by the Japanese Empire,
regional divisions of the National Middle School Championship began to
be held on the Korean peninsula in 1924. During Japanese colonial rule, a
total of twenty teams from Korea participated in the national tournament
held in Japan, but the Korean teams' records were less than impressive.

After liberation from Japanese colonial rule in 1945, Korean baseball was in the doldrums before being revived in the 1960s. Spearheading that rejuvenation was a group of Korean pro baseball players who were raised in Japan. In 1982, a six-team pro league was created in South Korea. In the 2008 Beijing Olympics, the Korean national team won the gold medal after beating Japan, the USA, and Cuba.

China is still a developing country when it comes to baseball. The baseball stadium built for the Beijing Olympics was taken down after the Games, and most Chinese sports fans don't pay much attention to baseball. But the phenomenal success of Yao Ming in the National Basketball Association (NBA) has had a notable crossover effect. China began to televise NBA games soon after Yao's 2002 debut, and the US baseball leagues are now recruiting promising young talent from China for their minor league systems, preparing to duplicate the NBA's success in China. Asia is quickly becoming the epicenter of the baseball world, with Japan's two consecutive championships in the World Baseball Classic, South Korea's Olympic gold, and Japanese players changing Major League Baseball to good effect.

This current globalization of baseball grows out of the game's remarkable history in Japan and other parts of Asia as a tool of war, peace, diplomacy, and commerce. From Albert Spalding to Babe Ruth to Hideo Nomo and now Ichiro, baseball shows itself less as an American transplant and more as a site for cultural commingling of all kinds. Furthermore, the game is becoming a truly global sport as reflected by the growing exchange of players between the USA and Japan and other parts of Asia. The challenge ahead will be understanding how to diffuse baseball into other developing countries and regions of the world where it remains a minor sport. Japan will continue as a major proponent of the global expansion of baseball, and has taken steps to expand the number of players and fans in developing countries and regions such as Africa through the donation of equipment and the service of coaches as part of foreign aid programs. And it is certain that the Japanese fans look forward to increased global coverage of the sport and to the greater representation of their athletes in baseball outside Japan.

NOTES

1. For a good general overview of the introduction of baseball to Japan, see Kimishima Ichiro, *Nippon Yakyu Soseiki* (Tokyo: Besuboru Magajinsha, 1972). For his study of early Japanese baseball, Kimishima was inducted into the Japanese Baseball Hall of Fame in 2009.

2. For the life and work of Hiraoka Hiroshi, see Suzuki Yasumasa and Sakai Kenji, *Besuboruto Okajoki: Nipponde Hajimete Kabuwo Nageta Otoko Hiraoka Hiroshi* (Tokyo: Shogakukan, 2005).

3. For differences between American baseball and Japanese baseball, see Ikei Masaru, "Baseball, Besubouru, Yakyu: Comparing the American and Japanese Games," *Indiana Journal of Global Legal Studies* 8 (2000), 73–79. Robert Whiting compares the national characters through studies of professional baseball: see, for example, Robert Whiting, *The Chrysanthemum and the Bat: The Game Japanese Play* (Tokyo: Permanent Press, 1977); *You Gotta Have Wa: When Two Cultures Collide on the Baseball Diamond* (New York: Macmillan, 1989). See also Donald Roden, "Baseball and the Quest for National Dignity in Meiji Japan," *American Historical Review* 85 (1980), 511–534.

4. For the summer high school baseball tournament, see *Asahi Shinbunsha*, ed., *Zenkoku Kotogakko Yakyu Senshuken Taikai Nanajunenshi* (Tokyo: Asahi Shinbunsha, 1989). For the Spring High School Baseball Tournament, see Mainichi Shinbusha, ed., *Senbatsu Kotogakko Yakyu Taikai Rokujunenshi* (Tokyo: Mainichi Shinbunsha, 1989).

5. For the Tokyo Big-6 League, see *Besuboru Magajinsha*, ed., *Tokyo Rokudaigaku Yakyu Hachijunenshi* (Tokyo: Besuboru Magajinsha, 2005).

6. For industrial league baseball, see *Mainichi Shinbunsha, Toshitaikio Yakyu Rokujunenshi* (Tokyo: Mainichi Shinbunsha, 1990).

7. For *Yomiuri Shinbun*'s role in professional baseball, see *Yomiuri Shinbun Hyakunenshi Henshuiinkai*, ed. *Yomiuri Shinbun Hyakunenshi* (Tokyo: Yomiuri Shinbunsha, 1976).

8. Joseph C. Grew, *Ten Years in Japan* (London: Hammond, Hammond, and Co., 1944), 208. For Babe Ruth's Japan tour, see Bob Considine, *The Babe Ruth Story* [1948] (New York: Signet NAL, 1992), 207–209; Leigh Montville, *The Big Bam: The Life and Times of Babe Ruth* (New York: Doubleday, 2006), 330–335.

9. The manager of the San Francisco Seals was Frank O'Doul. After 1931, O'Doul visited Japan several times, either as a player or a coach. He also brokered Babe Ruth's Japan tour, and the American tour of Japan's first professional team, the Dainippon Tokyo Baseball Club (forerunner to the Tokyo Giants) in 1935. For his contribution to US–Japanese baseball exchange, O'Doul was inducted into the Japanese Hall of Fame in 2002. For O'Doul, see Richard Leutzinger, *Lefty O'Doul: The Legend that Baseball Nearly Forgot. The Story of the Hall of Fame's Missing Star* (Carmel, CA: Carmel Bay, 1997).

10. The best biography of Yonamine is Robert Fitts, *Wally Yonamine: The Man who Changed Japanese Baseball* (Lincoln: University of Nebraska Press, 2008).

11. Charlie Manuel quoted in *Nikkan Sports*, October 31, 2008.

12. Robert Fitts, *Remembering Japanese Baseball* (Carbondale: Southern Illinois University Press, 2005) is based on the oral history of twenty-three players, including nineteen foreigners who played in Japanese professional baseball, such as Spencer and Blasingame. The book is illuminating of their relationship with Japanese baseball. The autobiography of Warren Cromartie, who played for the Yomiuri Giants between 1984 and 1989, is Warren Cromartie with Robert Whiting, *Slugging It Out in Japan: An American Major Leaguer in the Tokyo Outfield* (London, New York, and Tokyo: Kodansha International, 1991).

13. For Oh's biography, see Sadaharu Oh and David Falkner, *Sadaharu Oh: A Zen Way of Baseball* (New York: Times Books, 1985).

14. "Rookie in League of His Own." *New York Times*, May 3, 1995, B11.

15. For Nomo's impact on US–Japanese relations, see Ikei Masaru, "Nomo Hideo wo meguru Nichibei Kankei," *Shokun!* (September, 1995), 82–89.

16. For Ichiro's impact, see Masaru Ikei, "The Ichiro Effect," *New York Times*, July 9, 2001.

LEONARD CASSUTO

Interchapter: Roberto Clemente and Ichiro

Roberto Clemente and Ichiro Suzuki are the most prominent global baseball players of their generations, symbols of the game's international reach and appeal. Baseball has a deserved (and complicated) reputation as the national pastime of the United States, but the changing complexion of the major leagues during the past half-century ought to remind us that the game also travels among the cultures of the world.

Roberto Clemente was not the first Latino baseball player, but he became the flag-bearer for Latin America in the major leagues. Clemente grew up in San Juan, Puerto Rico, and joined the Pittsburgh Pirates in 1954. He spent his entire career in Pittsburgh, and in 1973 became the first Latin American player to be elected to the Baseball Hall of Fame.

No one who saw Roberto Clemente play will forget his smooth energy. Clemente was not big, but he was unusually forceful. At bat, his body would uncoil, swiveling and unleashing his pent-up momentum. When Clemente threw, he would wind up and throw himself forward, his arm a windmill. The ball would sail on a low, clothesline trajectory. To see Clemente throw a runner out at third base from hundreds of feet away in right field was a small piece of baseball poetry.

Clemente carried himself with a proud dignity that some observers took for haughtiness. Gestures like his insistence on being called "Roberto" (rather than "Bobby") conveyed his belief in the importance of his own example as a dark-skinned outsider, both black and Hispanic, a trailblazer who knew he was a role model. "Clemente was our Jackie Robinson," said Puerto Rican broadcaster and journalist Luis Mayoral. "He was on a crusade to show the American public what a Hispanic man, a black Hispanic man, was capable of."[1] Interviewed on television right after the Pirates won the World Series in 1971, Clemente chose to speak first in Spanish. It was, wrote Clemente biographer David Maraniss, "a simple moment that touched the souls of millions of people in the Spanish-speaking world."[2]

Figure 8. Roberto Clemente, sliding into home, 1955. © Bettmann/CORBIS.

Clemente died in a plane crash on December 31, 1972, personally accompanying a relief effort he had organized to bring supplies to Nicaragua after an earthquake there. He was 38, still an active player, and his physical skills, integrity, and self-sacrifice were suddenly frozen in time. Many honors followed, including the Roberto Clemente Award, given each year by Major League Baseball to a player who performs humanitarian work after Clemente's example. Today more than 200 public structures in Puerto Rico – not only ballfields, but also hospitals and schools – bear Clemente's name.[3]

Ichiro Suzuki is the first Japanese player to become a US major league superstar. After nine years with the Orix Blue Wave in Japan, he took advantage of the newly devised posting system (described in the previous chapter) to emigrate to a new country and a new team, the Seattle Mariners. An instant success upon his 2001 arrival, Ichiro broke a single-season record for most base hits in 2004 that had stood for eighty-four years.

Unlike many hitting stars, Ichiro is known for singles, not home runs. Rather than swinging for the fences (a gamble that also produces a high number of strikeouts), Ichiro seeks to place the ball artfully, using his footspeed to get on base. Once on base, he jangles the nerves of pitchers and infielders because of his threat to run. In this way, he reminds many observers of Jackie Robinson, whose exciting baserunning magnetized players and fans alike. Like Robinson, Ichiro makes interesting things happen when he comes to bat. Like Clemente, he's also a brilliant right-fielder. (He is shown fielding his position in spectacular fashion on the cover of this book.)

Also like Clemente, Ichiro is acutely aware of the image he projects, and of his foreignness in the major leagues. He chooses to be called simply "Ichiro," the single name reserved for only the most prominent cultural icons. Like another single-name celebrity, Madonna, Ichiro cultivates a distinctive charisma. "I think there's sexiness in infield hits because they require technique," he told the *New York Times* with self-conscious irony. "I'd rather impress the chicks with my technique than with my brute strength."[4] Ichiro's flamboyance extends to the field, where he decorates his movements with curlicues: little gestures at the end of a play that show that he's styling.

Ichiro has resisted assimilation into the star-making apparatus of American sports. He speaks English reluctantly, and for a number of years demanded an interpreter, even after his increasing English comprehension had become clear. He has limited need for American celebrity except on his own terms, for his fame in Japan has reached epic proportions. (It is said that a letter addressed simply to "Ichiro" in Japan will reach him.) More global ambassador than humanitarian, Ichiro has done more than anyone else to consolidate Japanese interest in the American major leagues. He has also made the Japanese game much more familiar to observers in the United States.

Roberto Clemente and Ichiro Suzuki share a sense of grace. Great athletes both, each invokes an individual sense of the dance on the field, a beauty of movement that one sees rarely, even in star players. This grace extends beyond the chalk lines marking the boundaries of the field. As self-conscious representatives of millions of players and fans outside the United States, these two players have demonstrated the possibilities of the global game, even as they've helped to fulfill them.

NOTES

1. Steve Wulf, "25 Roberto Clemente," *Sports Illustrated*, September 19, 1994. Available at http://sportsillustrated.cnn.com/vault/article/magazine/MAG1005692/index.htm.
2. David Maraniss, *Clemente: The Passion and Grace of Baseball's Last Hero* (New York: Simon and Schuster, 2006), 264.
3. *Ibid.*, 2.
4. Brad Lefton, "Mariners' Suzuki on a First-Name Basis with Records," *New York Times*, August 23, 2009, SP2.

12

ARTURO J. MARCANO AND DAVID P. FIDLER

Global baseball: Latin America

Introduction

Much of baseball's lore centers on the game's meaning in the United States. "Where have you gone, Joe DiMaggio? A nation turns its lonely eyes to you," sang Simon and Garfunkel. However, the US national pastime is a global game. As the focus on Japan and East Asia elsewhere in this volume suggests,[a] understanding baseball today requires a global perspective, but this perspective has to be more comprehensive than simply appreciating the skills of foreign players. This chapter analyzes the globalization of baseball in Latin America,[1] which has been the main source of foreign talent for Major League Baseball (MLB). In Latin America, the globalization of baseball has provided uplifting stories of players who emerged from Third World poverty to star in "The Show," as the American major league game is sometimes called. But it has also involved many problems MLB has struggled to address effectively in tapping into Latin America as a source of talent. This chapter explores the evolution of MLB's efforts to govern its activities in Latin America.

To begin, we detail the dominance of the Dominican Republic and Venezuela as sources of players for MLB. The prominence of Latin American players flows from MLB's efforts to globalize the market for baseball labor. The globalization of baseball operates differently in Latin America than in Asia and other regions, and a key difference is how MLB's recruiting efforts in Latin America predominantly target children. In response to criticism that it was operating a system that discriminated against and mistreated Latin American children, MLB has undertaken reforms, but, even as some past problems diminished in seriousness, MLB has had to confront new ones, such as abuse of performance-enhancing drugs by Latin American minor league players. Over the course of 2009–2010, MLB leaders have finally

---

[a] See "Global baseball: Japan and East Asia" in this volume, 155–167.

Table 12.1 *Foreign players in the major leagues*

Year	Total players	Foreign players	Percentage of foreign players
2010	833	233	28%
2009	818	229	28%
2008	855	239	28%
2007	849	246	29%
2006	813	223	27%
2005	829	242	29%
Average, 2005–2010			28%

Source: Major League Baseball

realized the need for more strategic and systemic reforms of MLB's Latin American activities, and this chapter analyzes the proposals suggested to achieve this outcome.

Latin American players in the major and minor leagues

Players from the Dominican Republic and Venezuela make up the vast majority of MLB's foreign players. From 2005 to 2010, foreign players constituted an average of 28 percent of major league rosters (see Table 12.1). Of this foreign contingent, Dominicans and Venezuelans predominate. Nationals from these countries represented 58 percent of all foreign players in the major leagues in 2009 and 62 percent in 2010.[2]

The proportion of foreign players in MLB's minor league system is even more striking (see Table 12.2). On average for the years 2005–2010, foreign players made up 47 percent of minor league rosters. Major League Baseball does not break down the number of nationals by countries for the minor leagues, but the Dominican Republic and Venezuela probably account for about 80 percent of the foreigners playing for MLB minor league teams.

The number of Latin American players in the major and minor leagues has been the cause of celebration and consternation. This contribution has raised the profile of Latin American players and reflects a sense that they are leaving behind discrimination and racism experienced in earlier decades. The importance of Latin American players to MLB also feeds the passion of Dominican and Venezuelan societies for baseball. In addition, Latin

Table 12.2 *Foreign players in the minor leagues of MLB*

Year	Total players	Foreign players	Percentage of foreign players
2010	7026	3370	48%
2009	6973	3335	48%
2008	7021	3356	48%
2007	6701	3098	46%
2006	6568	2964	45%
2005	N/A	N/A	45%
Average, 2005–2010			47%

Source: Major League Baseball

American prominence has inflated the sense of opportunity many Dominican and Venezuelan youngsters and their families believe MLB offers as a potential escape from poverty.

Others have looked at the Latin American presence with less enthusiasm. Gary Sheffield and Torii Hunter, both African American major leaguers, raised controversy by trying to explain why the presence of Latin American players had increased at the same time the number of African Americans in the major and minor leagues had been decreasing.[3] Their comments were less an attack on Latin American players than a criticism of MLB's efforts to reach out to African American youth, but the controversy highlighted the demographic shifts in major and minor league rosters that have taken place.[4]

Latin American participation in the major and minor leagues did not, of course, reach its current high level overnight. Three factors contributed to the emergence of the Dominican Republic and Venezuela as the dominant suppliers of foreign talent to the American major leagues. First, through military, political, economic, and cultural interactions with the United States, countries in Latin America were exposed to baseball, which, for various reasons, took root in societies in this region. Countries (including Cuba, the Dominican Republic, Mexico, Panama, and Venezuela) and territories (such as Puerto Rico) developed cultural attachments to baseball and began producing more talent earlier than other countries (such as Japan) that were exposed to baseball through relations with the United States.

The passion for baseball in many Latin American countries is reflected not only in their funneling of talent to MLB but also in the development of their own domestic professional leagues. The Dominican Republic, Mexico, Puerto Rico, and Venezuela all have professional leagues that play during the North American winter, with teams composed of domestically based players and players of different nationalities from the MLB major and minor leagues.[5] The teams that win league titles in these four countries participate in the annual Caribbean Series, which began in 1949.[6]

Second, MLB teams started searching for Latin American talent in the early twentieth century, threading the first filaments of a system that would develop to produce significant numbers of Latin American players in the major and minor leagues in the first decade of the twenty-first century. In earlier decades of recruiting Latin American talent, Cuban and Puerto Rican players were the most numerous, with the Puerto Rican Roberto Clemente being the most prominent star of this era. The Cuban revolution at the end of the 1950s cut off Cuba as a source, which gave MLB teams the incentive to look beyond Cuba in the Latin American region for prospects.

The third factor involves changes in the economics of MLB beginning in the 1970s that intensified efforts by its teams to recruit players from the Dominican Republic and Venezuela. With the abolition of the reserve clause, the start of free agency, and the later escalation in signing bonuses for top draft picks, MLB teams have faced increased labor costs. As a result, they have sought cheaper talent in the Dominican Republic, Venezuela, and elsewhere in Latin America. They increased their Latin American recruiting efforts, and, beginning with the first baseball academy developed in the Dominican Republic in 1987 by the Los Angeles Dodgers, started building training facilities and, later in the 1990s, operating a minor league system in the Dominican Republic and Venezuela. The inclusion of Puerto Rico in MLB's annual amateur draft in 1990 helped create more interest in the Dominican Republic and Venezuela, which continued to operate under a free-agency system.

The importance of the free-agency system in MLB's operations in the Dominican Republic, Venezuela, and other Latin American countries cannot be overstated. The efforts of MLB in other countries have not followed the free-agency path. For example, MLB teams have not historically been able to recruit players directly in Mexico. Rather, they have to negotiate with Mexican professional teams that have contractual rights to virtually all the players of interest to MLB teams. Similarly, MLB has arrangements with the Japanese and South Korean leagues that determine how MLB teams get access to Japanese and South Korean players. These formal processes prevent

MLB teams from signing players before they are contractually committed to teams in the leagues of those countries. As a result, Mexican, Japanese, and South Korean nationals who play for MLB teams are generally older and more experienced.

Under the free-agency system, MLB teams can recruit, sign, and train young prospects in the Dominican Republic, Venezuela, and other Latin American countries (for example, Panama, Colombia) who have not yet played professional baseball. Free agency gives MLB teams access to individuals who are younger, less educated, and less experienced than players subject to the MLB amateur draft (who must have finished high school) or those obtained from the Mexican, Japanese, or South Korean systems. These younger, less educated, and less experienced players often live in poverty.

Put another way, the targets of MLB recruiting in the Dominican Republic and Venezuela are children – defined by international human rights law as persons under 18 years of age – from impoverished backgrounds, who are less educated, less experienced, and more vulnerable than their counterparts in North America and East Asia. Many commentators have noted that MLB teams have an incentive to recruit many young prospects in order to find a small number with sufficient talent to make the minor or major leagues in the United States. The dynamics of the Latin American free-agency system thus propel MLB teams to go after children, whereas the approaches taken in the United States, Canada, Puerto Rico, Mexico, and Asia generally result in MLB teams signing a smaller number of adults with more education, experience, and economic means. Controversies involving age falsification by older Latin American players and their *buscones* (discussed below) confirm that, to MLB teams, younger Latin American players have more potential than older ones.

Any system through which business enterprises recruit and train children living in impoverished environments as sources of labor ought to be subject to heightened scrutiny, rules, and monitoring. Major League Baseball is a business that has globalized its markets for its products (for example, broadcast rights for games, licensed merchandise) and its pool of labor sources. Moral principles and national and international legal norms stress the vulnerability of children and the need for measures to protect them from harm, exploitation, and discrimination. Fulfilling these mandates requires governance strategies that protect children and promote their best interests. The next section of this chapter analyzes the evolution of MLB's efforts to develop and implement rules to ensure the health and welfare of children and the integrity of the globalization of baseball.

Governing the globalization of baseball in Latin America

When scrutiny of MLB's operations in Latin America began to increase in the late 1990s,[7] player recruitment and training went essentially unregulated by MLB. Observers have frequently described this environment as the "wild west" of professional baseball, in comparison to the highly regulated context found in the United States and Canada. In the late 1990s, MLB had only one formal rule it applied to teams operating in Latin America – the 17-year-old rule, which we will explain presently – and it had not established an office or other permanent presence in either the Dominican Republic or Venezuela despite the importance of these countries as suppliers of players. This lack of governance, rules, and institutions led to many problems for MLB that it has since been forced to address.

The 17-year-old rule sets an age limit for signing Latin American players. Major League Baseball adopted this rule in the mid 1980s to stop abuses stemming from teams signing 14-, 15-, and 16-year-old prospects in Latin American countries. Unfortunately, MLB teams have frequently violated the rule. In 2000, well over a decade after the 17-year-old rule's adoption, the Associated Press reported that "hundreds of underage boys are believed to have been signed clandestinely in Latin America every year by [MLB] scouts."[8] Such revelations raised questions about the teams' respect for MLB rules and the willingness of the Commissioner's Office to enforce the rule effectively.

Team employees might also be involved in practices that violate the purpose of the 17-year-old rule when they enter into agreements with *buscones* – individuals who train and then sell young players to MLB teams in return for a significant percentage of the player's signing bonus – for the services of players too young to sign officially. Here is a description of such a transaction:

> When Gayo [the Pittsburgh Pirates' scout] quietly asked how much cash it would take to sign the shortstop, Olivo [the *buscon*] replied $200,000. Gayo quickly countered with an offer of $80,000. Grinning, Olivo offered his hand ... The deal between Gayo and the *buscon* is not binding, as no player may officially be signed [under the 17-year-old rule] until July 2. But Gayo is confident it will stick, as his and Olivo's reputations are on the line ...[9]

Crucially, the 17-year-old rule did not prohibit MLB teams from inviting children not old enough to be signed to train in their academies until they were eligible to sign a contract. Teams routinely engaged in this practice, often enticing children to leave school to come to their academies. In response to criticism of the practice, the Commissioner's Office in 2001 prohibited teams from allowing unsigned prospects to stay in academies longer than thirty consecutive days. However, MLB teams continued to utilize their academies to recruit and train players who are too young to sign in ways that reveal this rule's weaknesses as a means of stopping teams from bringing younger children into the academies. A story on the Pittsburgh Pirates from 2008 described how some teams apply the rule: "MLB rules do permit the Pirates to 'hide' the player, even if he is unsigned, by housing him at their academy. The player can live and train there for a month, then spend 15 days at home, then go back to the facility for another month."[10] The rule actually mandates thirty days between visits to the same academy, so, if accurate, the news story reveals violations by MLB teams engaging in such practices with young, unsigned players.

Major League Baseball's attempts at regulation have not quelled concerns about a system that continues to target Latin American children as a source of labor. As part of its most recent thinking about reforms (see below), MLB officials indicated in 2010 that they are willing to consider increasing the age of eligibility of Latin American prospects to 18, which would be in line with the treatment of players subject to the amateur draft.[11]

Although the Dominican Republic and Venezuela supply much foreign baseball talent, and MLB teams have active and extensive operations in these countries, the MLB Commissioner's Office did not establish a permanent presence in either country until it opened its Dominican office in 2000. The office opened to address the problems being exposed about MLB operations in Latin America in the late 1990s, and its initial brief reflected the challenges MLB faced at that time:

- Monitor signings by teams in the Dominican Republic and other Latin American countries;
- Identify and investigate illegal signings;
- Insure compliance with the 17-year-old rule;
- Interact with and instruct scouts in the Dominican Republic and other Latin American countries to ensure that they understood the signing rules;
- Inspect academies in the Dominican Republic and Venezuela to ensure compliance with MLB standards; and
- Make recommendations on required improvements in the academies in the Dominican Republic and Venezuela.

Two initial projects the office undertook reveal how unregulated MLB activities in Latin America were when it opened. The first produced an official Spanish-language translation of the contract all minor league players must sign – the Uniform Minor League Players Contract (UMLPC). Even though MLB teams started recruiting in Latin America early in the twentieth century, it was not until 2001 that the Commissioner's Office translated the UMLPC into Spanish and required MLB teams to provide Spanish-speaking minor league players with the translated contract, and this action was undertaken only in response to criticism of the failure to give players contracts they could read.

The second project was to develop standards for MLB team academies in the Dominican Republic and Venezuela. When the Dominican office opened, MLB had rules regulating minor league facilities in the United States and Canada, but none for the Dominican Republic and Venezuela – despite the operation of facilities in these countries since the late 1980s. At the time the Dominican office was established, the quality of the housing, playing facilities, and professional staff (such as qualified trainers) was very uneven, with some teams providing good conditions and others forcing players to occupy sub-standard facilities without adequate professional oversight.

The living and playing conditions some Latin American children and young men had to endure were shocking. Our book, *Stealing Lives* (2002), details the mistreatment of one Venezuelan teenager and his teammates at the Dominican academy of the Chicago Cubs in the late 1990s.[12] Cubs officials angrily denied the teenager's story, but subsequent reporting by the *Chicago Tribune* confirmed the tale and added more evidence of mistreatment by the Cubs, including the revelation that inspections by the Dominican office concluded that Cubs facilities in the Dominican Republic and Venezuela continue to have serious problems after the time period covered in our book.[13]

Major League Baseball's Dominican office first issued standards for the Latin American minor league facilities in 2002, and one of its responsibilities has been to inspect academies and enforce compliance with these standards. The Commissioner's Office believes the standards have fixed the problem of poor living conditions, sub-standard playing facilities, and inadequately trained professional staff. However, news reports have suggested that some MLB teams continue to have problems with their Latin American facilities well after the standards were put in place and supposedly enforced by MLB. For example, before moving to an improved complex in 2004, the Minnesota Twins admitted that "we went from bad to worse to bad again" in terms of the quality of their Dominican academy.[14] In 2007 – five years after the standards were issued – the owner of the Pittsburgh Pirates ordered improvements to the Pirates' Dominican academy because he was "shocked" by an "aging, crumbling training facility" that "was so dilapidated, players were unable to improve their skills."[15]

Questions about implementation of academy standards have not, however, been the biggest problem for MLB's Dominican office in recent years.

Instead, the office has had to confront more problems associated with MLB's operations in Latin America – such as abuse of performance-enhancing drugs, age and identity falsification, and corruption by team employees – without an adequate staff of appropriately trained, experienced, and compensated professionals. In March, 2010, MLB fired the head of the Dominican office, whose tenure generated complaints of inadequate leadership, questionable judgment, nepotism, and corruption.[16] This firing marked the beginning of new reforms MLB plans to pursue in Latin America.

In 2003, the *Washington Post* exposed the serious problem of players in the Dominican Republic using chemical substances – including steroids meant for livestock – to enhance their prospects of signing with an MLB team.[17] The revelations about the use of performance-enhancing drugs (PEDs) by Dominican players included evidence that *buscones* were involved in plying prospects with PEDs to enhance signing bonuses. The pervasiveness of the problem made it impossible for MLB not to have known about it before the *Post* story appeared. Yet, MLB took no action before the *Post* exposed the crisis, despite having instituted a drug testing, prevention, and treatment program in 2001 for the minor league system in the United States and Canada. Initially MLB refused to adopt an equivalent program for its Latin American minor league system because officials at the Commissioner's Office said such a program would be too expensive and inconvenient.

This attitude angered many people, including New York Governor George Pataki, who, on July 15, 2003 – the date of the MLB All-Star Game – held a press conference to criticize MLB's double standards and ask it to develop a drug testing, prevention, and treatment program for MLB's Latin American minor league system.[18] Under pressure, MLB implemented a program for the Dominican Republic and Venezuela in 2004. However, the program and its implementation left many issues inadequately addressed, especially the lack of sufficient MLB staff devoted to the program and the failure to engage in effective educational efforts for Latin American players.[19]

Two other crises erupted for MLB's Latin American operations during the first decade of the twenty-first century: age and identity falsification by players and corrupt practices by MLB team employees. Much to their embarrassment and economic detriment, a number of MLB teams discovered that players signed for significant bonuses later turned out to be older than they had indicated or to have falsified their identities. After earlier declaring such irregularities to be infrequent, MLB eventually acknowledged that age and identity falsification had become a pervasive problem in the Dominican Republic. Age and identity falsification gained more attention under the post-9/11 heightened US scrutiny of visa applications and the escalating bonuses teams were paying top Latin American prospects. As with the abuse of PEDs, *buscones* were implicated in age and identity falsification, doubtless tempted by increased signing bonuses for Latin American players. The age and identify falsification problem led some to suggest genetic testing for Latin American players, a proposal that met with interest from teams but opposition from those worried about the privacy and other implications of DNA collection and testing by MLB.

Another crisis involving *buscones* in MLB's Latin American minor league system arose from revelations that employees of MLB teams were engaging in corrupt practices, such as skimming money off signing bonuses and participating in kickbacks with *buscones*. Chicago White Sox and Washington Nationals team officials were fired for their alleged involvement, and MLB began investigating employees of other teams for similar activities. It was widely understood that many team employees feared loss of access to prospects if they did not engage in skimming and kickback schemes with *buscones*. The Commissioner's Office eventually acknowledged that corruption involving MLB team employees had become prevalent in the Dominican Republic.

Despite the harm being caused by *buscones*, MLB had long maintained that it could not regulate their activities, and that only the Dominican government could do this. However, MLB did, in fact, start regulating team interactions with *buscones* by prohibiting teams from paying signing bonuses directly to them. Officials could have taken other actions, such as prohibiting teams from dealing with *buscones* with records of age and identity falsification, pushing PEDs to players, and financial corruption. They could have required *buscones* to register with the Dominican office before being permitted to engage in transactions with MLB teams. However, to move in these directions would require personnel and financial commitments to the Dominican office and Latin American minor league system, and MLB was not willing to make these commitments, even in light of the damage done to the health and welfare of children and professional baseball. The *buscones* feed off the incentives that MLB creates, so MLB has responsibilities for curbing the abuses *buscones* perpetrate against children – and against MLB's interests.

The Alderson ultimatum: strategic and systemic reform at last?

In light of the PED, age and identity falsification, and corruption problems, in May, 2009, MLB Commissioner Bud Selig appointed Sandy Alderson, a former executive for MLB teams and the Commissioner's Office, to chair a committee tasked with analyzing MLB's activities in the Dominican Republic. This committee issued its short-term recommendations for reforming MLB's

Dominican operations in September 2009. Although MLB has not publicly released this committee's report, news stories of Alderson's efforts to introduce the reforms in 2010 indicate that the committee has proposed significant changes. In addition, the committee is still thinking through recommendations for long-term reforms, including potentially expanding the draft to include the Dominican Republic, Venezuela, and other Latin American countries, and, as mentioned above, increasing the eligibility age to 18. In our decade-long involvement with these issues, these steps represent the first time we have seen the Commissioner's Office thinking strategically about systemic reforms to MLB's Latin American operations, as opposed to responding in ad hoc, reactive, and inadequate ways to adverse publicity about abuses and problems with MLB activities.

Judging from news reports covering Alderson's efforts to introduce the reforms in the Dominican Republic,[20] it appears that MLB wants to strengthen its anti-PED program significantly, especially through (1) mandatory testing prospects, (2) better education of players under contract and prospects who have not yet signed contracts, and (3) identifying individuals (for example, *buscones*) who provide PEDs to players. Initial indications suggest the new approach is having impact because thirteen of the top forty Dominican prospects in 2010 failed PED tests – failures which contributed to a reduction in "the number of elite Dominican teenager players being signed to contracts ... and the size of their signing bonuses."[21] In terms of age and identity falsification, MLB seems to want to improve record keeping of player ages and identities, perhaps by registering prospects on their first interactions with MLB teams through, for example, fingerprinting, document verification, and investigations coordinated centrally by MLB's Dominican office. After halting genetic testing on prospects in response to legal and ethical criticism, MLB has restarted using DNA tests under new guidelines that permit, rather than demand, prospects to submit DNA test information to confirm their identities.[22] The plan also apparently includes recommendations for measures to address corruption by team employees, including prohibiting employees found to have engaged in corruption from working within MLB. The reforms also target the *buscones* problem by recommending a registration system and educational outreach for *buscones*.

Stepping back from the proposed reforms, it is clear that their actual implementation will require unprecedented changes in how MLB oversees its activities in Latin America, including a significant increase in the responsibilities, personnel capabilities, technological assets, organizational structure, and financial resources of the MLB office in the Dominican Republic.[23] Under the reforms, the investment MLB makes in governance in that country would start to reflect the Dominican Republic's importance to

MLB as a source of labor. Strengthened governance would also move MLB away from its history of inadequate and reactive responses to problems its activities in Latin America generate.

During his initial talks in the Dominican Republic, Alderson also raised the possibility of expanding the draft to cover the Dominican Republic and beyond – a possibility that would become more likely if the proposed short-term reforms do not address the problems at issue. The prospect of an international draft as an answer to the problems with MLB's Latin American operations had been raised before (for example, during negotiations between MLB and the Major League Baseball Players Association that produced the 2003–2006 Basic Agreement), but the idea has not been seriously pursued. The possible expansion of the draft triggered opposition during Alderson's initial discussions in the Dominican Republic,[24] but Alderson did not take the draft option off the table in the face of criticism. In fact, Alderson criticized *buscones* for staging protests with their prospects against the reforms: "It was another example of kids being manipulated and victimized."[25] In short, Alderson has issued an ultimatum – the status quo cannot continue. As Alderson bluntly stated while he was in the Dominican Republic, "The system as it currently exists can't continue … If we don't clean up the abuses, I think there's a very strong likelihood there will be a draft."[26]

Conclusion

Whether MLB will effectively implement the short-term reforms the Alderson committee has proposed to date remains to be seen. In addition, any long-term reforms that the committee might recommend are not known. In light of the significance of the committee's recommendations, the Commissioner's Office should be more transparent about the committee's work, especially the details about the reforms the committee has recommended, by releasing the committee's deliberations, findings, and reports. Such transparency needs to extend to MLB's efforts to implement the reforms. The October, 2010 hiring of Alderson as the new General Manager of the New York Mets also raises questions about the future of the reforms Alderson has championed and whether the MLB Commissioner will appoint someone with the same credibility and determination as Alderson on these issues. Without effective implementation and sustained oversight of the new governance regime, the reforms will turn into wasted opportunities to transform a system that has not adequately protected and promoted the best interests of Latin American children into one that reflects the responsibilities MLB must shoulder as the center of gravity for the globalization of baseball.

NOTES

1. For purposes of this chapter, Latin America includes countries in the Caribbean, Central America, and South America.
2. The 2010 New York Mets' twenty-five-player roster, for example, contains fifteen foreign players: four Venezuelans; three Dominicans; three Puerto Ricans; two Japanese; and one player each from Canada, Mexico, and Panama.
3. "Sheffield Says Latin Players Easier to Control than Blacks," ESPN.com, June 3, 2007, http://sports.espn.go.com/mlb/news/story?id=2891875; and "Hunter Talks about Race," *ibid.*, March 11, 2010, http://sports.espn.go.com/los-angeles/ mlb/news/story?id=4983236. The percentage of African Americans in the major leagues declined from the mid 1980s to 8.2 percent in 2007. The percentage increased to 10.2 percent in 2009, the highest since 1995.
4. Major League Baseball has operated a program called Reviving Baseball in Inner Cities (RBI) since 1989 in an effort to introduce urban youth to baseball and provide opportunities to learn and play the game.
5. Many famous MLB players have participated in the Winter League over the years, including Barry Bonds, Greg Maddux, Willie Mays, Cal Ripken, and Pete Rose. The participation of MLB players in the Latin Winter League is governed by the Winter League Agreement, negotiated most recently in 2010 between MLB and the Latin professional baseball authorities.
6. Cuba participated in the Caribbean Series from 1949 to 1960, winning seven times; but its involvement stopped after the Cuban Revolution. Panama participated from 1949 to 1960 (winning in 1950), but did not when the Series was revived in 1970, after not being held from 1961 to 1969.
7. See Arturo J. Marcano and David P. Fidler, "The Globalization of Baseball: Major League Baseball and the Mistreatment of Latin American Baseball Talent," *Indiana Journal of Global Legal Studies* 6 (1999), 511–577; Samuel O. Regalado, "'Latin Players on the Cheap': Professional Baseball Recruitment in Latin America and the Neocolonialist Tradition," *Indiana Journal of Global Legal Studies* 8 (2000), 8–20; and Angel Vargas, "The Globalization of Baseball: A Latin American Perspective," *Indiana Journal of Global Legal Studies* 8 (2000), 21–36.
8. Associated Press, "False Pitches Crush Latin American Youngsters' Baseball Dreams," *The Star-Ledger Newark*, June 4, 2000.
9. Rob Biertempfel, "Gayo Leads Bucs in Dominican Republic," *Pittsburgh Tribune-Review*, May 10, 2009, www.pittsburghlive.com/x/blairsvilledispatch/ s_624453.html.
10. *Ibid.*
11. Melissa Segura, "Alderson Outlines Plans for Improving Dominican Operations," March 18, 2010, http://sportsillustrated.cnn.com/2010/writers/melissa_ segura/03/18/alderson.dominican/index.html.
12. Arturo J. Marcano and David P. Fidler, *Stealing Lives: The Globalization of Baseball and the Tragic Story of Alexis Quiroz* (Bloomington: Indiana University Press, 2002).
13. Gary Marx, "Clean Up Begins of a Sorry Mess," *Chicago Tribune*, June 29, 2003; and "Cubs Odyssey Was a Bad Trip, He Claims," *Chicago Tribune*, June 29, 2003.

14. Associated Press, "Twins are Worldly: Minnesota a Big Player in International Scouting," May 14, 2010, www.grandforksherald.com.

15. Biertempfel, "Gayo Leads Bucs in Dominican Republic."

16. Melissa Segura, "MLB Fires Top Latin America Executive Ronaldo Peralta," March 10, 2010, http://sportsillustrated.cnn.com/2010/baseball/mlb/03/10/mlb.exec.ousted/index.html.

17. Steve Fainaru, "Injecting Hope – and Risk: Dominican Prospects Turn to Supplements Designed for Animals," *Washington Post*, June 23, 2003, A01.

18. George E. Pataki, *Governor Supports Hispanics across America: Effort to Protect Hispanic Youth*, press release, July 15, 2003.

19. Arturo J. Marcano and David P. Fidler, "Fighting Baseball Doping in Latin America: A Critical Analysis of Major League Baseball's Drug Prevention and Treatment Program in the Dominican Republic and Venezuela," *University of Miami International and Comparative Law Review* 15 (2007), 107–201.

20. See, for example, Melissa Segura, "Alderson Outlines Plans for Improving Dominican Operations," March 18, 2010, http://sportsillustrated.cnn.com/2010/writers/melissa_segura/03/18/alderson.dominican/index.html; Jesse Sanchez, "Alderson Spearheads DR Effort," May 7, 2010, http://mlb.mlb.com/news/article.jsp?ymd=20100507&content_id=9864108&vkey=news_mlb&fext=.jsp&c_id=mlb; Michael S. Schmidt, "Dominican Prospects to Face Stricter Rules," *New York Times*, May 7, 2010. Available online at www.nytimes.com/2010/05/08/sports/baseball/08drugs.html; Sean Gregory, "Baseball Dreams: Striking Out in the Dominican Republic," *Time*, July 26, 2010, www.time.com/magazine/article/0,9171,2004099,00.html; and Dan Rather, "Dan Rather Reports: Field of Broken Dreams," Episode 533, October 19, 2010, www.hd.net/danrather_epguide.html.

21. Michael S. Schmidt, "Less Demand for Dominicans as M. L. B. Scrutiny Increases," *New York Times*, October 10, 2010. Available online at www.nytimes.com/2010/10/10/sports/baseball/10dominican.html.

22. Michael S. Schmidt, "DNA Testing of Prospects Continues Under New Rules," *New York Times*, October 9, 2010. Available online at www.nytimes.com/2010/10/10/sports/baseball/10testing.html.

23. Michael S. Schmidt, "Baseball Emissary to Review Troubled Dominican Pipeline," *New York Times*, March 10, 2010. Available online at www.nytimes.com/2010/03/11/sports/baseball/11dominican.html?emc=eta1.

24. Nick Collias, "Dominican Prospects Protest Reform," April 19, 2010, www.mlbtraderumors.com/2010/04/dominican-prospects-protest-reform.html.

25. Jesse Sanchez, "Venezuela Next Target for Clean-Up: MLB Pushing for Guidelines to Be Followed in Latin America," May 13, 2010, http://mlb.mlb.com/news/article.jsp?ymd=20100513&content_id=10017300.

26. Jeff Passan, "Alderson Addresses Dominican Corruption," April 22, 2010, http://sports.yahoo.com/mlb/news?slug=jp-dominican042210.

13

DAVID LUBAN AND DANIEL LUBAN

Cheating in baseball

Near the end of his life, Rogers Hornsby published an article in a men's magazine titled "You've Got to Cheat to Win in Baseball." Hornsby wrote, "I've been in pro baseball since 1914 and I've cheated, or watched someone on my team cheat, in practically every game. You've got to cheat."[1] Hornsby's confession was not a complete surprise. Revered as one of baseball's supreme hitters, he was also reputedly meaner than Ty Cobb, and absolutely devoted to winning at all costs. But Hornsby was not the only confessed cheater among the all-time greats, some with more likable reputations. Hank Greenberg described a season when he was managed by an expert sign-stealer. "I loved that. I was the greatest hitter in the world when I knew what kind of pitch was coming up."[2]

It is a truth universally acknowledged that in matters of supreme importance people cheat.[3] Baseball matters; you might say the rest follows. Today, when we talk about cheating in baseball, we automatically think of steroids, but it's important to understand that cheating is bigger than steroids, and in fact, as Thomas Boswell writes, cheating is baseball's oldest profession.[4] Even performance-enhancing drugs (PEDs) have a venerable history. Pud Galvin, one of the nineteenth century's greatest pitchers, downed an elixir of monkey testosterone before an 1889 game against Boston. Galvin won and drew a favorable comment from the *Washington Post*: "If there still be doubting Thomases who concede no virtue of the elixir, they are respectfully referred to Galvin's record in yesterday's Boston–Pittsburgh game. It is the best proof yet furnished of the value of the discovery."[5]

Before television and multiple umpires, cheating could be open and blatant. The great dead-ball slugger Sam Crawford reminisced that when he arrived in the big leagues at the turn of the twentieth century, only one umpire worked each game, and one umpire could never see everything. When the ump ran out to follow a hit to the outfield, the runner on second would sometimes skip third base on his way home. Crawford recalls Tim Hurst, a tough ump who once called Jake Beckley out at home while Hurst was watching a play at second. "What do you mean, I'm out?" Beckley roared, "They didn't even make a play on me." "'You big S.O.B.,' Tim said, 'you got here *too* quick!'"[6]

Crawford doesn't bother to mention the obvious: everyone in the ball-park except the umpire could see Beckley miss third base by fifteen feet. The same with John McGraw's tactic of holding runners on their base by grab-bing their belt.[7] It was totally out in the open, and McGraw did it only when the umpire was looking elsewhere. The blatancy of these tactics points to an important truth: fans understand cheating, and even condone cheating. That puts cheating – or at least the "right kind" of cheating – in an unusual moral category: wrongdoing that baseball lovers would rather have in the game than not.

The fact is that many of the most beloved and colorful stories in the annals of baseball involve cheating. Fans now know about sign-stealing by a man with a telescope in the New York Giants' center-field clubhouse, who relayed them to the dugout with an electric buzzer during the 1951 pen-nant race.[8] And fans laugh about Jason Grimsley's legendary 1994 burg-lary of a locked room in Comiskey Field – through the ceiling – to steal his teammate's corked bat before the umps who had confiscated it returned to inspect it. We love Don Sutton's reply when he was accused of using a for-eign substance on the baseball. "Not true at all," Sutton protested. "Vaseline is manufactured right here in the United States."[9]

In short, cheating belongs to the fabric of the game. Take the cheating out of baseball history and you take much of the pleasure out of baseball history. But cheating is also, well, *a form of cheating*. Thus we arrive at that favorite plaything of philosophers: a paradox. The label "cheating" is mor-ally loaded: by definition, cheating is wrong. By definition, wrong is what you cannot do. But far from becoming incensed by cheating in baseball, fans tolerate it and – truth be told – fans enjoy it. What's going on?

One explanation (which we don't completely buy) turns on the diffe-rence between amateur and professional ball. Pitcher and manager George Bamberger put it this way:

> We do not play baseball. We play professional baseball. Amateurs play games. We are paid to win games. There are rules, and there are consequences if you break them. If you are a pro, then you often don't decide whether to cheat based on if it's "right or wrong." You base it on whether or not you can get away with it, and what the penalty might be. A guy who cheats in a friendly game of cards is a cheater. A pro who throws a spitball to support his family is a competitor.[10]

We're skeptical that this can be the whole story. It may be the way that pros view cheating, but it doesn't explain why the fans go along. Pros may not decide whether to cheat based on right or wrong, but fans will argue rights and wrongs for years. Furthermore, we don't agree that right and wrong have no meaning in baseball, or only whatever meaning players choose to assign.

To begin with, no one seriously argues that moral rules stop at the diamond's edge – there are moral fundamentals just as basic on the ballfield as off, and not merely where cheating is concerned. A pitched ball can kill a man, and a pitcher who seeks an intimidation edge by headhunting has crossed a moral line. That would be true even if the official rules of the game allowed pitchers to intentionally drill the batter – which, by the way, they do not. The game's unwritten rules have always allowed plunking the batter below the neckline, or brushing him back with a high inside fastball – in fact, that's how teams enforce the code. But players and fans have always agreed that outright headhunting is beyond the pale, just as bribing umpires would be.

A better explanation than Bamberger's for the odd seductiveness of cheating in the eyes of fans has to do with our national love–hate relationship with formal rules and authority. At one level, Americans understand the importance of laws and extol the rule of law. At another level, we hate red tape and despise robotic rule-following. It's a cultural contradiction engraved in our national psyche. We know that we need speed limits and state troopers, but we speed all the time and we don't like troopers who ticket us. A moment's reflection on that flash of sullen anger everyone feels when they get pulled over for speeding explains a lot about why baseball fans boo the umpires. Of course, it makes sense that no one likes a blown call that hurts their team, but our love–hate relationship with the umps isn't reducible to their effect on our team's prospects; no ump who makes a game-deciding call ever earns respect from the winning team's fans equal to the anger from the losers.

At heart, few of us are legal formalists who put rules on a pedestal – which is not to deny that coaches all the way down to the T-ball level will lawyer the rules to death, furiously and volubly, to gain an advantage. Using the rule book to browbeat a Saturday-morning umpire in the Toddler League is just another way to disrespect the rule book. Rules in a book don't matter in and of themselves, even when we agree that they serve a laudable purpose. We tolerate rule-breaking as long as it's equal-opportunity and doesn't violate some deeper principle, and we admire the audacity of players who care more about the game than the rule book. Their attitude proves that they are playing with the passion the game deserves. If players never cheated, it would show that baseball doesn't deserve passion; in a curious way, cheating shows respect for the game. It's a certificate that fans are not wrong for caring about baseball so much. That is the deep meaning behind the old adage "if you ain't cheating you ain't trying." It's not to say that players who don't cheat don't care, which is surely untrue – only that if no players ever cheated, it would undermine our faith in the cosmic importance of the game.

At the same time, if cheating ruins the fairness of the contest it ruins the game. That's the fine line between "good cheating" and "bad cheating" (in the words of Derek Zumsteg).[11] A complex casuistry goes into drawing that line. Consider former Mets great Keith Hernandez's discussion of batters who peek behind them to see where the catcher is setting up – a trick that he admits that he used himself.[12] Under the unwritten players' code, peeking is a punishable offense: "If you get caught peeking you deserve to be drilled. It's as simple as that."[13] But Hernandez vigorously denies that peeking is cheating, because players do it out in the open. Hernandez distinguishes between tricks that give the other side a fair chance of catching you, and tricks that don't. Peeking is okay, and so is scuffing the ball; but corking your bat (which is undetectable to the eye) is not.

Hernandez's explanation is ingenious, but we don't think he has gotten to the heart of the difference between good and bad cheating. Here's our proposal. Some unwritten rules belong to the *natural law of baseball*: a code designed to maintain the balance between batter and pitcher, the basic balance that sets the entire texture of the game. If the batter knows in advance where the pitch is going, he can set up for it, and that throws the balance out of whack. So the no-peeking rule isn't just a rule of respect, it's a rule designed to maintain the balance of the game. "Bad" cheating is rule-breaking that threatens the balance, and in that way threatens to make baseball a worse game.

"Natural law" sounds awfully scholastic – if not downright spooky – for the spit and sweat of the ballfield. But we are not talking about the Ten Commandments or philosophical deductions. As we define it, the natural law of baseball consists of whatever rules (written or unwritten) make the game the best it can be, given the dimensions of the ballfield, the physics of the thrown or batted ball, and the evolving skills and limits of the players. It derives more from aesthetic considerations, and the intuitive sense that the fan has of what makes good baseball, than from abstract a-priori rules. A game in which the batter–pitcher balance shifted so much that baseball games had football scores could still be competitive – as we see in beer league softball – but it wouldn't be baseball. Every coach in third-grade ball understands that eventually, no matter how bad the pitcher, the umpire must call some strikes. That's part of the natural law of kids' ball – otherwise batters never swing, fielders lose interest and play with the dandelions in the outfield, and the game is ruined. Here, unlike in professional baseball, the emphasis shifts from what makes the game good for fans to what makes it good for players – but the core principles remain the same: the batter–pitcher contest must stay tense, unpredictable, and absorbing. The pitcher must hold enough of an edge that the burden lies on the offense to prove its mettle, but not so much that batters become a negligible threat.

We'd like to emphasize that the "natural law of baseball" is not the same thing as the players' unwritten code of conduct, about which there has been a spate of recent books.[14] Mostly, this unwritten code has to do with respect, not fairness, and breaking those rules isn't cheating. The code's basic rule is to avoid showing up the other team's players; in Sparky Anderson's words, "I will always respect the other foxhole." (Not that Anderson always viewed ballgames as battles. He also saw respectful conduct as compassion for pros struggling to stay in the big leagues: "Don't do it to the man. He's got a family, too.") [15] Football-like victory dances are unthinkable, but the unwritten code of respect covers more subtle offenses as well. You don't run aggressive plays like base-stealing or the hit-and-run in the late innings of a blowout victory, although players may disagree about how big an advantage counts as a blowout. You don't bunt to break up a no-hitter, and you don't swing on a 3–0 pitch when your team has a big lead. These strictures are in the players' code to protect against dishonor and disrespect, not unfairness.

But not all the unwritten rules are about chivalry. Consider, one last time, the no-peeking rule. Plainly, peeking is a way for batters to get an edge on the pitcher, not a way to show the pitcher up. That makes peeking an issue of fairness, not honor.

What it means to break the rules: the case of steroids and other performance-enhancing drugs

The biggest questions in recent years, of course, have revolved around steroids and other PEDs. Where do they fit into the moral universe of baseball cheating? Do they violate moral rules, rules of fairness, or the natural law of baseball? These drugs raise several distinct issues, some ethical but others not – and some genuine, while others are not. Let's start by looking at the arguments for banning PEDs.

Health

The most basic reason for banning steroids is that they are bad for you. The health effects are nasty enough to clamp down on. But the health argument has nothing to do with cheating, and it may not get at what most bothers fans about PEDs.[a]

To see this, imagine a fantasy world in which someone invents a steroid substitute that isn't bad for you, and markets it under the name Anodyne (or rather Anodyne®). Maybe Anodyne is even good for you, in the mild way that flossing twice a day is good for you – and Anodyne is as potent as steroids at building muscles, relieving inflammations, and speeding recovery from injuries. Now, every player can have monster muscles and greater baseball longevity, while fighting gum disease at the same time. With the invention of Anodyne, the health argument is off the table. It seems overwhelmingly likely that fans would still object to Anodyne, regardless of the health argument. The question is why.

Nature versus nurture

Many fans harbor a deep-seated conviction that baseball should be a test of skills unaided by artifice. When he finally confessed to steroid use, Mark McGwire insisted that he used them only to bounce back from injuries, not to increase his strength. "I did this for health purposes," McGwire said. "There's no way I did this for any type of strength use."[16] The hair-splitting casuistry was worthy of a medieval theologian, since of course McGwire *knew* that the drugs would also increase his strength even if that's not why he took them. But his public-relations instincts were impeccable: recovering from injury isn't an enhancement, because a healthy body is a natural body; muscles from a bottle are an artificial enhancement, and McGwire sensed that we don't like enhancements.

Unfortunately, the nature-versus-nurture argument doesn't hold water. Advanced training techniques, vitamins and other legal supplements, painkillers, physical therapy, and Tommy John surgery (in which a surgeon grafts a tendon into a pitcher's elbow joint to replace a torn ligament) are all artifice. For that matter, so is a lifetime of good health care that gives today's 40-year-old a body that a grizzled, battered old-timer would have envied at the age of 30. (Don't forget that until 1930 the average life expectancy of a white male American was under 60.) Even though some old-school players resisted advanced training techniques – John Kruk's immortal line "I ain't an athlete, lady, I'm a ballplayer" typifies the attitude – the nature–nurture distinction makes no sense in the world of modern sports medicine.

---

[a] The health argument is especially relevant to PED use by prospects, and figures in MLB's evolving Latin American policies. See Chapter 12, "Global baseball: Latin America," 181.

Aesthetics

Muscleman baseball is ugly baseball, because it glorifies the home run. (Remember the famous Nike commercial from the late nineties: "Chicks dig the long ball."[17]) Aesthetically, the homer is the least interesting play in baseball, for an obvious reason: it puts the ball beyond play. The moment the swing is over, the home run becomes baseball without baseball playing. It's like a tennis match with too many aces – or, more to the point, a high school fast-pitch softball game where the dominant pitcher fans eighteen of twenty-one batters. There's a fascination to the display of raw power, but it dumbs down the game and quickly wears thin.

That's not to deny that homers add indispensable spice to the game – *but only when they're rare.* That brief moment where finesse becomes irrelevant in the face of *force majeure* is awesome and humbling, the way the mystery of death is awesome and humbling. And the sudden switch in focus from team to individual, where one player neutralizes nine with a swing of the bat, appeals to our love of heroes, our rugged individualism. It's John Wayne versus a gang. It's a close-up in the midst of wide-angle shots. All this is good – provided that homers remain few and far between. By making homers commonplace, steroids debase the game. As we already discussed, isn't the aesthetic argument as good as any when baseball is concerned? Aesthetics plays a large role in the natural law of baseball.

On examination, though, this aesthetic argument has holes. For one thing, it leads to the conclusion that Babe Ruth debased the game rather than elevated it. (Ty Cobb, among others, argued this, but it's unlikely that many contemporary fans would agree.) For another, most steroid users aren't star power hitters, but journeymen clinging to the big leagues by their fingernails. Even at the peak of steroid use, the major leagues averaged fewer than 2.5 homers per game – higher than in other eras, but hardly enough to transform the nature of the game.[18] In any case, the argument that performance enhancers are cheating would be the same if players started using a drug that increases speed rather than power, thereby leading to a more "aesthetic" game with steals, triples, and running grabs instead of home runs and cautious pitching. The debate about steroids is *not* first and foremost about the aesthetics of the game.

Unfair pressure on nonusers

The real trouble is that once some players start muscling up and recovering more quickly, it pressures other players to join the arms race (and legs race, and chest race). That's where the genuine worry about cheating comes in: users gain an unfair advantage over nonusers, and no player should be under pressure to become a user.

In the end, we favor the ban on PEDs, because when it comes right down to it, they aren't all that anodyne, and the pressure they put on nonusers really is unfair. Sabermetrician Bill James disagrees, and thinks that some day we will all be extending and enhancing our lives with chemicals, and we might as well bow to the inevitable.[19] Along the same lines, a few years ago, a distinguished team of bioethicists made headlines by defending cognitive-enhancing drugs. But they were appropriately cautious about the risks, and one of the authors explained that in his view "Better-working brains produce things of more lasting value than longer home runs."[20] (No comment.)

All these arguments have to do with the future: should we ban steroids and other PEDs at all? But most of the steroids debate has revolved around the past: what should be done with the past steroid users, their records, their Hall of Fame chances, and our overall mental scorecard of their careers?

We are inclined to be very lenient toward the steroid users of the past. In our view, Major League Baseball (MLB) made its bed and has been desperately trying to avoid lying in it. Elementary common sense suggests that everyone in the Commissioner's Office and the baseball press knew in 1998 that Mark McGwire and Sammy Sosa were on steroids, but they made the decision to look the other way because it was good for business and made for a compelling story. Now we see many of the same parties adopting shamelessly self-righteous poses and scapegoating the players for playing by the rules that the higher-ups implicitly endorsed.

The most plausible story about Barry Bonds and his turn to steroids is that he started during or shortly after that 1998 season. He had had another typical and superb Bonds year (.303 average, 1.047 OPS, 37 HR, 122 RBI, 28 steals) that went totally unnoticed – he finished eighth in the National League Most Valuable Player voting that year. According to the reporters who broke the Bay Area Laboratory Co-Operative (BALCO) steroids story, Bonds grew irate at the media adulation given to the obviously enhanced McGwire and Sosa – players not close to his equal as pure ballplayers – and decided he could outdo them.[21] This is a concrete illustration of how baseball's blatant unwillingness to confront its own devils created incentives for others to use PEDs. These incentives were of course even stronger for players who weren't trying to go from superstars to super-duperstars, but who were struggling just to stay in the majors.

Before condemning the steroid users as cheats, we should consider how widespread steroid use was. Bill James estimates the number of steroid users in the heyday of PEDs as somewhere between 40 and 80 percent – a wide range, to be sure, but in line with other estimates. "It seems to me," James continues, "that the argument that it is cheating must ultimately collapse under the weight of carrying this great contradiction – that 80% of the players are cheating against the other 20% by violating some 'rule' to which they never consented, which was never included in the rule books, and for which there was no enforcement procedure."[22]

Taken to its logical conclusion, James's argument would lead us past the idea that "the roiders were cheating, but we can forgive them in some cases" to the idea that the roiders weren't cheating at all. For the reasons we've already given, we don't go that far. (And of course, the argument wouldn't apply going forward, now that there are clearcut rules and scrutiny and enforcement procedures about PEDs.) But there is merit to James's overall point that steroid use in an environment of tolerance is a venial, not a mortal, baseball sin.

Perhaps the real source of the outrage over steroids is that it was a rare case where the fans' understanding of the natural law of baseball diverged from the players'. Some prominent players, to be sure, refused to take PEDs and even spoke out publicly against them. (Frank Thomas comes to mind.) But indications are that even those players who were not thrilled about the prevalence of PEDs in baseball viewed the issue with resignation or grudging acceptance. The same goes for coaches, front office personnel, and – at least for a while – the media. Fans, on the other hand, had little knowledge of the scope of steroid use, despite what many must have suspected. In the late 1990s, when baseball was still struggling to regain popularity in the wake of the 1994 strike, both MLB and the media were happy to keep fans in the dark and milk the publicity of the McGwire–Sosa home run chase. Given this disconnect between the baseball world and the fans, it was hardly surprising that fans felt blindsided when revelations about steroid use began to trickle out.

Another reason for the anger about PEDs, of course, is the central importance that baseball attaches to its numbers, far more than in any other sport. Any real baseball fan need only hear numbers like 56, .406, or 714 to think of DiMaggio, Williams, and Ruth respectively, and home run records have always been particularly sacrosanct.[b]

But baseball would benefit if it removed its records from their pedestal, and stopped correlating numbers with all-time greatness. It may be helpful in this regard to take a look at the leaders in pitching wins (career totals or, more strikingly, single-season).[23] Wins, as a stat, is enormously skewed

---

[b] For a fuller discussion of the role of statistics in discussions of baseball greatness, see "Babe Ruth, sabermetrics, and baseball's politics of greatness" in this volume, 33–44.

toward old-timers: only two of the top ten in career wins – Greg Maddux and Roger Clemens – played in the last forty years, and Warren Spahn is the only other member of the top ten who was even born in the twentieth century. The single-season win totals are even more dramatically skewed: all of the top 100 single-season win totals came in the dead-ball era, particularly the nineteenth century, when 40-win seasons were common. "Old Hoss" Radbourn's 59 wins in 1884 give a sense of the workloads these pitchers were accumulating; or consider our old friend Pud Galvin's 1883 campaign, when he went 46–29, throwing a complete game in 72 out of his 75 starts, for a preposterous 656 innings pitched.

Because the changing standards of pitcher workloads are so obvious, and because credited wins depend on many factors outside a pitcher's control, baseball fans have learned not to take wins too seriously as a measure of all-time pitching prowess. No one suggests that Pud Galvin was better than Greg Maddux because Galvin won ten games more in his career – or that Galvin's 1883 season was twice as good as Pedro Martinez's 1999 season (46 wins to 23). We realize that the dead-ball era was an exceptional time in terms of pitchers' ability to accumulate wins, so we adjust accordingly.

We suspect that part of the reason people are so agitated about the "should-their-records-count" issue – and the steroids issue more generally – is an unwillingness to let go of the importance attached to home run records the way we've already done with wins. Many people want to believe that even if other statistics like wins are context-dependent, home runs offer a "pure" measure of offensive performance that allows us to impartially compare players across historical contexts. (Hence the hullaballoo when Ruth's career and single-season home run records were broken by Hank Aaron and Roger Maris – there's a strange fear that this is tantamount to allowing that Aaron and Maris were better than Ruth.)

A healthier approach would be to recognize that, just as the dead-ball era was an outlier in terms of wins, the steroid era was an outlier in terms of home runs, and leave it at that. It simply does not make sense to say that Barry Bonds's records shouldn't count, just as it would not make sense to say that Cy Young's records (such as his career total of 511 wins, unreachable in today's game) shouldn't count. Rather, we should take these records with a (large) grain of salt – and recognize that, just as Pud Galvin's win totals don't make him a better pitcher than Greg Maddux, similarly Sammy Sosa's home run totals don't make him a better slugger than Mickey Mantle. This is a far better solution than making mere statistics so hallowed and sacrosanct, and thus forcing baseball to enforce protective standards of purity that it cannot possibly hope to meet.

The great political philosopher John Rawls once wrote a letter to a friend explaining why baseball is the perfect game:

First: the rules of the game are in equilibrium: that is, from the start, the diamond was made just the right size, the pitcher's mound just the right distance from home plate, etc., and this makes possible the marvelous plays, such as the double play. The physical layout of the game is perfectly adjusted to the human skills it is meant to display and to call into graceful exercise. Whereas, basketball, e.g., is constantly (or was then) adjusting its rules to get them in balance.[24]

Rawls's history is inaccurate. In fact, baseball has adjusted its rules many times – often in response to new forms of unfairness that creative scoundrels like John McGraw devised.[c] And as we've seen, both players and umpires supplement the rule book with an unwritten code that changes as the game evolves. But Rawls's basic idea is right. The rules that matter are the rules that keep baseball as near to perfect as can be. Breaking those rules is cheating; breaking the lesser rules is simply good dirty fun.

NOTES

1. Jason Turbow (with Michael Duca), *The Baseball Codes: Beanballs, Sign Stealing, and Bench-Clearing Brawls: The Unwritten Rules of America's Pastime* (New York: Pantheon, 2010), 186–187.
2. Lawrence Ritter, *The Glory of Their Times: The Story of the Early Days of Baseball Told by the Men Who Played It*, enlarged edn. (New York: Quill, 1984), p. 322.
3. Our apologies to Jane Austen.
4. Thomas Boswell, *How Life Imitates the World Series: An Inquiry into the Game* (New York: Doubleday, 1982), 198.
5. Robert Smith, "A Different Kind of Performance Enhancer," NPR, March 31, 2006, www.npr.org/templates/story/story.php?storyId=5314753.
6. Ritter, *The Glory of Their Times*, 322.
7. Derek Zumsteg, *The Cheater's Guide to Baseball* (Boston, MA: Houghton Mifflin, 2007), 8–9.
8. Joshua Harris Prager, "Inside Baseball: Giants' 1951 Comeback, the Sport's Greatest, Wasn't All It Seemed," *Wall Street Journal*, January 31, 2001, A1.
9. www.baseballlibrary.com/features/matchuppitcher.php?with=Sutton_vs_Wynn.
10. Boswell, *How Life Imitates the World Series*, 199.
11. Zumsteg, *The Cheater's Guide*, xiv.
12. Just to be clear: there is no formal rule against peeking. It belongs to the players' code, not the Rules of Major League Baseball.

[c] For an overview of baseball's evolving rules in this volume, see "The Rules of Baseball" (9–20), with the account of the gradual legalization of overhand pitching and the responses to that change being especially instructive (12–15).

13. Keith Hernandez and Mike Bryan, *Pure Baseball: Pitch by Pitch for the Advanced Fan* (New York: HarperCollins, 1994), p. 127.

14. In addition to Turbow, there is Paul Dickson, *The Unwritten Rules of Baseball* (New York: HarperCollins, 2009); and Ross Bernstein, *The Code: Baseball's Unwritten Rules and Its Ignore-at-Your-Own-Risk Code of Conduct* (Chicago: Triumph Books, 2008).

15. Murray Chass, "When It Comes to Stealing, Yankees Can't Get past First Base," *New York Times*, April 6, 1993. Available online at www.nytimes.com/1993/05/16/sports/notebook-when-it-comes-to-stealing-yankees-can-t-get-past-first-base.html?scp=1&sq=sparky%20anderson%20cripples&st=nyt&pagewanted=2. Anderson was referring specifically to swinging on a 3–0 pitch against a struggling pitcher when your team has a large lead.

16. Dave Sheinin, "Baseball Slugger Mark McGwire Admits to Using Steroids," *Washington Post*, January 12, 2010.

17. www.metacafe.com/watch/72233/nike_chicks_dig_the_long_ball/.

18. Until the early 1990s, the average exceeded two in only one season, and even in the postwar era it has often been below one. See http://en.wikipedia.org/wiki/File:MLB_HR_and_SB_rates.png.

19. Bill James, "Cooperstown and the 'Roids," www.actapublications.com/images/small/PressReleases/Cooperstownandthe'Roids_F2.pdf.

20. Bernadette Tansey, "Experts Urge Wider Use of Brain-Boosting Drugs," *San Francisco Chronicle*, December 8, 2008, quoting Stanford law professor Hank Greely. The bioethicists' paper is Henry Greely, Barbara Shahakian, John Harris, *et al.*, "Towards Responsible use of Cognitive-Enhancing Drugs by the Healthy," *Nature* 456 (December 11, 2008), 702–705.

21. See, for instance, Mark Fainaru-Wada and Lance Williams, "The Truth about Barry Bonds and Steroids," *Sports Illustrated*, March 13, 2006. Available online at http://sportsillustrated.cnn.com/vault/article/magazine/MAG1116081/index.htm.

22. James, "Cooperstown and the 'Roids."

23. www.baseball-reference.com/leaders/W_career.shtml; and www.baseball-reference.com/leaders/W_season.shtml.

24. John Rawls, "The Best of All Games," *Boston Review* 33 (March/April, 2008). Available online at http://bostonreview.net/BR33.2/rawls.php.

LEONARD CASSUTO

Interchapter: Pete Rose

Confession, writes the literary theorist Peter Brooks, is a social act. It binds the penitent to society by making his deeds public, and enables the granting of redemption, the idea of which originates on high, but which is mediated through society. "The process of rehabilitation and reintegration," says Brooks, starts only when one says, "I did it." Though the authority of confession originates with the Catholic Church, which made the act mandatory in 1215, there's nothing denominational or even specifically religious about the power of confession in western culture today. Its influence suffuses our morals and law – indeed, our entire social world.[1]

The centrality of confession to baseball's recent off-the-field drama says a lot about the game and its place in US culture. The ordeal of Pete Rose, one of baseball's most notorious figures in recent times, shows how baseball clings doggedly to the memory of innocence long lost. Baseball draws on that innocence to invoke a special kind of moral authority that it still tries to exert despite the game's evolution into a media-driven big business.

Pete Rose once personified baseball virtue. Nicknamed "Charley Hustle," he played with vivacious intensity, and set an all-time record for base hits. Rose would sprint when he needed only to walk, and led his teams by his hard-charging example for over twenty years. He even became a player-manager, a dual role rarely seen in the sport. But Rose's desire to compete extended beyond the basepaths. A well-known gambler on other sports, Rose violated one of baseball's most sacred taboos when he bet on the outcome of baseball games. (Such an activity threatens the fair outcome of the game even when one bets on one's own team to win – for Rose's bets on a given day could have influenced his managerial decisions on other days. For example, he might rest his best players today to increase his chances of winning a game he'd bet on tomorrow.)[2]

In baseball, any hint of gambling reflexively summons the specter of the infamous Chicago "Black Sox," eight of whom conspired with gamblers to throw the 1919 World Series. Those eight Chicago players were banned from baseball for life. Since that scandal, Major League Baseball has strictly forbidden any associations with gambling, even forbidding Mickey Mantle years later from lending his name to a casino long after his retirement as a player. So Rose's transgression was extreme.

The most famous of the 1919 Black Sox, "Shoeless Joe" Jackson, admitted his guilt under oath, and his story subsequently took on a life its own. One of baseball's classic anecdotes – which was reported at the time and so may be based on truth – takes place outside the Chicago courthouse where Jackson gave his testimony in 1920. "Say it ain't so, Joe," a young boy begs, but Jackson replies, "I'm afraid it is." Jackson has become a tragic figure in baseball history. A functionally illiterate country boy who became a star before his career abruptly ended, Jackson played various exhibitions after he left the major leagues, and lived mostly in obscurity until his death in 1951. Advocates have taken up his cause in the years since his banishment from the major leagues, seeking posthumous rehabilitation and a place for him in the Baseball Hall of Fame. Certainly Jackson's afterlife as a baseball martyr owes something to his swift confession and lifelong penitence.[a]

When John M. Dowd, an independent counsel retained by Baseball Commissioner Bart Giamatti, found that Pete Rose had bet on baseball, Giamatti took Rose to court in 1989. To head off a trial, Rose agreed to a permanent ban from the game. The ban meant that he could no longer appear in any official capacity at any Major League Baseball event, and he was marked ineligible for the Baseball Hall of Fame.

But withal, Rose didn't admit wrongdoing. Quite the opposite: he stubbornly and repeatedly declared his innocence, even in the face of the overwhelming evidence that Dowd presented in his report. Rose stonewalled for years against demands for public confession, appealing to fans for support as he applied for reinstatement from a changing cast of Baseball Commissioners who succeeded Giamatti. In time he became something of a huckster, selling his name in settings as tacky as professional wrestling events. He also sold his autograph without reporting the income, and served time in prison for tax evasion in 1990.

In a 2004 book, *My Prison without Bars*, Rose finally admitted to betting on baseball – and in the same breath again requested reinstatement. The belated confession made little impact, and Commissioner Bud Selig left Rose's banishment in place. In 2007 Rose tried another tack. "I bet on my team every night," he insisted – which would have meant that his bets would

---

[a] Jackson is also the sympathetic hero of one of the best known novels about baseball, W. P. Kinsella's *Shoeless Joe* (1982), which was adapted for the movies as *Field of Dreams* (1989). Both versions of the story are discussed elsewhere in this volume; see 112, 114, 118, and esp. 122–123.

not have affected his managerial decisions from day to day. Dowd again contradicted him.[3] This brief flurry changed nothing, and today Pete Rose remains a baseball exile, gnashing his teeth at the sport's gates, but with nothing of interest left to say.

We call for confessions, Brooks says, "yet we are suspicious of them."[4] Indeed, Rose is a distinctly suspect confessant. His admission, made only after prolonged punishment and with a payoff clearly in mind, does not suggest repentance. His confession therefore doesn't do what it's supposed to do, which is to create the possibility of redemption.

But why should we care about redemption in this context? Other sports don't traffic in such concepts. Very few of today's basketball fans even know about the gambling scandal of the late 1940s and early 1950s that resulted in thirty-two arrests and the disgrace of the City University of New York's championship basketball team. When professional basketball expelled a referee, Tim Donaghy, in 2007 for betting on games and then officiating in such a way as to affect point spreads, the enforcement procedure was mechanical, and success was measured by the results: no one else was implicated, the game went on, and all was well. All sports have rules. Football bans steroids as baseball does, and when a football player is caught using them (as happens from time to time, often with star players), he's suspended for a certain number of games. Then he comes back, and all goes on as before. In baseball, a steroid user is marked for life. Steroid use in baseball, like gambling, is not simply a matter of a broken rule. It stands as a moral failing: a sin.

The difference here between baseball and other sports is the difference between culpability and guilt. Culpability is external, and is assigned as part of the rules of the game. Guilt is internal, and measures the culprit's moral health. Alone among other sports, baseball claims a sense of morals that connects to its ancient claim as the national pastime. "Baseball, hot dogs, apple pie, and Chevrolet," ran a successful mid-1970s advertising campaign. That jingle points to the cultural centrality of baseball. So does the appearance of the President of the United States to throw out the first ball at the beginning of each season.[b]

Only in baseball would the debate take place over whether Shoeless Joe Jackson and Pete Rose belong in the Hall of Fame. That baseball assigns sin and judges the sincerity of the penitent points to its unique status in American sport. Guardians of baseball's morals – both official and self-appointed – protect them with an obsessive sense of purity. But what does

---

[b] One could also point to the role that baseball played during World War II, both within and outside the military, as a morale builder. See "Baseball and war" in this volume, 81–93.

"national pastime" mean these days? What has it ever meant? The following two chapters will address this question.

NOTES

1. Peter Brooks, *Troubling Confessions: Speaking Guilt in Law and Literature* (Chicago and London: University of Chicago Press, 2000), 3.
2. John M. Dowd said in 2002 that he believed that Rose may also have bet against his own team: "Report: Dowd says Rose 'Probably' Bet against Team," ESPN.com, December 12, 2007, http://static.espn.go.com/mlb/news/2002/1212/1475769.html.
3. Dowd said that Rose usually bet on his team to win, but not always when certain pitchers pitched: "Rose Admits to Betting on Reds 'Every Night,'" ESPN.com, March 16, 2007, http://sports.espn.go.com/mlb/news/story?id=2798498.
4. Brooks, *Troubling Confessions*, 3.

14

ANDREW ZIMBALIST

Baseball's economic development

Major League Baseball (MLB) is a closed league. Owners and teams can only enter with the permission of the existing club members. Other US team sports leagues are organized the same way. US sports fans tend to think that this is the only way to organize a sports league.

Fans of world soccer know otherwise. English and European soccer leagues, among others, are open. Anyone with the motivation and money can enter a team in a low-level league, and that team can then work its way up to the top league, such as the Premier League in England. In England, teams get promoted to the next-highest league if they finish in the top three in their league, or demoted if they finish in the bottom three. In open, promotion/relegation leagues teams have a hard time extorting stadium and other subsidies from host cities, because the number of teams in a particular metropolitan area is determined by market forces. London today, for instance, has six teams in the twenty-team Premier League.

The early years

United States leagues owe their closed structure to William Hulbert, founder of the National League (NL) in 1876. Attempting to improve upon the chaotic and corrupt first professional league – the National Association of Professional Base Ball Players, (NAPBBP), 1871–1875 – Hulbert insisted upon a league with solid organization, tight discipline, and a strong central authority. During the NAPBBP years, players had too much control, did too much carousing, and jumped teams too frequently, and in Hulbert's view, all that had to change. Hulbert kicked unreliable teams and miscreant players out of his league and secretively introduced baseball's player reserve system in 1879.[a]

---

[a] For an account of the NAPBBP and the formation of the leagues that is tied to rule formation, see "The rules of baseball" in this volume, 9–20, esp. 17–19.

Hulbert and his successors also had to beat back rival leagues. Hulbert's National League had little branding and benefited from few barriers to entry; that is, stadiums were spartan, urban land was plentiful, there were no media contracts, and player salaries were low. New leagues sprang up practically every year. The NL managed either to defeat or merge with its would-be competitors. One especially compelling challenge came from the American Association (AA) in 1882.

According to some reports, each of the AA team owners owned either a pub or a brewery. Small wonder, then, that the AA distinguished itself from the NL by allowing beer to be sold at the ballpark. Some referred to the AA as the "beer and whiskey circuit." Thus, the AA aggressively sought a mass popular base – a tactic that Hulbert eschewed. Hulbert wrote to an associate in 1881: "You cannot afford to bid for the patronage of the degraded, if you are to be successful you must secure recognition by the respectable ... The sole purpose of the League, outside of the business aspect, is to make it worthy of the patronage, support, and respect of the best class of people."[1] Hulbert's views looked back to the sport's origins in the 1840s as a leisure-time activity for the genteel classes, promoting good fellowship and reinforcing social standing.

Luckily for baseball's business future, Hulbert's elitist notions were put in check by competition from the AA. The AA's policy innovations – cutting ticket prices from 50 cents to 25 cents, selling beer, and permitting Sunday play – encouraged mass spectatorship for baseball and helped to set the foundation for the sport's identity as the national pastime.

Hulbert proved to be a hard realist who knew that the NL needed to make accommodations with its competitors. Prior to his death in 1882, Hulbert initiated a mutuality pact with the AA to provide protection for each league's player reserve system and recognition of each other's territorial rights.

Another serious challenge came from the Players League in 1889. Each time a rival league surfaced, the competitive pressures in the labor and product market threatened to wrest control of labor from the NL – for instance, by diminishing the player reserve system, which indentured players to the team that originally signed them. Any such loss of control over labor, the NL feared, would cause player salaries to rise. After defeating both the Players League and the AA in 1891, the NL extended its player reserve system to cover all players on each team (instead of the five that it covered when introduced in 1879).

The next major challenge to the NL came from Ban Johnson's American League (AL), which before the 1901 season declared its intention to be a major league; that is, to hire the top player talent and establish its own deals with subordinate leagues. Competition for players between the AL and the NL promptly heated up. AL teams attracted some of the NL's top stars, including Cy Young and Napoleon Lajoie. Despite the defection of these stars, the NL still outdrew the AL at the gate by a small margin in 1901. In 1902, however, the AL attracted a reported 2.21 million fans compared to the NL's 1.68 million.[2] The postseason salary wars between the AL and NL picked up full force following the conclusion of the competition in 1902. The leagues decided it was in their best interest to call a truce and work together, which they did in January, 1903 – creating the modern monopoly of baseball, as we know it today.

The modern era

The new dual-league structure of organized baseball required a new constitution (known as the "National Agreement.") The leagues were to be governed by a National Commission, consisting of the President of the AL (Ban Johnson), the President of the NL (Harry Pulliam), and a third Commissioner (Garry Herrmann), selected by the first two. The third member was designated as Chairman of the National Commission. His term was renewed on a yearly basis.

With the reserve clause in place and the absorption of the only rival league with the 1903 agreement, the baseball monopoly had relatively clear sailing through its first decade. As the urban share of the US population grew from 40 to 46 percent between 1900 and 1910, major league attendance increased from 4.75 million fans in 1903 to 7.25 million in 1909. Team revenues soared, while player salaries languished. As late as 1914 the average player salary was only $1,200 (roughly $25,500 today).[3]

Most of the business of baseball's National Commission until 1912 concerned the movement of players between major and minor league teams and player fines or suspensions, but then stronger challenges arose.

The first came from the formation in September, 1912 of the Fraternity of Professional Baseball Players of America. This incipient union embodied the growing disgruntlement of players, who saw a booming industry with little growth in their salaries. Within a few months the Fraternity signed up 288 players, each paying $18 annual dues. The Fraternity's momentum accelerated during a spring 1913 salary confrontation between some star players and their teams. Most visible was the holdout of Ty Cobb. Cobb had won five consecutive batting titles, the last three (between 1910 and 1912) with averages of .385, .420 (a modern major league record at the time, and still the second-highest batting average since 1900), and .410. Meanwhile, Cobb's salary was stuck at $9,000 throughout this period. Cobb asked for

$15,000, a figure that still would not have been the highest in baseball. The Tigers' owner, Frank Navin, refused to budge on his offer to Cobb. When Cobb refused to report, Navin suspended him. The National Commission did Navin one better, putting Cobb on the ineligible list. Following threats from two members of Congress from Cobb's home state of Georgia to look into baseball's possible violation of the country's antitrust statutes, and Cobb's coming to terms with Navin at $11,332, the National Commission reinstated Cobb after levying a token fine of $50. The Fraternity continued to bring grievances before the Commission for the next four years, but the Commission refused to give formal standing to the Fraternity and generally would not allow the Fraternity's president, David Fultz, to appear before it.

In 1914, though, the challenge from the Fraternity took a back seat to the Federal League (FL). The FL was founded in 1913 as a minor league, but in August of that year announced that it would seek status as a major league. Hoping to take advantage of the players' disgruntlement, the FL repudiated the reserve clause and in its stead offered players long-term contracts. While only 18 players jumped to the FL in 1913, their salaries doubled on average. Despite Ban Johnson's threat to permanently banish those who jumped to the FL, higher salaries lured an additional 221 players (including 81 major leaguers) to the FL during 1914 and 1915.[4] The AL and NL responded by raising salaries. Cobb's salary, for instance, rose to $20,000 in 1915. According to one account, the average pay of 20 major league regulars practically doubled from $3,800 in 1913 to $7,300 in 1915.[5] The National Commission also permitted covert collusion between the major and minor leagues to hide talent from the FL.[6]

The competition for players and fans led to losses for both established leagues. Attendance at NL and AL games dropped from 6 million in 1913 to 4.1 million in 1914. According to one account, together these two leagues lost some $10 million.[7] Even larger losses were suffered by the FL, which began with smaller cash reserves.

With the National Commission doing all it could to block FL access to both major and minor league talent, the FL's only real hope appeared to be to pursue litigation. In January, 1915, the FL's lawyers filed an antitrust suit against the AL and NL club presidents and the National Commission in the US District Court of Northern Illinois for denying the FL access to baseball's labor markets.

This was the circuit of judge Kenesaw Mountain Landis, who eight years earlier had earned a reputation as a vigorous enforcer of the 1890 Sherman Antitrust Act. It turned out, however, that Landis, ever quixotic and capricious, had more loyalty to baseball than he did to the fight against monopoly power. Landis tipped his hand early on in the trial when he asked one of the FL attorneys: "Do you realize that a decision in this case may tear down the very foundation of the game?"[8] When FL lawyers attempted to present evidence about exploitation in baseball's labor market, Landis asserted: "As a result of thirty years of observation, I am shocked because you call playing baseball labor."[9] Landis told the parties that he would take the case under advisement, knowing full well that the FL's financial situation was too precarious for it to hang on long. Sure enough, after waiting almost a year, in November, 1915, the FL and organized baseball reached a settlement. It included $600,000 total compensation divided unequally among several FL owners, while two FL owners were allowed to buy into NL or AL clubs.

The disappearance of one-third of major league jobs and the absence of competition meant, of course, that the clubs again had the upper hand over their players. Salaries not surprisingly dipped in 1916. The Fraternity president, David Fultz, then called upon players to refuse to sign contracts for 1917 and to prepare to strike. In January, 1917, Fultz held talks with the American Federation of Labor's Samuel Gompers about joining that union's ranks. Talk was easier than action, however. As January drew to a close, some players began to sign contracts and the union ranks withered. Fultz had overplayed his hand. The Fraternity faded and the National Commission had yet another victory.

The Commission's ascendance, however, was not to last. After President Wilson declared war on Germany in April, 1917, hundreds of players were drafted for the war effort. The major league clubs proceeded to raid the minors in order to restock their rosters. Minor league operators, meanwhile, found their players being siphoned away both to the armed forces and to the major leagues. Despite the increased demand for minor leaguers, draft prices were fixed in the National Agreement. To make matters worse, the US economy entered a period of war-driven, double-digit inflation.

With the troops returning home before the 1919 season, the minor league operators felt it was time to recover their standing. They appealed to the majors for higher prices for their drafted players. When the majors refused, the minors broke ranks and suspended the majors' draft and optional-assignment rights. The National Commission tried to restore the status quo *ex ante*, but failed. The National Commission also failed to resolve individual player disputes, provoking both increased rancor between the NL and AL and power struggles among members of the Commission itself. The revelations of the 1919 World Series being intentionally thrown by players on the Chicago White Sox – the infamous Black Sox Scandal – made it clear that the game needed a new governance structure.[10]

The Commissioner and the antitrust exemption

In January, 1921, organized baseball adopted a new National Agreement that articulated the role of an all-powerful Commissioner who would protect the interests of all of baseball's constituencies – owners, players, fans, and host cities. Judge Kenesaw Mountain Landis became the first Commissioner, a job he held for the next twenty-three years.

Less than a year-and-a-half after the creation of the Commissioner's Office, baseball was granted an antitrust exemption by the US Supreme Court. The Court found that baseball was not involved in interstate commerce and, therefore, the Sherman Antitrust Act did not apply to it.[11] This judicial exemption was matched by a de facto monopoly over the entire spectator team sports industry, because baseball in effect had the field to itself – the National Football League (NFL) was just emerging in the 1920s and did not reach maturity until the late 1950s, and the National Basketball Association did not begin until the 1940s, and did not reach its current level of popularity until the 1980s.[b]

Thus, the baseball industry developed in an artificial environment that featured the presumption of an omnipotent Commissioner, lack of competition from other team sports, a judicially conferred antitrust exemption, and a labor market characterized by the player reserve system that restricted player movement from team to team. These insulated, uncompetitive circumstances resulted in passive and inefficient team ownership. Industry magnates had little incentive to market their product or make innovations in the game's structure. Indeed, other than lifting the color bar in 1947 (which Landis had delayed for several years), baseball stayed basically the same from the 1920s until the 1950s, with the same sixteen teams playing in the same twelve cities. The advancing reality of population growth and dispersion, however, brought an era of itinerant franchises beginning in the 1950s, a development explored in more detail elsewhere in this volume.[c] The would-be rival Continental League provoked baseball's first expansion by two teams in 1961, and New York Yankee dominance motivated the introduction of the reverse-order amateur draft (in which the team with the worst record chooses first) in 1965. In 1966, Marvin Miller came in as the executive director of the players' union and inspired the successful drive to abolish baseball's reserve clause.[12]

---

[b] For a discussion of football's ascendance in the late twentieth century, see "Baseball and mass media" in this volume, 230ff.

[c] See "Baseball and the American city" in this volume, 95–106.

The advent of free agency

Following the Curt Flood case, and the Messersmith and McNally arbitration cases, baseball grudgingly yielded to free agency in the player market after 1976.[d] Now, with the advent of market-based player salaries and new cost pressures, the industry would be called upon to conduct itself like a real business. It was not up to the challenge.

Bowie Kuhn, Commissioner from 1969 to 1984, was preoccupied with maintaining a coalition of discordant owners large enough for him to hold on to his lucrative job. Most owners believed that Charlie Finley, the wacky owner of the Oakland A's, was bad for the game, so to appease them Kuhn repeatedly punished Finley by defying economic logic and not allowing Finley's player trades.

Meanwhile, the owners could not agree on a constructive reform of the players' market. The lowest common denominator, the only position for which there was a consensus, was to fight energetically to preserve the reserve clause. So, after arbitrator Peter Seitz ruled in favor of Messersmith and McNally in his December, 1975 decision, the owners brought suit first in US district court and then in appeals court, losing both times. The owners reluctantly acknowledged reality in their new collective bargaining agreement with the players, but then spent the next twenty years attempting to undermine free agency – still the only goal they could agree upon.

After an aborted and costly effort by owners to lower player salaries via collusion in the mid and late 1980s, relations between the owners and players' association reached a nadir. In 1990, the owners were intent on breaking the union and locked the players out of spring training camps. The new Commissioner at the time, Fay Vincent, decided that it was imperative to repair relations with the union. He hired former player agent Steve Greenberg as his Associate Commissioner and forced the owners to end their lockout and sign a new labor agreement which, to the owners' disgruntlement, did not curtail free agency rights. The frustrated owners forced Vincent to resign in 1992 and hired one of their own, Bud Selig, owner of the Milwaukee Brewers, to be their "acting" Commissioner.

In doing so, the owners essentially jettisoned the myth of the omnipotent Commissioner who would stand above the game and look after everyone's interests. It was now time to be like other businesses and be run by a CEO, who managed things on behalf of the owners. This change opened up great

---

[d] For a fuller account of these momentous changes, see, in this volume, the interchapter on Jackie Robinson and Curt Flood (76–80); and the interchapter on Andy Messersmith, Charlie Finley, and George Steinbrenner, immediately following this chapter (216–220).

economic potential for the industry, but it took a while for the opportunities to be realized.

Growing inequality

Beginning in the late 1980s, the economic disparities among the teams were growing sharper.[13] The advent of regional sports channels and the introduction of new, retro-design, downtown stadiums, together with a reduction of over 65 percent in the new shared national television contract, deepened the divide between the high- and low-revenue teams. An economic study committee concluded that the owners would not be able to solve the game's financial difficulties without finding new ways to share revenue among the teams.

At the owners' meeting in December, 1992, the magnates voted fifteen-to-thirteen to reopen the 1990 labor agreement. Dick Ravitch, the owners' hired negotiator, called Don Fehr, executive director of the players' association, with the message that he should prepare for urgent talks. Fehr prepared, but Ravitch didn't call back. The 1993 season got underway in April and there was still no call from Ravitch. The apparent reason for the delay was that the owners couldn't agree with one another over the plan they would present to the union. They did agree in concept that the salary system and revenue sharing should be linked, but they couldn't agree on the details of either.

Ravitch had been spending his time trying to get the owners to trust each other. If there was to be revenue sharing, the owners had to accept one another's reports on their team revenues. So, step one was to get the owners to open their books to each other. Ravitch couldn't get the owners to take that first step. Meanwhile, baseball's rules stipulated that any new revenue sharing had to be approved by three-quarters of the owners – thus creating an internal impasse.

In August, 1993, hoping to forge a revenue sharing consensus, Ravitch summoned the barons to a bucolic resort in Kohler, Wisconsin. The two-day enclave at Kohler was the most rancorous and destructive that anyone in attendance could remember. At the time, there was only a minimal sharing of local team revenues: American League teams shared 20 percent of gate receipts with the visiting team and the National League teams shared less than 5 percent. In addition, there was a negligible sharing of cable television revenues in the American League.

In preparation for the Kohler meetings, eleven high-revenue teams began caucusing weeks in advance, as did a larger group of low- and medium-revenue teams. At Kohler, because of the acrimony, the two caucuses could not meet together. Ravitch, Bud Selig, and others had to carry messages back and forth. Selig described the atmosphere at Kohler in no uncertain terms: "I'd never seen anything like that. It wasn't just bad. It was vile. Kohler, Wisconsin was probably the most painful three days I'd ever been through. Everybody else who was there, including George W. Bush [the principal partner of the Texas Rangers ownership group at the time], had never seen anything like it."[14] The high-revenue clubs had a rallying cry at Kohler: "You're not going to put your hands in my pockets." Notwithstanding Acting Commissioner Selig's nonstop therapy sessions with the more choleric owners, the magnates continued to feud. Many, however, began to sense that the game itself was being threatened by their disunity. They understood that some accommodation, some compromise had to be made. One final stimulus that pushed the high-revenue owners to accept revenue sharing was the coming expiration of the National League's television agreement. The small-market owners threatened not to sign a renewal, which, pursuant to US copyright law, meant that teams would only be able to televise their home games in the local markets.

Although tempers eventually calmed a bit, the owners were still not ready to discuss revenue sharing at their September, or December, 1993 meetings. They did, however, finally take it up again at their special meeting in Chicago in January, 1994. This time the owners split into three caucuses. Ravitch put forward a plan that included both increased revenue sharing and an added salary cap. The plan received twenty of the twenty-one votes it needed to pass. Nevertheless, the owners were heartened by their near-accord and agreed to meet again in the warmer climes of Fort Lauderdale, Florida ten days later. There they struck an historic compromise: the high-revenue clubs would share $58 million with the low-revenue clubs, contingent on the players accepting a salary cap. The underlying notion was that whatever the high-revenue clubs lost in revenue sharing, they would gain in lower player salaries via the new limit on team salaries.[15] Of course the players were not consulted, and proved to have other ideas. Thus, the owners traveled to the precipice only to strike a deal with each other that was premised on an unrealistic expectation of what they could get from the players' association. It took the owners a few more months before they could agree on sufficient details on their proposal to be ready to go to the bargaining table with the players – something they had urgently called for a year-and-a-half earlier.

This inauspicious process culminated in the strike of 1994–1995, the most devastating work stoppage in US sports history. The strike was ended by the felicitous decision of then-US district court judge, Sonya Sotomayor, who found the owners guilty of unfair labor practices. Fans, however, were alienated by the long strike, and annual attendance dropped by 20 percent after baseball resumed at the end of April, 1995.

Revenue sharing

The ensuing 1996 labor accord contained baseball's first revenue sharing agreement. The plan carried perverse incentives, but it at least marked the baseball owners' first step toward the "league-think" philosophy of the NFL, which places the greater good of the league ahead of that of individual teams. By the last year of the agreement in 2002, the high-revenue teams were sharing a total of $165 million with the low-revenue teams, compared to only $23 million in 1995.

The longevity heroics of Cal Ripken, the steroid-aided power displays of Mark McGwire and Sammy Sosa in 1998, the prodigious record-setting of Barry Bonds in 2001,[e] the building of several new stadiums, and, remarkably, the inauguration of baseball's first central office marketing department together led to a magnificent growth spurt for the industry. Revenues grew at over 14 percent a year between 1995 and 2002.

Both the owners and the players were chastened by the ill will and negative effects engendered by the 1994–1995 strike. Moreover, the owners seemed to be turning the corner financially and the players' average salary surpassed $2 million. The militant days of Marvin Miller unionism had long passed, and the players, with their lofty salaries, were in no mood to risk shortening their already-brief careers and further alienating the fans. Thus, the conditions in 2002 were ripe for the two sides, in spite of themselves, to reach baseball's first collective bargaining agreement without a work stoppage.[16] Ultimately, this is precisely what they did, but not before they had engaged in some of their ritualistic and counterproductive shenanigans.

In early 1999, Commissioner Selig appointed a blue ribbon panel to study the state of the game's economics and make recommendations for its reform. The panel issued its report in July, 2000 and, most observers believed, it was to form the basis for the owners' position in the coming labor negotiations. Yet it was not until six months after the report's release that Selig dispatched Paul Beeston, baseball's Chief Operating Officer (COO), and Rob Manfred, Vice-President for labor relations, to begin bargaining with the players' association. The two sides had twenty-three productive meetings between February 28 and June 20, 2001. When the June 20 meeting adjourned, the

---

[e] The exploits of McGwire, Sosa, and Bonds – and their contentious aftermath – are explored in more detail elsewhere in this volume, in "Babe Ruth, sabermetrics, and baseball's politics of greatness" (39–42); and "Cheating in baseball" (189–195).

players' association and Beeston, who had kept Selig updated on the progress of the talks, thought they had reached an accord that only needed a final stamp of approval from the Commissioner's Office.

However, the players' association not only did not hear from Beeston in the coming days, it also did not hear from the Commissioner's Office again about substantive bargaining until December, 2001. The probable explanation for this setback and new delays was the disunity among the owners. When the owners finally returned to the bargaining table, they came again with onerous demands that proved unacceptable to the union.

Labor peace

Several months of frantic bargaining ensued, ending in a last-minute agreement on August 30, 2002, the strike deadline the players had set. The two sides played out their bluffs as long as they could without stopping the game once again. Many fans and commentators were relieved by the accord, declaring that baseball had entered a new era of maturity and labor peace.

So baseball gained a labor peace of sorts, but it still lacked a well-designed labor agreement. The new revenue sharing system contained perverse incentives: it levied a marginal tax rate on the top-revenue teams of 40 percent and on the bottom-revenue teams of 49 percent. This provided a stronger disincentive for the weak teams to spend money to improve their on-field performance, and, other things being equal, would have made competitive outcomes more unlikely. Baseball already had a competitive balance problem, and this agreement seemed likely to aggravate it. By 2006, the high-revenue teams were transferring $326 million a year to the low-revenue teams, and many low-revenue owners were putting the money in their pockets rather than spending it on acquiring new talent. According to the labor agreement, the Commissioner was supposed to ensure that the transfers were spent on improving on-field performance, but Commissioner Bud Selig and his family owned the Milwaukee Brewers, a low-revenue team (until they sold it in January, 2005), and showed no interest in enforcing this provision.

High-revenue teams were therefore being penalized for their entrepreneurial success, while low-revenue teams were rewarded for their managerial lassitude and ineffectiveness. The perversity of baseball's revenue sharing system is dramatized by a comparison of the Philadelphia Phillies and the Boston Red Sox. The Phillies inhabited the country's fourth largest (and largest unshared) media market, played in a new, publicly subsidized stadium, and yet were receiving around $5 million in transfers annually from Major League Baseball (MLB) – while the Red Sox, in the nation's sixth largest media market, but with baseball's twenty-first largest television territory, in a privately funded ballpark, were paying over $55 million into the system.[17] The Phillies were being rewarded for their failure and the Red Sox were being penalized for their success.

Baseball again avoided a work stoppage in reaching its 2006 collective bargaining agreement. With the sale of the Washington Nationals for $450 million; the sterling success of Major League Baseball Advanced Media (MLBAM), baseball's Internet company; growing attendance; new ballparks; and the emergence of team-owned regional sports networks, the industry was rolling in money. Compromise and peace are easier under these auspicious circumstances. The owners and players even succeeded in rationalizing the incentive system in the new agreement, by introducing a uniform and lower marginal tax rate of approximately 31 percent and basing over one-third of the sharing on a fixed revenue concept. Baseball's revenues continued to rise at double-digit rates; franchise values have soared (some reaching near $1 billion); and the average player salary, which stood at $51,501 in 1976, had risen to $3.2 million by 2008.

Governing the game

Yet the problem of owner disunity in baseball, while it has receded, has not gone away. Commissioner Selig knows that he must navigate very perilous waters to avoid another Kohler-style blowup. The leadership style he has evolved in consequence is rather autocratic and manipulative. Teams are informed of policy matters on a need-to-know basis only. Meetings of all the owners together are held to a minimum, and open discussion is generally avoided. Selig works one-on-one with each ownership group, discourages communication among the owners, and, like a politician, makes it clear that if they support his initiatives, he will be more supportive of their needs in the future.

Thus, baseball has developed a relatively functional governance process. While it works for the time being, it is held together by skillful jockeying by the Commissioner's Office. It appears to threaten to break apart with any serious provocation. Baseball's coordination issues, then, have been corralled, but they have not been solved.

Nonetheless, the effective centralization orchestrated by Selig and his COO Bob Dupuy has permitted the modernization of baseball management. Since the strike of 1994–1995, the game has continuously made innovations: the increase to three divisions and the wild-card playoff qualifier within each league; the first marketing department in MLB's central office; interleague play; the posting system accord with Japanese baseball that allows for orderly transfer of players between the two leagues;[f] the promotion of youth baseball, particularly in the inner cities; the Internet marketing agreement and MLBAM, an entertainment industry pioneer in developing the business use of the Internet and mobile communications; the World Baseball Classic (in which national teams meet quadrennially in a brief tournament); and the MLB Network, among others.

The future

Baseball's post-1995 growth spurt has not been painless, however. The ongoing steroid scandals have damaged reputations, raised issues of honoring baseball records, and soured some fans on the game. Major League Baseball has responded firmly, but the issues have remained as names have leaked out from the list of 104 players who tested positive in 2003. In the future, new chemical compounds will frustrate testing protocols and gene doping likely will become an option. The performance-enhancing drug problem will be with baseball and other sports for decades to come. There is no short-term solution, only long-term vigilance.

A related conundrum has emerged with baseball's internationalization. Baseball's revenues from media and merchandise sales in Japan well exceed $100 million annually and the game relies increasingly on international talent, especially from the Caribbean. In April, 2009, out of 818 players on major league active rosters and disabled lists, 229 (or 28 percent) were from outside the United States, 81 of them from the Dominican Republic and 52 from Venezuela; out of 6,973 minor leaguers, 3,335 (or 47.8 percent) were foreign-born. Players from the Caribbean are a cheaper source of talent. Eager teams have set up camps in the Dominican Republic and elsewhere, and worked with street agents to identify the most promising young players.[g] These efforts have spawned a largely unregulated and corrupt players' market, which includes falsification of birth records and seemingly widespread use of steroids. It is not a simple matter for MLB to set up and implement testing and training protocols in foreign countries.

The success and growth of MLBAM has also exacerbated old tensions about centralization versus decentralization. Its live online streaming of out-of-market games has created a new centralized revenue stream that is shared equally across all clubs, even though certain clubs are responsible for most

---

[f] For more on the posting system and Japanese baseball generally, see "Global baseball: Japan and East Asia" in this volume, 155–167.

[g] For a more detailed account of the personnel relations between the American major leagues and the Caribbean, see "Global baseball: Latin America" in this volume, 171–184.

of this revenue. In 2009, MLBAM began to stream the games of some teams in-market. Here again, revenue from a team's local market that used to belong to the local club ends up being shared in part with the other twenty-nine clubs. Some clubs believe that the central office's encroachment on their market in this way not only eats into their revenue, but also diminishes their incentives to innovate. This struggle will continue to be played out.

The financial collapse of 2008–2009 in the US and world economy constitutes another challenge. While the downturn ended in late 2009, economic malaise is likely to persist for some time. Revenue streams that were growing reliably will dissipate and MLB will have to learn to live with much slower growth. In such an environment, the more constructive labor relations that have emerged since 1995 will be put to the test.

All of these challenges are better met when MLB has intelligent leadership. Bud Selig's strong and effective hand will not be around much longer, and baseball will need to fashion new mechanisms for effective governance.

As a closed, monopoly league, not subject to the normal rigors of competition, baseball's economy languished for decades. Insulated from outside competition, the industry's conduct depended heavily on its internal, largely dysfunctional governing structures. The advent of free agency in 1977 and the jettisoning of the myth of the omnipotent Commissioner who represented all of the game's constituencies began a process of modernizing MLB's management.

In the end, baseball, like all team sports leagues, has moved toward the American ideal of free enterprise. Yet it has also been constrained by the special feature of a sports league. The outcome of on-field competition must be uncertain in order to entice and maintain fan interest. Teams come from markets of very different sizes and conditions, but they all go to the same players' market to hire talent – giving an advantage to big city clubs. This tension yields agreements to constrain the free market (for example, revenue sharing, luxury taxes, salary caps in some leagues) and inevitable strife among the owners. Managing this process and planning for the sport's future is a delicate and difficult task – one that baseball cannot avoid. The coming decade will prove to be interesting both on and off the field.

NOTES

1. Stefan Szymanski and Andrew Zimbalist, *National Pastime: How Americans Play Baseball and the Rest of the World Plays Soccer* (Washington, DC: Brookings Institution Press, 2006), p. 33.
2. Each league had eight teams, although the AL did not have a team in New York until 1903.
3. Andrew Zimbalist, *Baseball and Billions: A Probing Look into the Big Business of Our National Pastime* (New York: Basic Books, 1994), 9.

4. Competition from the FL also facilitated nonsalary gains for the players. The Fraternity presented the AL and NL owners with a list of seventeen demands in January, 1914. Several were met, including: owners agreed to pay for players' uniforms (except shoes) and travel expenses to spring training, owners agreed to provide written notification and explanation of suspensions or releases and promised nondiscrimination against Fraternity members, and owners agreed to provide all players with written contracts. While modest concessions, they were important steps toward recognizing that players had some legal rights.

5. Harold Seymour, *Baseball: The Golden Age* (New York: Oxford University Press, 1971), 205–207.

6. Robert F. Burk, *Never Just a Game: Players, Owners, and American Baseball to 1920* (Chapel Hill: University of North Carolina Press, 2000), 203.

7. David Voigt, *American Baseball*, 3 vols., Vol. II (University Park: Pennsylvania State University Press, 1983), 117.

8. Cited in Burk, *Never Just a Game*, 208.

9. Zimbalist, *Baseball and Billions*, 9.

10. See Andrew Zimbalist, *In the Best Interests of Baseball? The Revolutionary Reign of Bud Selig* (Hoboken, NJ: Wiley, 2006), Chapters 2–3 for more detail.

11. For further discussion, see Andrew Zimbalist, *May the Best Team Win: Baseball Economics and Public Policy* (Washington, DC: Brookings Institution Press, 2003), Chapters 1–3.

12. The story of this struggle is told by many authors. See, for instance, Marvin Miller, *A Whole Different Ball Game: The Sport and Business of Baseball* (New York: Carol, 1991); and Zimbalist, *Baseball and Billions*.

13. The revenue disparity between the top and bottom teams was below $20 million in the late 1970s. By 1985, the gap was around $30 million and by 1991 the differential had increased to over $60 million. At time of writing, despite extensive revenue sharing, the gap exceeds $300 million.

14. Quoted in Zimbalist, *In the Best Interests of Baseball?*, 141.

15. There was, of course, also the hope that the new revenue sharing would improve the league's competitive balance and financial stability.

16. By this time baseball had a remarkable and unenviable record dating back to 1972 of suffering either a strike or a lockout each time an old labor agreement expired. Following the agreement in 2002, union head Don Fehr asserted: "All streaks come to an end sometime, and this one was long overdue" (quoted in Zimbalist, *In the Best Interests of Baseball?*, 164).

17. This was the second highest amount in MLB. The highest was the Yankees at around $77 million in 2006. By 2008, the total transfer from the high-revenue to the low-revenue teams had increased to around $400 million, and the Yankees' contribution had grown to over $120 million. The Red Sox were still second, contributing over $80 million net.

JONATHAN LEWIN

Interchapter: Andy Messersmith, Charlie Finley, and George Steinbrenner

When the Kansas City Athletics moved to Oakland after the 1967 season, Senator Stuart Symington of Missouri called Oakland "the luckiest city since Hiroshima."[1] Athletics owner Charlie Finley was brash, cheap, and constantly interfering with the running of his last-place team. But Oakland would turn out to be lucky after all, at least for a while. The team, now known as the A's, would become the only franchise besides the New York Yankees to win three consecutive World Series, from 1972 to 1974. But when the economic landscape of baseball drastically changed, Finley would preside over the destruction of his team, while another brash and meddling owner, the Yankees' George Steinbrenner, would take advantage of the new topography to restore his franchise to glory.

Unlike most owners, Finley served as his own general manager. Finley had a great eye for talent, but his hands-on approach, which once included firing his manager twice in one night, hurt his team in other ways. When first baseman-outfielder Ken Harrelson criticized Finley's actions in 1967 as "bad for baseball,"[2] Finley abruptly released Harrelson, who ended up getting a big raise to join the pennant-contending Boston Red Sox a few days later. Harrelson announced that he would send Finley "a thank-you note and a dozen roses."[3]

In retrospect, Harrelson's experience showed the potential value of player free agency, but he had become a free agent only because of Finley's caprice. All players were permanently bound to their teams through the reserve clause, which was upheld by the Supreme Court in 1922 when it ruled that baseball was exempt from antitrust laws.

Under the reserve clause, teams could unilaterally renew a player's contract for one year. Both owners and players believed that each renewal created a new contract that could be renewed, meaning that the team held the player's rights in perpetuity. But Marvin Miller, who became head of the baseball players' union in 1966, felt that the wording of the reserve clause meant that a player was bound to his team for just one additional year after the conclusion of his contract. Even after the Supreme Court ruled against outfielder Curt Flood's attempt to overturn the reserve clause in 1972,[a] Miller sought a test case – a player who would agree to remain unsigned for a full season.

Meanwhile, the owners worried about just such a test of the reserve clause and by the growing number of holdouts in general. They offered a concession for labor peace: salary arbitration. The owners approved arbitration over vehement objections and dire warnings from Finley.

When salary arbitration first appeared in February, 1974, Finley's A's had won the previous two World Series, but still had baseball's second-lowest payroll. Finley had gone through bitter salary disputes with players such as Reggie Jackson and Vida Blue, who briefly retired at age 22 rather than accept Finley's offer. But now his stars had the chance to be paid like those on other teams. Nearly a third of the cases heard in the first round of salary arbitration were from Oakland.

During the 1974 season, Finley continued to battle with his players over money. He refused to pay pitcher Catfish Hunter part of his salary because it was in the form of an annuity and therefore not deductible that year. After the season, arbitrator Peter Seitz ruled that Hunter's contract was terminated. Hunter, the best pitcher in baseball at the time, was now free to sign with any team.

George Steinbrenner had bought the Yankees the previous year. The once-dominant franchise had not been to a World Series since 1964, and had lost its position of primacy in the nation's largest market to the New York Mets. In 1974 the Mets outdrew the Yankees for the eleventh straight season. Now Steinbrenner saw an opportunity to help his team on the field and at the gate. Though officially suspended from baseball over his conviction stemming from illegal campaign contributions to Richard Nixon's 1972 presidential campaign, Steinbrenner could still authorize his staff to do what it took to sign Hunter.

On December 31, 1974, Hunter became a Yankee. His new five-year, multimillion-dollar contract raised his average annual compensation sevenfold. Hunter's example showed players what free agency could do. In 1975, six players began the season without signed contracts. By August, five of the six had signed for nice raises offered by increasingly nervous team owners. But the sixth holdout would change baseball history.

Andy Messersmith did not set out to bring free agency and untold riches to major league baseball players. "I never went into this for the glory and

---

[a] See "Interchapter: Jackie Robinson and Curt Flood," this volume, 76–80.

betterment of the Players Association," Messersmith would later say. "At the start it was all personal."[4]

After Messersmith had a falling-out with Los Angeles Dodgers general manager Al Campanis, the star pitcher feared that Campanis would trade him to another team. So Messersmith refused to sign his 1975 contract unless it contained a no-trade clause. The Dodgers eventually offered Messersmith, who had made $90,000 in 1974, a three-year deal worth over half a million dollars. "The money was incredible, but they wouldn't bring the no-trade to the table," Messersmith said. "Now I understood the significance of what this was all about. I was tired of players having no power and no rights."[5]

But union leader Miller wanted a backup in case the Dodgers eventually signed Messersmith. Veteran pitcher Dave McNally had left the Expos in June with a sore arm and did not think he could pitch anymore. But McNally had never signed a contract for 1975. Unworried about possible retribution since he was planning to retire anyway, McNally, a former team union rep himself, agreed to be part of Miller's test case, so he passed up a lucrative contract offer from the Expos designed to pre-empt that possibility. (McNally later followed through on his plan to retire.)

In October, 1975, Oakland's three-year run as World Series champions came to an end when they lost in the playoffs to Boston. After the final game, Oakland stars Jackson, Joe Rudi, Rollie Fingers, and Sal Bando together told Boston's ownership that they were sick of playing for Finley's A's and hoped to come to the Red Sox.

On December 23, 1975, arbitrator Seitz issued a sweeping ruling in favor of Messersmith and McNally. Seitz declared that "no contractual bond" existed between the two players and their now-former teams.[6] After almost a century, the reserve clause was dead.

"I didn't do this for myself," Messersmith said. "I'm making lots of money. I did it for the guys sitting on the bench who couldn't crack our lineup. These guys should have an opportunity to go to another club."[7]

That same winter, the owners tried to blackball Messersmith. They refused to bid on him, except for a few token offers for $50,000. Rumors started that Messersmith had a sore arm. Messersmith was forced to look into pitching in Japan or Mexico.

Next, the owners locked the players out of spring training before the 1976 season began. They demanded that free agency be limited to players with ten years' experience, a level reached by only 4 percent of their number. The two sides eventually agreed to require six years of service for free agency, which was more of a victory for the players than the owners realized, because more free agents might have flooded the market.

Just after the start of the 1976 season, Atlanta Braves owner Ted Turner signed Messersmith to a three-year deal for $1 million, along with a no-trade clause. In Oakland, Finley's star players were all demanding long-term contracts at much higher salaries. At the start of the season, Finley traded Jackson to the Baltimore Orioles. When Finley failed to sign his other stars, he tried to trade them as well. Just before the June 15 trading deadline, Finley changed his strategy. Now he would sell his players. Rudi and Fingers went to the Red Sox for $1 million each and Blue went to the Yankees for $1.5 million.

Summoned to Commissioner Bowie Kuhn's office over the sales, Finley told Kuhn, "Commissioner, I can't sign these guys. They don't want to play for ol' Charlie. They want to chase those big bucks in New York. If I sell them now, I can at least get something back." His goal, he said, was to "sign amateurs and build the team again, just the way I did to create three straight World Series winners."[8] Unmoved, Kuhn voided Finley's player sales on the grounds that they undermined baseball's "integrity" and its "competitive balance."[9] In response, Finley called Kuhn the "village idiot."[10]

The first crop of free agents hit the market after the 1976 season. The biggest star available was Reggie Jackson. The Yankees' Steinbrenner set out to win Jackson over, squiring him around Manhattan in his limo and sending him flower sprays and telegrams that said "We want you." When Jackson went to Chicago to meet with other teams, Steinbrenner followed him, camping out in Jackson's hotel lobby on Thanksgiving Day. Steinbrenner's aggressive pursuit of Jackson made him a Yankee. Jackson said of the Yankee owner, "he hustled me like a broad."[11]

In the first two seasons of widespread free agency, George Steinbrenner's Yankees won the World Series.

With most of his stars fleeing via free agency after the 1976 season, Charlie Finley's A's finished in last place in 1977. The decimated A's were soon being compared to a minor league team and were nicknamed the Triple A's. In 1980, Finley sold the team.

Andy Messersmith, who had won nineteen games the season before he became a free agent, would win only eighteen more games in the remaining four years of his career. Messersmith finished his career with the Dodgers, the team he never wanted to leave. Miller later wrote: "The Dodgers and the rest of the baseball establishment fought to keep [Messersmith] a Dodger; all that Andy had wanted was a no-trade provision so that he *could* remain a Dodger for the rest of his career." If the Dodgers had agreed to the no-trade contract, Miller felt that it "very well could have prevented – or at least postponed – free agency."[12]

In 1976, the average major league baseball player's annual salary was $52,300. By 1980, it was almost $144,000.

In 2009, the average baseball salary was $3,240,000.

NOTES

1. Geoffrey C. Ward and Ken Burns, *Baseball: An Illustrated History* (New York: Alfred A. Knopf, 1994), 432.
2. Brent Musburger, "The Charlie O. Finley Follies," *Sports Illustrated*, September 4, 1967.
3. *Ibid.*
4. John Helyar, *Lords of the Realm: The Real History of Baseball* (New York: Ballantine Books, 1994), 163.
5. *Ibid.*, 164.
6. *Ibid.*, 179.
7. Ward and Burns, *Baseball: An Illustrated History*, 435.
8. Helyar, *Lords of the Realm*, 204.
9. *Ibid.*, 206.
10. Marvin Miller, *A Whole Different Ball Game: The Inside Story of Baseball's New Deal* (New York: Simon and Schuster, 1991), 377.
11. Helyar, *Lords of the Realm*, 224.
12. Miller, *A Whole Different Ball Game*, 253.

15

CURT SMITH

Baseball and mass media

However vague and selective memory may be, baseball coverage began with print, added radio and television, and thus ferried the game to far-away homes, stores, and cars. As early as 1859, writers – "scribes," in the age's argot – described amateur teams playing at the White Lott, or Ellipse, between the White House and Washington Monument. Deem them Coronado, or Cortez. In 1861, Abraham Lincoln became President, playing hooky to watch ball on the Ellipse. By the 1880s, amateur pitcher William Howard Taft pined for the major leagues, settling for Lincoln's post. In 1909, Taft saw his first game as President. "It was interrupted by cheering," read *The Washington Post*, "which spread from the grandstand to the bleachers as the crowd recognized him."[1] At 300 pounds, he was hard to miss.

Lincoln and later Taft governed as America turned from wilderness to settlement, agrarian to manufacturing, Eastern Seaboard to Westward-Ho. In 1876, nearly eight in ten lived on farms or in towns that relied on agriculture. By 1900, cities had surged in the industrial postwar boom. In one part of lower Manhattan, nearly 1,000 persons an acre filled tenements. To succeed, they needed to learn English. The best way was to read.

Daily newspapers – New York had twelve in 1930 – "provided the main opportunity to learn the new [English] language and practice arithmetic," said Leonard Koppett of *The New York Times*. Having emigrated from Russia at age 5, Koppett called baseball "the essential and dominant feature of my Americanization."[2] Few dreamt that another sport might pass it, or radio and TV would eclipse print.

In Portland, Maine, or Oregon, early-twentieth-century tykes hit fungoes, traded the American Tobacco Company four-color playing cards, and studied "baseball edition" scores on a paper's front or back page. In a mining town near Birmingham, Mel Allen's home lacked indoor plumbing, electric light, and telephone. Mom and Dad read catalogues to their young son and future New York Yankees' announcer. "[It's] how I learned baseball," said

Allen, "and to read before kindergarten."[3] The game was, in a sense, umbilically tied to the Republic.

Most cities had at least one morning and afternoon paper. For those keeping score, the geometry of the diamond drew periodicals like *The Saturday Evening Post*, *Collier's*, and the monthly *Baseball Magazine*. Print's vines circled the pastime's trellis: for example, Reach's and Spalding's *Annual Baseball Guide* and weekly *Sporting Life*, and the St. Louis-based *The Sporting News* (*TSN*). Bylines became as personal as a reader's Uncle Ted.

In 1913, J. G. Taylor Spink, 25, joined his father's *TSN*. Next year, *père's* death made *fils* publisher, editor, and advertising manager. Spink wrote a column, stories, and editorials; sent the paper abroad to US troops in World Wars I and II, and made it "The Bible of Baseball." Each major and many minor league teams had a regular correspondent. Spink chose a yearly All-Star team and manager, executive, and player of the year. Many feared his half-curse and half-command.

Born Daniel Markowitz, Dan Daniel wrote more stories for *The Sporting News* than anyone, under the byline "By Daniel." At 21, Fred Lieb became a longtime Spink correspondent, covered each World Series between 1911 and 1958, and christened Yankee Stadium "The House That Ruth Built." By mid-century, power in New York began to gravitate to TV, film, and ad men. Previously, it belonged to baseball writers, their personae as famous as their names.

Grantland Rice – "Grannie," the venerable courser of the press box – died one month after finishing his 1954 memoir, *The Tumult and the Shouting*. Damon Runyon, the Salieri of the short story, inspired the musical *Guys and Dolls*, but was better known for sportswriting. Ring Lardner's "Alibi Ike" and "You Know Me Al" series buoyed *The Saturday Evening Post*. John Kieran wrote the first "Sports of the Times" column and headlined network radio/TV's *Information Please*. Heywood C. Broun played checkers with pitching great Christy Mathewson, was a *New York Herald-Tribune* World War I correspondent, and wrote the syndicated column "It Seems to Me."

Other columns orginated beyond the Hudson, including Detroit's Harry G. Salsinger's "The Umpire," Philadelphia's James Isaminger's "Tips from the Sporting Ticker," and John Carmichael's *Chicago Daily News* "The Barber Shop." At 12, Bob Broeg took tickets at Sportsman's Park in St. Louis. Later he typed a *TSN* column, edited *St. Louis Post-Dispatch* sports, and gave the Cardinals' star hitter Stan Musial a sobriquet – "Stan the Man".

In 1923, Babe Ruth whacked Yankee Stadium's first homer. "On a low line it sailed, like a silver flame, through the gray, bleak April shadows, and into the right-field bleachers," Rice wrote, "and as the crash sounded, and the white flash followed, fans rose en masse in the greatest vocal cataclysm baseball has ever known."[4] Florid prose masked an underside. A reporter's job was hardscrabble: more papers, with more "running" edition takes. Many were ill-schooled; food, drink, and other costs team-bought and team-paid. The quid pro quo could be coverage: writer as hack and flack.

Ruth ran around, swore heavily, and drank: alone, with strangers, and with friends. His fast-lane life was largely covered up, not covered – a vivid contrast to today. As *Sports Illustrated* later wrote, a pact of silence fueled "America's great *divertissement*."[5] Few complained, not knowing what they missed.

George Eastman called color photography "a mirror with a memory." The same applied to black and white. Pictures dotted the *Famous Sluggers Yearbook* and Whitman's *All American Girls Baseball League*. A 1939 photo of Yankees' skipper Joe McCarthy, hat off, and Lou Gehrig, head bowed, dying, wed nobility and tragedy. The cartoonist could warm cold type, too. For a century each *TSN* cover was illustrated. In 1966, seeing its first full-cover color photo, the longtime reader felt like planets had realigned.

In 1920, "sound in the round" joined brush, lens, and print.[6] At Cleveland's League Park, Tom Manning stood behind home plate, pointed a megaphone, and bayed player names. The public address Voice soon added starters, substitutions, and scoring rules. That election night, KDKA Pittsburgh debuted commercial radio. On August 5, 1921, Harold Arlin, 26, bought a Forbes Field seat, used a telephone as microphone, and launched baseball play-by-play. Often the transmitter failed, or crowd noise silenced Arlin. "We didn't know if we were talking to anyone," he said, or "if we'd do more ball."[7]

Arlin voiced the Pirates through 1924, sporadically and laconically. Growing up in Georgia, broadcaster Ernie Harwell grasped radio's theater of the mind. Say a batter hit to right-center field: "Mentally, you saw it all at once – base runners, fielder chasing, shortstop relay, catcher bracing. Radio showed you everything, once the announcer spoke."[8] Harwell delineated America's two favorite sports. Football was "better packaged for TV's screen"; baseball, the imagination.

In 1921, Grantland Rice aired the "wireless"'s first World Series, KDKA feeding WJZ (later WABC) Newark and WBZ Springfield, Massachusetts. Arlin and Tommy Cowan gave half-inning bulletins, linked by telephone to a reporter in New York's Polo Grounds. Next season Rice and W. O. "Bill" McGeehan "for the first time carried the Series ... to great crowds [5 million] throughout the eastern section of the country," said the *Times*. "Amplifiers connected to radio instruments ... made radio listeners feel as if they were in the grandstand. Cheers could be heard throughout the land."[9]

Then, in May, 1923, a 24-year-old piano player on lunch break from jury duty entered New York's A. T. & T. Building, won a WEAF audition, and that fall did Series "color" commentary. By Game Three, replacing McGeehan on play-by-play, radio's first great name began a transcendent reign. Graham McNamee covered foreign visits, coronations, and at least ten sports. Each broadcast began "How do you do, ladies and gentleman of the radio audience?" and ended, "This is Graham McNamee speaking. Good night, all."[10]

Ultimately, McNamee aired twelve straight World Series, conceding "being an entertainer first and broadcaster second." Irked, Lardner wrote: "I don't know which game to write about, the one I saw today or ... heard McNamee announce."[11] Such bile evinced fear of radio. Why read if you could hear for free?

In 1925, one in ten Americans owned a radio. Two in three did by McNamee's 1934 World Series *au revoir*. *Literally*, change was in the air. Fred Hoey aired Boston's Braves and Red Sox. In Detroit, wrote Bob Latshaw, "There wasn't an afternoon the Tigers played that anyone could escape Ty Tyson."[12] The first daily mikeman, Chicago's Hal Totten, called the first game (April 23, 1924) of the first station (WMAQ) to air an entire home schedule (the Cubs'). "America's northeast quadrant got regular-season radio because every team was there," said Mel Allen. "Elsewhere, you just got the [World] Series."[13]

Until 1966, the Commissioner of Baseball, radio/TV network, and sponsor (usually the Gillette Safety Razor Company) chose announcers for baseball's twin tiaras: the World Series and All-Star Game. Chicago's Bob Elson aired twelve Series (tying Totten and McNamee) and ten All-Star Games: also the 1929–1941 Cubs and 1929–1941 and 1946–1970 White Sox; and baseball's first on-field interview in 1930, with Philadelphia A's manager Connie Mack.

"[Baseball Commissioner Kenesaw M.] Landis said it was OK to run a wire from the booth," said Elson. "At first players were antsy. Before long they got the swing."[14] In 1939, Gillette bought exclusive rights to air the Series. Elson entered the Navy in 1942. A year later Franklin Roosevelt asked the now-nicknamed "Old Commander" to broadcast the Fall Classic: the "only time," said Chicago TV's Jack Brickhouse, "that a President pulled rank to get a uniformed baseball guy home."[15]

By then, an announcer knew how to describe a game he never saw. A Western Union Simplex telegraphy machine operator at the park sent data to a studio: b1l meant ball one, low; s2c, strike two called. Eureka! A Voice could *recreate* "play-by-play," wrote *The Sporting News*, "within three seconds of the time it occurs."[16] A pencil tapping wood simulated bat on ball. A sound track mimed background murmur. Using Simplex telegraphy from Cincinnati, Pat Flanagan told Cubs listeners, "If you want these out-of-town games regularly, write and tell us."[17] Next day, 9,000 did.

In 1935, four Des Moines, Iowa stations aired the Cubs *live*. A fifth, WHO, recreated. Once, its wire stopped, Ronald "Dutch" Reagan nearly switched to other programming. "Then I thought, 'If we put music on people'll turn to another station doing it in person.'" What to do? Make a big *to*-do. "Fouls don't make the box score, so for seven minutes I had Billy Jurges set a record" for most foul balls. Pitcher Dizzy Dean tied a shoe. Rain neared. A fight began. "None of this happened, but at home it seemed real." Finally the wire revived, the future President laughing. Years later he revealed its text: "Jurges popped out on the first ball pitched."[18]

Most used sound effects to hide being in studio. Baseball's Diogenes put the mike adjacent to the telegraph, amplifying its dot-dash. Walter Lanier "Red" Barber was the first poet-reporter: the mound, a "pulpit"; booth, "catbird seat"; a "rhubarb [fight] is on the field." The Mississippian aired thirteen Series as well as regular-season games from 1934 to 1966. He also lit National Public Radio's 1981–1992 *Morning Edition*, and won broadcasting's Pulitzer, the George Foster Peabody Award. Red was a distant cousin of poet Sidney Lanier. Hearing, you could tell.[19]

By 1938, thirteen major league teams, including Barber's Cincinnati Reds, used radio. The exception: New York City's Yankees, Giants, and Brooklyn Dodgers, completing a self-imposed five-year ban. "They'd thought radio would hurt attendance," said Barber, "so they banned all coverage."[20] In 1939, Cincinnati's Larry MacPhail, knowing better, became Dodgers head and brought Barber to Brooklyn's Ebbets Field.

That May 17, Bill Stern announced baseball's first televised game: Princeton at Columbia. On August 26, NBC aired TV's first pro sports event to about 400 sets in the New York area. "[Reds and Dodgers] players were clearly distinguishable," Harold Parrott wrote, "but it was not possible to pick out the ball."[21] It *was* possible to pick out Barber, in the second deck, hawking Ivory Soap, Mobil Gas, and General Mills. Making history, he was flying blind. "No monitor, only two [Ebbets Field] cameras, and I had to guess [its direction] from which light was on."[22]

"All sports had been on paper," said Harwell. "Now more daily [news] came from a box."[23] Unchanged: many teenagers still left school to become a sportswriter. Changing: African American and some white writers increasingly denounced baseball's color scheme, Roger Kahn later noting, "The grass was green, the dirt was brown, and the ball players were white."[24] Commercial radio was unconcerned, content to air the Drake Relays, Vanderbilt Cup Race, Kentucky Derby, and, above all, World Series.

In 1942, Allen read a *TIME* article hours before the Series opener. In US drug stores, "lunch wagons, barbershops, parlors, and pool halls, over 25 million radio listeners will cock their ears to listen to three men [Allen,

Barber, and Bill Corum] – the [Series'] sportscasting trio."[25] At 2 pm, Allen called the first pitch, "terrified. I bumble along before I get my wits." Eventually, he broadcast 21 Series, 24 All-Star Games, and nearly 3,000 Twentieth Century Fox film newsreels and short subjects: to a Baby Boomer, baseball at high tide.

"Especially on the weekend, the [movie] house'd have a double feature," said Allen.[26] The newsreel filled intermission: Hearst, Pathé, United Press, and largest, Fox. Allen wrote and spoke script in studio: "This is your Movietone reporter," heard twice-weekly by up to 80 million viewers. *Sports Illustrated* called him "the most successful, best-known, highest-paid, most voluble figure in sportscasting, and one of the biggest names in broadcasting generally."[27]

Allen and Barber shared six World Series from 1940 to 1952, and also the first Hall of Fame Ford C. Frick Award (1978) for Broadcast Excellence. Often likened to each other, they differed, too. Red was white wine, crêpes Suzette, and bluegrass music. Mel was hot dogs, beer, and the United States Marine Band, a greenhouse decorating his voice. Allen's "How about that!" turned national idiom. Barber juxtaposed "bases FOB [full of Brooks]," Carlyle, and Thoreau.[28]

"Either way you got greatness,"[29] said Tennessean Lindsey Nelson, join-ing Dixie's postwar Russ Hodges and Harwell in New York. Harwell was asked "why so many baseball broadcasters [were] Southern. My answer: We grew up in a storytelling atmosphere" of oral density and a siren past. "On the porch Dad and Mom and Uncle Fred and Aunt Ethel talked about the local banker and beauty parlor operator and who married whom,"[30] their rhythm that of big league radio, mythy and sweetly rural.

Radio had been an immovable object. In 1946, Americans owned 56 mil-lion receivers versus 17,000 TV sets. The next year NBC televised its first Series, with three cameras, on four eastern outlets. Slowly, video became an irresistible force, 10,000 sets a day sold by the mid 1950s. They beamed a work in progress. "Nothing was easy," said Allen. "For example, you could only tape TV by shooting its actual picture [kinescope]."[31]

Some adapted better than others. Ironically the greatest beneficiary was another sport.

Pro football had once resembled pro wrestling – except that wrestling had a more established niche. In time, that would change.

For now, print, cartoon, and picture freeze-framed more than ever a fluid swing, ballet in the shortstop hole, a collision at the plate. Willard Mullin created the Brooklyn Bum. Dodgers photographer Barney Stein bared pitcher Ralph Branca, desolate after Bobby Thomson's 1951 pennant-winning homer. Dell released *Baseball Stars*; NBC, *Complete Baseball* Magazine;

Time Inc., *S.I.*'s first issue in 1954. *Baseball Digest* became a still-running monthly. In 2011, *Street & Smith's Baseball Yearbook* will turn seventy.

Each medium proved indestructible, if not immutable. Photo and illustration have never been more widely or easily reproduced than today. Likewise, radio remains a sonata versus television's still life. In 1949, the *New York Sun* scored NBC TV's World Series coverage: "None of the infield plays or outfield catches could be seen."[32] On Mutual Radio, the Dodgers–Yankees opener's last-inning climax *could*. "Look at him grin! Big as a slice of watermelon!," Barber punctuated Tommy Henrich's game-winning home run. A record 67 percent of all US homes with radio heard baseball's Montagues and Capulets.

Nelson grasped why the announcer counts. First, "You're the producer, salesman, writer, star."[33] Second, even pre-free agent Voices lasted years with a club – in Vin Scully's case, sixty-two! – becoming the team's face and sound. Some etched a region; others evoked time standing still; all were your ears and eyes. Finally, rhetoric navigated a sea of dead air. In a three-hour game, the ball may be in play eight to nine minutes. "Football and basketball carry the announcer," said the Bay Area's Hank Greenwald. "The announcer carries baseball."[34]

Prewar radio reached mostly big league cities. By the 1950s and 1960s, it reached thousands of farms and towns. Bob Wolff kept Washington's wretched Senators from seeming the Atlantis of the American League. Harwell dubbed his 1960–1991 and 1993–2002 Detroit Tigers "Tiges" and a double play "two for the price of one." Bob Prince's home run call, "You can kiss it good-bye!" defined the Pirates. Milo Hamilton said "Holy Toledo!" for seven different teams. Cardinals flagship KMOX wed Jack Buck ("That's a winner!"); Joe Garagiola, the Bob Hope of the resin bag; and Harry Caray ("It might be! It could be! It is!" he hailed a homer. "*Holy Cow!*").

In 1950, Scully, 22, debuted in Brooklyn. In 1953, its Bums lost their seventh straight World Series.[35] On October 4, 1955, Scully pronounced on NBC: "Ladies and gentlemen, the Brooklyn Dodgers are the champions of the world!" Brevity cloaked emotion: "If I'd said another word at that very instant, I'd have broken down and cried."[36] In 1958, the team fled to Los Angeles Memorial Coliseum, so huge that many brought transistor radios to *hear* what they couldn't *see*. In 1959, 93,103 fans feted crippled Roy Campanella, "asked in silent tribute [on signal] to light a match," Scully said. The result was "thousands and thousands of fireflies ... a sea of lights at the Coliseum."[37] The lay Voice draws dots. Scully's lingo linked them: "twilight's little footsteps of sunshine"; "he catches the ball gingerly, like a baby chick falling from the tree." If, as Greenwald said, "the announcer carries baseball," the best climbed a peak of place and mood as baseball endeavored to elevate its coverage.

The 1946 Yankees were first to air each wireless game *live*. In 1949, forging radio's Liberty Broadcasting System, Gordon McLendon, 30, a.k.a. The Old Scotchman, eyed America west of the Mississippi and south of Virginia. A year later, 458 outlets heard Liberty's recreated *Game of the Day*. Before long, attendance-wary owners forbade Western Union to participate, stopping Liberty's heartbeat. In 1950, older (born 1935) and larger (nearly 700 stations) Mutual began its own *Game of the Day*, aired each day but Sunday, announcer Al Helfer on location. By 1954, having traveled "four million miles, I counted it" for Mutual,[38] he resigned.

In 1961, the major leagues swelled to eighteen clubs, killing *Game of the Day*. "Suddenly," said Helfer successor Van Patrick, "stations were switching to the new expansion teams."[39] A Jazz Age and Depression listener had heard radio baseball invent itself. Now, a mid-century viewer saw television do the same.

Like 1920s radio, Chicago was television's early capital, having one of every ten US sets by 1947. Next year WGN Channel 9 aired each White Sox and Cubs home game *live*, which was "practical because they weren't home at the same time," Brickhouse said. "We did whichever was. Continuity made fans."[40] New York's WPIX and WOR put baserunner and closeup cameras near each dugout and above first and third base. In 1951, WGN introduced the center-field camera, today seen on every telecast. Six years later it debuted on NBC's World Series, the first in "living color."

In 1948, Harwell became the sole Voice ever traded for a player: Brooklyn's Cliff Dapper. October 3, 1951 brought another first: a sports event telecast nationally. "Surely I'd get *immortality*," Harwell joked of CBS's Dodgers–Giants decisive playoff game. "Instead I get *anonymity*." Hodges' radio call, taped by a listener, eclipsed Harwell's national TV debut: "There's a long drive! It's going to be, I believe! The Giants win the pennant! The Giants win the pennant! The Giants win the pennant! The Giants win the pennant! Bobby Thomson hits into the lower deck of the left-field stands! The Giants win the pennant! And they're going crazy! They are going crazy! Oh-ho!"

Next day NBC began television's first coast-to-coast World Series. In 1952, the network started a five-year, $7 million exclusive contract: each game, said the research firm J. A. Ward, seen wholly or in part on every other TV set. Until 1977, local-team mikemen aired Series radio/television. "The Yankees were always in it," said Nelson, "so Mel was, too," working each Fall Classic from 1947 to 1963.[41] Movietone headlined: "Mel Allen

Relives Series Thrills." To many in the bijou, he was as familiar as actor Jimmy Stewart.

From 1947 through 1965, Gillette anchored "America's greatest sports event: the World Series" on NBC TV. Life "stopped," recalled *Brooklyn Bridge* creator Gary David Goldberg. "Everyone followed the game – farmers, factory workers, of course kids," smuggling radios into class.[42] Even in Canada, the Series iced hockey. "Learning scores by sign signal," said future Bob Hope humor writer Doug Gamble, "only added to the drama."[43]

On October 13, 1960, 12-year-old Bill Glavin left school in Albany, New York, at 2.50 pm, his Yanks leading Pittsburgh 7–4 in the World Series' seventh game. Glavin's bus stopped at a corner, a friend updating him through the window, "9–7, Pirates, in the eighth." New York tied the score at 9. Arriving home, Glavin saw Bill Mazeroski's ninth-inning blast give Pittsburgh the game, 10–9, and Series. "I don't know a person who doesn't know where they were when that ball left the park," he said.[44] To a Boomer, the Series tie still binds.

As we have seen, network radio belatedly added regular season to October coverage. Network TV soon followed suit. In 1953, ABC began Saturday's *Game of the Week*, blacked out within fifty miles of a big league city. Unvexed, the network had an 11.4 rating (i.e., 11.4 percent of all households with a television). In 1955, moving to swanker CBS, *Game of the Week* attracted a staggering 80 percent of sets in use, adding a Sunday telecast in 1957. Announcer Dizzy Dean sang *The Wabash Cannonball*, dubbed the cosmos *pod-nuh*, and razed English as no one again is likely to. A batter "swang." A runner "slud." A hitter was "standing confidentially at the plate." Outlanders loved Ol' Diz's 300 pounds, string tie, and Stetson – the whole rustic goods.[45]

In 1960, all three networks aired a record 123 games, auguring the current level of Fox, ESPN, and TBS exposure, their response warmer then. Dean closed down Pleasantville twice weekly. "Football fans watch regardless of team," said former ABC executive Edgar Scherick.[46] "On TV, baseball isn't telegenic," needing a Voice *surpassing* team. Dean was the first ex-player to become a Voice, fusing Ma Kettle, Billy Sunday, and Tennessee Ernie Ford. He was "an original," said Nelson. "Maybe network sports never took off without Diz's lead."[47]

Technology helped. In 1956, CBS's Frank Chirkinian devised an earplug – or IFB (Intercepted Feed Back) – to connect the announcer, director, and producer, smoothing on-air flow. Optical-turned-magnetic sound clarified a sound track. Videotape made recording almost instantly airable. On July 17, 1959, TV crossed a dividing line, never looking back. In the ninth inning, starting pitcher Ralph Terry yielded his first hit of a game at Yankee Stadium.

Videotape recently had let the home team air postgame highlights. On a whim, Allen asked director Jack Murphy about reshowing the hit. "It took a few minutes," Mel said, "but it was the first-ever replay."[48]

Dean didn't need instant replay. Football did, finding it nirvana. Run play. Review. Run next play. Football is "an *analyst's* sport," said NBC blue-chip announcer Bob Costas. "Baseball's different. Not every pitch is *worth* replay. Baseball's conversation. Tell me about the guy sitting down at the end of the dugout. Is he a character? Does he give guys the hot foot? Does he come from a small town in Arkansas?"[49] Dean actually did, before he began "commertating." Sadly, few so grasped baseball broadcasting's essence at its 1950s peak.

America once drove, read, hit the beach on Sunday: anything but watch the tube. (Diz was the exception.) Then, in 1956, CBS launched weekly coverage of the National Football League (NFL). Ironically, the NFL's rise began in baseball-crazed New York after the Dodgers' and Giants' 1958 California exit created a print/electronic void.[*a*] Filling it, the football Giants sold Madison Avenue on what Scully had described as "nothing but a bunch of pot-bellied longshoremen."[50] Baseball's decline as Big-Game America began with its split Big Apple.

Some Dodgers and Giants fans went underground. Others forswore baseball for a time, or for life. In 1956, *Sports Illustrated* wrote, "To your average balding, loose-bellied sedentary American male, [baseball] is something to read about, to talk about, to listen to on radio, to watch on television. It occupies an extraordinarily large part of his time."[51] Just two years later, 50 million people viewed NBC's Giants–Colts "Greatest Game Ever Played," fueling pro football's surge.

Like the screen, football's scrimmage line is rectangular, each player viewed at once. Every play *moves*: thus, *engages*. Unlike baseball's, both football teams move simultaneously, suddenly and second-guessably. In a 1964 Lou Harris poll, baseball routed football, 2–1, as America's favorite sport. By 2010, *The Wall Street Journal* wrote: "It isn't often that Major League Baseball can claim a victory over the NFL."[52] Added *The Washington Post*: "Nothing in sports seduces Americans the way the National Football League does."[53] Football eclipsed baseball over time, not overnight.

In 1962, NFL Commissioner Pete Rozelle got Congress to exempt football from monopoly charges. He put every team in a package, sold its rights to CBS, and shared the bounty equally. By 1965, baseball, envious, gave ABC *Game of the Week*, now aired everywhere. Merle Harmon succeeded

---

[*a*] For more on the departure of the Giants and Dodgers, see "Baseball and the American city" in this volume, 95–105.

Diz as Voice, but ratings tanked. A year later NBC bought exclusivity, enforcing uniformity. Network broadcasters had included a variety of greats: Allen, Barber, Buck, Dean, Nelson, and Wolff. Curt Gowdy replaced them all, announcing the World Series, All-Star Game, and *Game of the Week* by himself.

"As spectacle, [TV] baseball suffers," Harry Caray wrote, noting "the time span between pitches."[54] The pace lags. A camera can lose the ball. Only remote shots show the entire field. Gowdy's "just the facts, ma'am" style cloaked twelve World Series, fifteen All-Star Games, professional and college football, and the Emmy Award-winning *The American Sportsman*, this versatility earning him sportscasting's first Peabody Award for radio/TV excellence. Gowdy was fair and accurate, but was felt by some too Paleozoic for a nascent anything-but-bore-me age.

In 1950, 4 million homes had owned a television. Ten years later, 44 million homes – 88 percent – did. Network TV beamed each NFL game, available in every home. By 1968, network baseball covered just 28 games: 23 *percent* of 1960's total. Meanwhile, individual clubs averaged 53 locally broadcast games compared to 1960's 43 on outlets dispersed and decentralized, selling – this is crucial – the local team, not the national game.

"Not many years ago ... baseball [was] an American institution," wrote the *Journal*. "If you weren't enthusiastic about it, you risked being considered unpatriotic. Not now." In 1968, "football passed baseball as the top favorite sport," pollster Harris said.[55] That December the baseball owners fired Commissioner William D. Eckert, essentially shooting the messenger. As Harris said: "The problem is that baseball has become too dull."

In 1962, the expansion first-year New York Metropolitans won 40 games and lost 120. "They played for fun," said Nelson, leaving NBC that year to work Mets local TV/radio. "They weren't capable of playing for anything else."[56] New York finished last every year through 1968. Napoleon said, "Ability is fine, but give me commanders who have luck." In 1969, the Miracle Mets gave new Commissioner Bowie Kuhn luck, albeit briefly.

On October 16, NBC's Gowdy, incredulous, blared "The Mets are the world champions!" New York City Mayor John Lindsay recalled "the sheer enormity of the thing." For a time, baseball benefited from New York's trickle-down publicity effect. The sheer *improbability* of the thing helped, too: the Mets, Number One! Since then, as we shall see, some notable baseball events have sired a temporary big league high. Inevitably, the effect wore off, lacking the traction forged by football's each-Sunday presence.

The 1959 World Series drew a composite three of four viewers; by the 1970s, the number dropped to one in two. In September, 1970, ABC launched *Monday Night Football*, giving the NFL a presence on all three major TV networks. Baseball responded by fit and start. On October 13, 1971, 60 million watched the first-night Series game. In 1973, NBC began a limited Monday baseball series to middling ratings and reviews. More auspicious was NBC's and ABC's 1976–1979 joint pact to share the All-Star Game, Series, and League Championship Series (LCS, a new playoff, added in 1969). For a while interest rode a magic carpet weaved by the 1975 Red Sox–Reds Classic, watched at least partly by a then-record 124 million viewers.

"No event helped baseball more than that Series," said Buck. Its Everest was Carlton Fisk's twelfth-inning Game Six-winning Classic-tying home run, hit at 12.34 am. In 1998, *TV Guide* termed the blast the "greatest sports TV moment of all time." Harry Coyle, director of NBC, "kept the scoreboard camera on Fisk, creating one of the medium's most famous reaction shots. As if in a trance, the catcher bounced up and down near home plate, willing" and pushing and praying "it to stay fair. And when the ball obeyed … he leaped into the air and began his trot around the bases, both fists raised."[57]

Fisk's reaction shot transformed sports coverage. "Since then," said Coyle, "everything's up-close, not just the play but people's response." Baseball left TV's critical list, hoping to combat football. The problem, as filmmaker Geoff Belinfante said, was "baseball's lack of credibility." Roone Arledge, ABC's sports head, launched *Monday Night Baseball*, flaunting Voices Al Michaels, Bob Uecker, and Howard Cosell. More successful was baseball's old friend the wireless.

In 1976, CBS Radio bought All-Star Game, LCS, and World Series rights, pining to show "how to sell the game. I think it's only play-by-play that counts," said senior vice-president Dick Brescia, tapping Scully, who declined to dumb down.[57] Through 1982, Scully's All-Star Game and World Series broadcasts averaged 48 million listeners – one in three Americans 18 years or older. In 1985, Brescia began a radio *Game of the Week*, hiring Gowdy, Harwell, Buck, Jerry Coleman, and Harry Kalas, but not Mel Allen, the latter busy with baseball's first TV highlight series. *This Week in Baseball* (*TWIB*) began June 12, 1977, with Allen hosting. "Today highlights bombard Direct TV, ESPN, and local-team affiliates," said the Entertainment and Sports Programming Network (ESPN) stylist, Jon Miller. A quarter-century earlier *TWIB* had stood alone. "Growing up [outside Detroit]," said the Yankees' Derek Jeter, "it was the only chance to see other players besides our home team" – a link to the outside.

This Week in Baseball tied together "stuff on each team, a feature, and bloopers," said producer Belinfante, creating sport's most popular TV serial.

"We'd get a 6 to 7 rating, rivaling [syndication's] *Wheel of Fortune*."[58] In 1964, the Yankees had fired Allen, near his peak as an institution: he virtually vanished for a decade. *TWIB* now resurrected his career, voice-overing games culled from around the country. Many appeared on a *new* friend: cable television.

Cable enlarged baseball variety: thus, possibility. In 1968, White Sox owner Arthur Allyn began daily coverage of Chicago's first ultra-high-frequency (UHF) free cable TV outlet (WFLD). *Pay* cable was around the corner – or was it? Cable systems specked just a few US markets. In 1976, Ted Turner bought the Atlanta Braves, upped their TV schedule, and renamed WTCG Atlanta coast-to-coast SuperStation WTBS. In 1982, the Braves won thirteen straight games to begin their season: "the 'two-by-four,'" said Voice Ernie Johnson, "that hit America between the eyes."[59] In Valdez, Alaska, a Braves Fan Club chapter pooled cash, bought a screen, and named its bar "The Braves Lounge." WTBS households leapt 7,000 percent in a decade. Other SuperStations rose: WOR, WPIX, Harry Caray's WGN. Each team now uses basic subscription cable, wired in nine out of ten homes, to beam much or all of its schedule.

Cable's birth inaugurated a still-running quarrel: should it supplement, or supplant, network coverage? All but one World Series between 1975 and 1981 featured New York, Boston, and/or Los Angeles, drawing at least half the TV audience. Their cachet temporarily helped other markets, too. In 1980, 130 million watched all or part of the Kansas City–Philadelphia World Series. Baseball even briefly topped Gallup's sports preference poll for the first time since 1968. *Sports Illustrated* proclaimed "Baseball's Golden Age," not saying if it was real gold, or fool's.

In 1976, Joe Garagiola replaced Gowdy on *Game of the Week*. In 1983, Scully succeeded *him*, Garagiola doing color. (Bob Costas and Tony Kubek aired a backup *Game*.) Eventually, baseball's TV prosopopeia aired twenty-five Series and eighteen no-hitters, got a star on the Hollywood Walk of Fame, and won a lifetime Emmy Achievement Award. In 2009, the American Sportscasters Association named Scully "top sportscaster of all time," playing English like Jascha Heifetz had a violin.

In 1986, Bill Buckner's error at first base famously concluded Game Six of the World Series: "Here comes Knight! And the Mets win it!," Scully said, his usually singsong voice alight with feeling. Game Seven's audience share routed *Monday Night* football's, 55 to 14 percent, wooing 81 million of the curious and devoted: still the most-watched baseball game of all time. In 1988, injured Kirk Gibson, homering, won a riveting and pivotal Series opener. Said Scully: "In a year that has been so *improbable*, the *impossible* has happened," memory jarring in baseball's free-fall ahead.

Commissioner Kuhn's weekday-night and weekend-day World Series game schedule had served laborers and children since 1972. Unsatisfied, Kuhn's successor Peter Ueberroth made the 1985 Fall Classic an all-night game affair. Short-term, higher ratings helped the bottom line. Long-term, the move presaged a quarter-century of tunnel vision. "Is baseball serious about engendering a love affair with the next generation when children are in bed, preparing for school?" the *Chicago Tribune*'s Bob Verdi later wrote.[60] In 1989, NBC killed the afternoon *Game of the Week*. "Ueberroth could'a kept us and another network," mused Costas, "but he only cared about cash," namely CBS's $1.04 billion bid for 1990–1993 broadcast exclusivity. No longer would Saturday hinge, as Scully said, on "pull[ing] up a chair."

Game of the Week's end showed baseball going back to its sad-sack late 1960s and early 1970s future. CBS's mere sixteen-game regular season meant you could visit Tibet, a Madonna movie, or Arthur Murray's, but not see weekly ball. Coverage largely vanished for the 30 percent of homes without local and/or cable, owners presumably expecting the other 70 percent to buy a team cap, shirt, or jacket. Interest shrank, baseball no longer so wed to America as when Japanese soldiers in World War II cried, "To hell with Babe Ruth!"

"What startles me is that in the '40s and '50s baseball had DiMaggio, Williams, and Jackie Robinson," said future Commissioner Bud Selig in 1994, "That kind of dominance [of public consciousness] by today's players doesn't exist."[61] Increasingly, the pastime braved a guttural culture antithetical to its middle-brow and middle-class DNA. Baseball might have become a refuge from taunt and trash talk. Instead, a sweetly unhip sport moronically panted to have boomboxes screech and hip hop blare.

Game of the Week had been available in every home. By contrast, baseball's 1990–1993 $400 million pact with ESPN limited exposure to six homes in ten. In one sense, cable's Atlas became baseball's window, beaming *Baseball Tonight*, *SportsCenter*, *Sunday Night Baseball*, All-Star Game *Home Run Derby*, World Baseball Classic, and the new Division Series (or DS, another postseason round, begun in 1995 to precede the LCS). In another sense, the window blurred.

"We got baseball because CBS didn't want a *Game of the Week*," said *Sunday Night*'s Miller, in effect succeeding Scully as baseball's national Voice.[62] "The weekend's over, you come back from the beach, and there we are." ESPN forecast a 5.0 1990 rating (7 million of 140 million homes). The first year averaged 3.0. Noncable America got too little baseball; cable-wired America, too much, initially five ESPN games a week. By 1993, 40 million *fewer* saw all or part of the World Series than in 1980. Minus a regular-season foundation, the postseason slip-slid away.

"What's dumber than the dumbest football owner? The smartest baseball owner," Baltimore Orioles and football Washington Redskins owner Edward Bennett Williams once asked rhetorically.[63] Formerly *Game of the Week*'s NBC lead-in, *TWIB* moved to weaker outlets. A players' strike aborted the 1994–1995 schedule, killing the World Series for the first time since 1904. "It gave folks an excuse," said Ernie Harwell, "to leave a sport they'd cooled on anyway." Miscoverage dimmed even the benefit of surprise. The 1996–2000 Yankees took four Series in five years. Arizona won a classic 2001 Classic. Wild-card playoff teams from Anaheim, Florida, St. Louis, and Boston won a title, the Red Sox' first since 1918's Yankee (26th Division) entered France. Each event gave baseball a bounce, but no lasting rise.

Paraphrasing F. Scott Fitzgerald, some announcers "beat on, boats against the current" of contemporary decline. In particular, minority radio/TV Voices tardily began to rise. In 1971, ex-All-Star first baseman Bill White became play-by-play's first African American. He knew the stakes: failure might sink others. Instead, such commentators as Harold Reynolds, Darrin Jackson, and Gary Matthews followed. In 1977, White became the first African American to call a World Series. In 1997, Latina Broadcasting Company's Jaime Jarrin aired Colombian Edgar Renteria's Series-winning hit to 35 million listeners, as many as heard Scully on CBS. At Cooperstown, Buck Canel and Felo Ramírez now flank Jarrin in the Hall's radio/TV wing. Eleven teams strut Spanish-speaking networks, reaching America's fastest-growing minority. Their appeal is the sport's exception, not the rule.

In 1994, baseball inked a two-year NBC–ABC pact. "The Baseball Network" began each July, had no national or day coverage, and carried the DS and LCS playoffs only into areas of "natural" (i.e., local) interest. What league you saw depended on where you lived. *Sports Illustrated* wrote: "Yes, sir, that's baseball: America's regional pastime." Scully's television *Game of the Week* was weekly, national. In 1996, new TV network Fox began a sixteen-game random, regional schedule. Fox and NBC split the postseason and All-Star Game. Joe Buck, Jack's son, became the Series' youngest Voice since the 25-year-old Scully in 1953.

Unlike Scully, the younger Buck seemed lukewarm about his sport. "Baseball takes forever," he said. Since a viewer "doesn't have the patience to put into it, it's asking a lot to watch."[64] Those watching met a tsunami of technology. The "Fox Box" aped a computer page, listing score, inning, outs, balls, strikes, and men on base. Fox miked managers, players, walls, and bases. A catcher's mask camera etched the pitcher–batter duel. ESPN begot the K Zone, bat track, first official's replay call, and BaseCam. Every network had slow motion, stop-action, and telestrators – an analyst's magic pen – drawing diagrams. Booth monitors helped see and call the ball.

Internet technology helped each team build a website under the mlb.com aegis. The American Journalism Review – ajr.com – accessed every base-ball program, including Baseballlibrary.com, ESPN.com, and Fastball.com. As numerous morning and afternoon papers died or shrank in ad inches and circulation, people surfed more, often snared by ESPN's octopus. CBS Radio's network had been baseball's largest since 1950s Mutual. In 1997, ESPN outbid it for exclusivity. "They paid a bundle," said CBS's Frank Murphy. "Our clearance [98 percent of affiliates carried *Game of the Week*] didn't count."[65]

In 1998, ESPN TV's still-major-league-highest audience (9.5 rating) saw Mark McGwire tie Roger Maris's single-season home run record.[b] Since then, new "entertainment options" – Direct TV, iPod, DVD, CD, text-messaging – have split the viewing pie. A welcome baseball hit was 2009's MLB Network's dazzling 24/7 debut in 50 million homes, sport's largest ever cable startup. The network mixed highlight, interview, play-by-play, and archive. Its sole flaw was not its fault: mostly the converted, not convertible, watched.

In 2006, junking the Braves, the renamed TBS network began national regular- and postseason baseball. ESPN telecast to Commissioner Selig's "growth markets": Japan, China, Puerto Rico. Elsewhere, interest stalled. In 1960, Gallup said, baseball led football, 39 to 17 percent. By 2009, it trailed by 43 to 11 percent.[66] "The majors want cash [2010 revenue neared a record $7 billion], glad to have 10 people see 10 games," said Harwell. "The NFL wants cash and exposure: 100 people seeing a given game."[67] Dallas Cowboys owner Jerry Jones explained: "The most popular *TV* sport is by definition *America's* most popular sport."[68]

In 2009, TBS's Division Series coverage drew a scant 9 percent of foot-ball's each-Sunday 60 million. Black Sunday was October 18. NBC's Bears–Falcons regular-season football routed TBS's Phillies–Dodgers LCS playoff game: even LA's *sans*-NFL-team market preferred football to its Dodgers! In 1952, each World Series contest averaged one in two US viewers; 1980, one in five; 2009, one in *sixteen*. Meanwhile, 2010's Super Bowl lured one in three (106.5 million viewers): TV's all-time most watched show. In the post-1990s multimedia world, each non-football sport's network audience has dipped, but baseball's most of all.

In 2009, baseball acknowledged falling traffic at its official website. *Street & Smith's Sports Business Daily* "most marketable athletes" list barely notes baseball players. Hollywood once meant baseball's *Pride of the Yankees*, *The Natural*, and *Field of Dreams*. Football's 2009 *The Blind Side* recently

---

[b] For more on the McGwire–Sosa duel, see "Babe Ruth, sabermetrics, and baseball's politics of greatness" in this volume, 39–42; and "Cheating in baseball," 189–195.

became the all-time highest-grossing film about sports. An NBC executive said: "For baseball, the long-term trend is bad."[69]

Baseball disagrees, noting attendance higher than any other US sport's: a record 79.5 million paid admissions in 2007, and 73.1 million in a 2010 recession. A deeper look tells a different story. The total includes tickets *sold*, not *used*: consider empty seats in spring and fall. Moreover, it counts *many of the same people over and over again.* According to *The Wall Street Journal*, thirty big league teams average 15,000 full season tickets: almost half of all seats sold. Millions more buy smaller ticket packages or see a handful of games, bulging repeat attendance.

As football's pool swells, baseball's stagnates. "Vision could change this," says Costas. "Today baseball has a role in America, but not nearly what it should."[70]

Senator Eugene McCarthy once said that "Baseballs never absolutely go out of bounds."[71] Why does baseball today seem out of bounds to many? To find out, in December, 2009 Selig appointed a fourteen-member "special committee for on-field issues," which floated, said *Sports Illustrated*, a "floating realignment," the most cuckoo scheme since The Baseball Network: teams "moving from division to division at the start of each year" – Flying Dutchmen, seeking parity.[72]

To Selig, the problem was the payroll-rich Yankees. (If so, explain baseball's golden 1950s, dominated by the same team.) In truth, the problem is the product, stupid. The game that wooed for a century is too seldom played, or shown. Below, five lessons to make baseball over.

First, announcing counts. "We didn't have models to copy" growing up, said Harwell. "Today guys train at radio school and college," sounding robotic and alike. Past Voices relied largely on language to entertain. Most now lack "background to paint word-pictures,"[73] mocking Churchill's *mot* that "words are bullets you use as ammunition."

Second, TV/radio partnership demands promotion. Network carriers seem to view baseball, quoting Ring Lardner, like "a side dish they decline to order."[74] Like NBC in the 1980s, they should confer attention and respect.

Third, spurn Social Darwinism – survival of the richest. "Football sells itself," said NFL Films' David Plaut, "no matter who's on TV."[75] Baseball relies on a few marquee teams. On regular-season network/cable coverage, any club can appear up to twenty-seven times a year. Invariably, the Red Sox, Yankees, and perennial also-ran but beloved Cubs do. By comparison, some teams appear only once or twice. A sport is no stronger than its weakest franchise.

Fourth, quicken a glacial pace of play that even big league umpire Joe West recently termed "a disgrace." America stormed Normandy, split the atom, and reached the moon. Baseball won't enforce the strike zone, keep a batter in the box, or uphold a bases-empty rule mandating a pitch every twelve seconds. A 1–0 game routinely tops three hours. Game Seven of the 1960 Series recorded nineteen runs in two hours and thirty-six minutes. As culture becomes more impatient, baseball becomes more inert.

Fifth, intimacy works. Describing Fenway Park, director Harry Coyle once hailed its "great TV" coverage, each park copying the home plate shot: low, yet above an angled backstop. New stadiums put the booth above luxury suites, turning players into TV ants. Worse, vertical guy wire/mesh screens obstruct the camera. Falling ratings are no coincidence. We rarely watch what we cannot see.

At their best, radio and TV sing a sonnet upon baseball's heart. So: hire harmonic Voices. Make baseball less unslow motion. Move the weekend Series to afternoon. Make Fox's *Game of the Week* truly national. Angle the backstop. Make Fenway's the model for each park's camera coverage. For what *not* to do, see any post-mid-1990s park. For what *to* do, see baseball *circa* 1960.

Shortly after World War II, Pope Pius XII said that America "has a genius for splendid and selfless action."[76] Putting baseball's media house in order would be self-interested. It would also be splendid and overdue.

NOTES

1. Curt Smith, *Storied Stadiums: Baseball History through Its Ballparks* (New York: Carroll and Graf, 2001), 95.
2. Curt Smith, *What Baseball Means to Me: A Celebration of Our National Pastime* (New York: Warner Books, 2002), 128.
3. Curt Smith, *The Voice: Mel Allen's Untold Story* (Guilford, CT: The Lyons Press, 2007), 9.
4. Smith, *Storied Stadiums*, 139.
5. Robert Creamer, "The Great American Game – 1956," *Sports Illustrated*, April 12, 1956, 29. Available online at http://sportsillustrated.cnn.com/vault/article/magazine/MAG1130845/index.htm/.
6. For a fuller historical account of baseball broadcasting, see Curt Smith, *Voices of the Game: The Acclaimed Chronicle of Baseball Radio and Television. From 1921 to the Present* (New York: Simon and Schuster, 1992).
7. Curt Smith, interview with Harold Arlin, September 12, 1984.
8. Curt Smith, *Voices of Summer: Ranking Baseball's 101 All-Time Best Announcers* (New York: Carroll and Graf, 2005), 88.
9. Smith, *Voices of the Game*, 8.
10. *Ibid.*, 12.
11. *Ibid.*
12. Smith, *Voices of Summer*, 25.
13. Curt Smith, interview with Mel Allen, October 5, 1990.

14. Smith, *Voices of Summer*, 18.
15. *Ibid.*, 18.
16. *Ibid.*, 13.
17. *Ibid.*
18. *Ibid.*, 14.
19. For more on Red Barber, see Red Barber and Robert Creamer, *Rhubarb in the Catbird Seat* (Garden City, NY: Doubleday, 1968).
20. Curt Smith, interview with Red Barber, June 10, 1988.
21. Smith, *Voices of Summer*, 39.
22. *Ibid.*, 39.
23. Curt Smith, interview with Ernie Harwell, April 15, 2000.
24. Roger Kahn, *The Boys of Summer* (New York: HarperCollins, 2000), xviii.
25. Smith, *The Voice*, 39.
26. *Ibid.*, 56.
27. Huston Horn, "Baseball's Babbling Brook," *Sports Illustrated*, July 9, 1962. Available online at http://sportsillustrated.cnn.com/vault/article/magazine/MAG1073994/index.htm/.
28. For more on Mel Allen, see Smith, *The Voice*.
29. Curt Smith, interview with Lindsey Nelson, June 8, 1986.
30. Smith, *Voices of Summer*, 88.
31. Smith, *The Voice*, 56.
32. *Ibid.*, 67.
33. Curt Smith, interview with Lindsey Nelson, October 22, 1986.
34. Smith, *Voices of Summer*, 4.
35. For more on Vin Scully, see Curt Smith, *Pull up a Chair: The Vin Scully Story* (Washington, DC: Potomac Books, 2009).
36. *Ibid.*, 46.
37. *Ibid.*, 75–76.
38. Smith, *Voices of Summer*, 68.
39. *Ibid.*, 70.
40. *Ibid.*, 82
41. Smith, interview with Lindsey Nelson, June 8, 1986.
42. Smith, *The Voice*, 164.
43. *Ibid.*, 163.
44. *Ibid.*, 162.
45. For more on Dizzy Dean, see Curt Smith, *America's Dizzy Dean* (St. Louis, MO: The Bethany Press, 1978).
46. Smith, *Voices of the Game*, 144.
47. Curt Smith, interview with Lindsey Nelson, November 13, 1985.
48. Smith, *The Voice*, 120,
49. Smith, *Voices of Summer*, 393.
50. Smith, *Pull up a Chair*, 4.
51. Creamer, "The Great American Game," 28.
52. Matthew Futterman, "MLB Sponsors Outperform the NFL," *Wall Street Journal*, April 10–11, 2010, W7.
53. Michael Wilbon, "It's the Most Wonderful Time of the Year," *Washington Post*, September 5, 2007. Available online at www.washingtonpost.com/wpdyn/content/article/2007/09/03/AR2007090301053.html/.

54. Smith, *Voices of the Game*, 300.
55. *Ibid.*, 299.
56. Smith, *Voices of Summer*, 140.
57. *Ibid.*, 439.
58. Smith, *The Voice*, 200.
59. Smith, *Voices of Summer*, 249.
60. Smith, *The Voice*, 223.
61. Curt Smith, interview with Bud Selig, July 7, 1994.
62. Smith, *Voices of Summer*, 340.
63. Smith, *Pull up a Chair*, 172.
64. *Ibid.*, 190.
65. *Ibid.*, 196.
66. Gallup poll, 2009. The NFL led each 2009 demographic. Harris also put football ahead, 31 percent to 16 percent, its largest margins among 25- to 29-year-olds, $35,000 to $75,000 earners, and blacks. Women preferred football by two-to-one. In white suburbia, baseball was overwhelmed. According to Nielsen Media Research, football boasted nineteen of 2009's twenty most watched sports events. Regular-season viewers dwarfed 2008 Presidential election voters, 225 million to 131 million. The NFL led every sport in video game sales, licensed garb, Fantasy Camp players, and unique Internet users.
67. Smith, interview with Ernie Harwell.
68. Curt Smith, interview with Jerry Jones, January 18, 2009.
69. Curt Smith, interview on condition of anonymity, December 10, 2009.
70. Curt Smith, interview with Bob Costas, February 10, 1999.
71. Smith, *What Baseball Means to Me*, 154.
72. Tom Verducci, "Selig: Committee Considering Radical Realignment Plan," *Sports Illustrated*, March 9, 2010. Available online at http://sportsillustrated. cnn.com/2010/writers/tom_verducci/03/09/floating-realignment/index.html/.
73. Smith, *Voices of Summer*, 393.
74. Smith, *Pull up a Chair*, xv.
75. Curt Smith, interview with David Plaut, May 25, 2004.
76. Smith, *Voices of the Game*, 565.

A GUIDE TO FURTHER READING

Allen, Dick. *Crash: The Life and Times of Dick Allen*. Boston, MA: Ticknor and Fields, 1989.

Angell, Roger. *Game Time: A Baseball Companion*. New York: Harcourt, 2003.

Bedingfield, Gary. *Gary Bedingfield's Baseball in Wartime*, www.baseballinwartime. com.

Block, David. *Baseball before We Knew It: A Search for the Roots of the Game*. Lincoln: University of Nebraska Press, 2005.

Briley, Ron. *Class at Bat, Gender on Deck, and Race in the Hole*. Jefferson, NC: McFarland, 2003.

Bryant, Howard. *The Last Hero: A Life of Henry Aaron*. New York: Pantheon, 2010.

Shut Out: A Story of Race and Baseball in Boston. Boston, MA: Beacon, 2003.

Bullock, Steven R. *Playing for Their Nation: Baseball and the American Military during World War II*. Lincoln: University of Nebraska Press, 2004.

Crepeau, Richard C. *Baseball: America's Diamond Mind, 1919–1941*. Lincoln: University of Nebraska Press, 2000.

Cromartie, Warren with Robert Whiting. *Slugging It Out in Japan: An American Major Leaguer in the Tokyo Outfield*. London, New York, and Tokyo: Kodansha International, 1991.

D' Antonio, Michael. *Forever Blue: The True Story of Walter O'Malley, Baseball's Most Controversial Owner, and the Dodgers of Brooklyn and Los Angeles*. New York: Riverhead Books, 2009.

Dewey, Donald. *The 10th Man: The Fan in Baseball History*. New York: Carroll and Graf, 2004.

Dewey, Donald and Nicholas Acocella. *Total Ballclubs*. Toronto: Sport Classic Books, 2005.

Dickerson, Gary E. *The Cinema of Baseball: Images of America, 1929–1989*. Westport, CT and London: Meckler, 1991.

Echevarría, Roberto González. *The Pride of Havana: A History of Cuban Baseball*. New York: Oxford University Press, 1999.

Edelman, Rob. *Great Baseball Films*. New York: Citadel Press, 1994.

Elias, Robert. *The Empire Strikes Out: How Baseball Sold US Foreign Policy and Promoted the American Way Abroad*. New York: The New Press, 2010.

Erickson, Hal. *Baseball at the Movies: A Comprehensive Reference, 1915–1991*. Jefferson, NC and London: McFarland, 1992.

Fitts, Robert. *Remembering Japanese Baseball: An Oral History of the Game.* Carbondale: Southern Illinois University Press, 2005.

Flood, Curt with Richard Carter. *The Way It Is.* New York: Trident, 1971.

Freedman, William. *More than a Pastime: An Oral History of Baseball Fans.* Jefferson, NC: McFarland, 1998.

Gems, Gerald R. *Sport and American Cultural Imperialism.* Lincoln: University of Nebraska Press, 2006.

Gershman, Michael. *Diamonds: The Evolution of the Ballpark from Elysian Fields to Camden Yards.* Boston, MA: Houghton Mifflin, 1993.

Gmelch, George, ed. *Baseball without Borders: The International Pastime.* Lincoln: University of Nebraska Press, 2006.

Good, Howard. *Diamonds in the Dark: America, Baseball, and the Movies.* Lanham, MD and London: Scarecrow Press, 1997.

Gutman, Dan. *Banana Bats and Ding-Dong Balls: A Century of Baseball Inventions.* New York: Macmillan, 1995.

Halberstam, David. *October '64.* New York: Fawcett, 1994.

Hall, Donald. *Fathers Playing Catch with Sons: Essays on Sport (Mostly Baseball).* New York: Farrar, Straus, and Giroux, 1984.

Heaphy, Leslie. *The Negro Leagues, 1869–1960.* Jefferson, NC: McFarland, 2003.

Helyar, John. *Lords of the Realm: The Real History of Baseball.* New York: Ballantine Books, 1994.

Holway, John. *Blackball Tales.* Springfield, VA: Scorpio Books, 2008.

Hye, Allen E. *The Great God Baseball: Religion in Modern Baseball Fiction.* Macon, GA: Mercer University Press, 2004.

Jamail, Milton H. *Full Count: Inside Cuban Baseball.* Carbondale: Southern Illinois University Press, 2000.

Venezuelan Bust, Baseball Boom: Andres Reiner and Scouting on the New Frontier. Lincoln: University of Nebraska Press, 2008.

Jamieson, Dave. *Mint Condition: How Baseball Cards Became an American Obsession.* New York: Atlantic Monthly Press, 2010.

Kashatus, William. *September Swoon: Richie Allen, the '64 Phillies, and Racial Integration.* University Park, PA: Penn State University Press, 2005.

Klein, Alan. *Sugarball: The American Game, the Dominican Dream.* New Haven: Yale University Press, 1991.

Lanctot, Neil. *Negro League Baseball: The Rise and Ruin of a Black Institution.* Philadelphia: University of Pennsylvania Press, 2008.

Lester, Larry. *Black Baseball's National Showcase: The East–West All-Star Game, 1933–1953.* Lincoln: University of Nebraska Press, 2002.

Marcano, Arturo J. and David P. Fidler. "Baseball's Exploitation of Latin Talent." *North American Congress of Latin America Report on the Americas* (March–April, 2004), www.nacla.org.

"Fighting Baseball Doping in Latin America: A Critical Analysis of Major League Baseball's Drug Prevention and Treatment Program in the Dominican Republic and Venezuela." *University of Miami International and Comparative Law Review* 15 (2007), 107–201.

Stealing Lives: The Globalization of Baseball and the Tragic Story of Alexis Quiroz. Bloomington: Indiana University Press, 2002.

McGimpsey, David. *Imagining Baseball: America's Pastime and Popular Culture.* Bloomington: Indiana University Press, 2000.

Miller, Marvin. *A Whole Different Ball Game: The Sport and Business of Baseball.* New York: Carol, 1991.

Morris, Peter. *A Game of Inches: The Stories Behind the Innovations that Shaped Baseball.* 2 vols. Vol. I: *The Game on the Field.* Chicago: Ivan R. Dee, 2006.

  A Game of Inches: The Stories behind the Innovations that Shaped Baseball. 2 vols. Vol. II: *The Game behind the Scenes.* Chicago: Ivan R. Dee, 2006.

Oh, Sadaharu and David Falkner. *Sadaharu Oh: A Zen Way of Baseball.* New York: Times Books, 1985.

O'Keeffe, Michael and Teri Thompson. *The Card: Collectors, Con Men, and the True Story of History's Most Desired Baseball Card.* New York: William Morrow, 2007.

Okkonen, Marc. *Baseball Uniforms of the Twentieth Century: The Official Major League Baseball Guide.* New York: Sterling, 1991.

O' Neil, Terry. *The Game Behind the Game: High Pressure, High Stakes in Television Sports.* New York: Harper and Row, 1989.

Patterson, Ted. *The Golden Voices of Baseball.* Champaign, IL: Sports Publishing, 2002.

Peterson, Robert. *Only the Ball Was White.* Oxford: Oxford University Press, 1992.

Powers, Ron. *SuperTube: The Rise of Television Sports.* New York: Coward–McCann, 1984.

Regalado, Samuel O. "'Latin Players on the Cheap': Professional Baseball Recruitment in Latin America and the Neocolonialist Tradition." *Indiana Journal of Global Legal Studies* 8 (2000), 8–20.

Robinson, Jackie. *I Never Had It Made.* New York: HarperCollins, 1995.

Schraufnagel, Noel. *The Baseball Novel: A History and Annotated Bibliography of Adult Fiction.* Jefferson, NC: McFarland, 2008.

Seymour, Harold. *Baseball: The Early Years.* New York: Oxford University Press, 1960.

Shapiro, Michael. *The Last Good Season.* New York: Broadway Books, 2003.

Shieber, Tom. "The Evolution of the Baseball Diamond," in *Total Baseball*, ed. John Thorn and Pete Palmer with Michael Gershman, 4th edn. New York: Viking, 1995, 113–124.

Smith, Curt. *Pull up a Chair: The Vin Scully Story.* Washington, DC: Potomac Books, 2009.

  Voices of Summer: Ranking Baseball's 101 All-Time Best Announcers. New York: Carroll and Graf, 2005.

  Voices of the Game: The Acclaimed Chronicle of Baseball Radio and Television. From 1921 to the Present. New York: Simon and Schuster, 1992.

Sullivan, Kathleen. *Women Characters in Baseball Literature: A Critical Study.* Jefferson, NC: McFarland, 2005.

Szymanski, Stefan and Andrew S. Zimbalist. *National Pastime: How Americans Play Baseball and the Rest of the World Plays Soccer.* Washington, DC: Brookings Institution Press, 2006.

Tana, Kyle. "Realities behind America's Favorite Pastime: The Dominican Republic's Cheap Labor Bazaar for the Major Leagues." *Council on Hemispheric Affairs,* www.coha.org/realities-behind-america's-favorite-pastime-the-dominican-republic's-cheap-labor-bazaar-for-the-major-leagues/.

Triumph Books. *The Official Rules of Major League Baseball*. Chicago: Triumph Books, 2010.

Tygiel, Jules. *Baseball's Great Experiment: Jackie Robinson and His Legacy*, 25th anniversary edn. New York: Oxford University Press, 2008.

Past Time: Baseball as History. Oxford: Oxford University Press, 2000.

Vargas, Angel. "The Globalization of Baseball: A Latin American Perspective." *Indiana Journal of Global Legal Studies* 8 (2000), 21–36.

Ward, Geoffrey C. and Ken Burns. *Baseball: An Illustrated History*. New York: Alfred A. Knopf, 1994.

Wasch, Adam G. "Children Left Behind: The Effect of Major League Baseball on Education in the Dominican Republic." *University of Texas Review of Entertainment and Sports Law* 11.1 (2009), 99–124, http://ssrn.com/abstract=1571479.

Westbrook, Deeanne. *Ground Rules: Baseball and Myth*. Urbana: University of Illinois Press, 1996.

White, G. Edward. *Creating the National Pastime: Baseball Transforms Itself, 1903–1953*. Princeton: Princeton University Press, 1996.

Whiting, Robert. *The Chrysanthemum and the Bat: The Game Japanese Play*. Tokyo: Permanent Press, 1977.

The Meaning of Ichiro: The New Wave from Japan and the Transformation of Our National Pastime. New York and Boston, MA: Warner Books, 2004.

You Gotta Have Wa: When Two Cultures Collide on the Baseball Diamond. New York: MacMillan, 1989.

Wood, Stephen C. and J. David Pincus, eds. *Reel Baseball: Essays and Interviews on the National Pastime, Hollywood and American Culture*. Jefferson, NC and London: McFarland, 2003.

Zimbalist, Andrew. *Baseball and Billions: A Probing Look into the Big Business of Our National Pastime*. New York: Basic Books, 1994.

Circling the Bases: Essays on the Future of the Sports Business. Philadelphia: Temple University Press, 2011.

In the Best Interests of Baseball? The Revolutionary Reign of Bud Selig. Hoboken, NJ: John Wiley, 2006.

May the Best Team Win: Baseball and Public Policy. Washington, DC: Brookings Institution Press, 2003.

INDEX